Andrew J. Cannon

Lessons from the Australian Constitution

WORLDS OF LAW

Foundations and Intersections

edited by

Andrew J. Cannon
and
Thomas Lundmark

Volume 1

LIT

Andrew J. Cannon

Lessons from the Australian Constitution

An Introduction to the Australian Legal System

LIT

Bibliographic information published by the Deutsche Nationalbibliothek
The Deutsche Nationalbibliothek lists this publication in the Deutsche Nationalbibliografie; detailed bibliographic data are available in the Internet at http://dnb.d-nb.de.

ISBN 978-3-8258-0667-5

A catalogue record for this book is available from the British Library

Auslieferung/Verlagskontakt:
Fresnostr. 2 48159 Münster
Tel. +49 (0)251–62 03 20 Fax +49 (0)251–23 19 72
e-Mail: lit@lit-verlag.de http://www.lit-verlag.de

Distributed in the UK by: Global Book Marketing, 99B Wallis Rd, London, E9 5LN
Phone: +44 (0) 20 8533 5800 – Fax: +44 (0) 1600 775 663
http://www.centralbooks.co.uk/acatalog/search.html

Distributed in North America by:

Transaction Publishers
New Brunswick (U.S.A.) and London (U.K.)

Transaction Publishers
Rutgers University
35 Berrue Circle
Piscataway, NJ 08854

Phone: +1 (732) 445 - 2280
Fax: + 1 (732) 445 - 3138
for orders (U. S. only):
toll free (888) 999 - 6778
e-mail:
orders@transactionspub.com

LESSONS FROM THE AUSTRALIAN CONSTITUTION

Dr Andrew J Cannon[1]

AUTHOR'S NOTE

I express my gratitude for the continuous support from Jan Bailey and our daughters Alissa and Eleanor.

I acknowledge and thank Professor Thomas Lundmark who invited me to participate in the excellent Fachspezifische Fremdsprachenausbildung für Juristinnen und Juristen (FFA) at the Westfälische Wilhelms-Universität Münster and who suggested I convert my lecture materials into this text. Thanks to all the friendly staff at the FFA and the enthusiastic students I have taught. I acknowledge the South Australian Law Foundation Fellowship, which made possible my first visit to Germany in 1999 to pursue my interest in comparative studies of court systems, and Professor Helen Gamble who mentored my studies at that time. Patrick North and Lauren Bacon, my associates[2], researched some recent High Court cases for me. John Bailey and Martin White made helpful suggestions on the text.

This text is not a comprehensive explanation of Australian constitutional law. It is intended to explain the power relationships in a common law federation, and the common law judicial method, and I have focussed on topics of general interest for those purposes. For those interested in a more comprehensive discussion of Australian constitutional law I recommend Blackshield and Williams *Australian Constitutional Law and Theory: Commentary and Materials,* second edition The Federation Press (1998) Leichhardt NSW, which I used as one of my primary sources in writing this text. I have not discussed the State constitutions, which use the same basic model as the Commonwealth of Australia Constitution, but without the federal aspect.

One purpose of the FFA program is to learn familiarity with legal language and some of the specialised words in the text have been footnoted and included in the glossary.

[1] Adjunct Professor of Law, University of Münster, Germany, Adjunct Associate Professor, Flinders University School of Law, Deputy Chief Magistrate and Senior Mining Warden for the State of South Australia.

[2] A graduate lawyer who works with a judge for experience.

FOREWORD

The Australian constitutional arrangement is an interesting blend of the English monarchical model, with power constrained by unwritten conventions, and the United States federal written model. The author draws lessons from these sources to identify and elucidate the electoral process, separation of powers, the freedom of the press, the independence of the judiciary, and the key protections of a civil society.

This book is not just an introduction to the Australian Constitutional legal arrangements, rather it uses strategic examples to ground chosen topics in reality and to explore their legal implications. The author recognises that a constitution reflects its community and to explain this gives a perceptive insight into Australia's sometimes uneasy development from its white British roots to a multicultural society in which 40% of Australians or their parents were born in another country. Australia is today coming to terms with its original Aboriginal inhabitants, who were dispossessed and largely excluded for many years from the Australian federation.

Australia has managed this development with little legal trauma and few constitutional amendments, with the most significant constitutional changes being brought about by the decisions of the High Court of Australia. This is revealed in an excellent discussion of the common law case method of developing the law by interpreting, distinguishing and, where the occasion demands, overruling earlier authorities. There is a most insightful discussion of the extent that judges shroud the real policies behind their decision making, and the desirability of revealing and discussing those policy considerations, rather than pretending to make decisions on the basis of 'black letter law'. In the process the author discusses topics of interest beyond the Australian context, such as race, immigration, the change of interpretation to meet the needs of war and industrial relations.

It is revealing for any student of federal arrangements to see how the careful protection of State rights in the Australian federation has been ineffective to prevent a substantial shift of power to the central authority due to the special needs of wartime, financial reality, and judicial interpretation undermining the original balance of power.

The author, quite appropriately, emphasises the judicial arm of government. He peels away the pretences of the judicial system to find its source of legitimacy as an unspoken pact with the powerful in society to preserve their influence by providing an orderly dispute resolution system. This leads to a discussion, again by an instructive example, of the importance of credible methods of judicial appointment and judicial independence once appointed. Judicial control over administrative arrangements is also addressed. Finally, the author compares the common law and Civilian judicial methods, and persuasively argues that much of the way a court system operates is determined by the way legal costs are calculated and paid.

In all there is much of interest here for legal scholars and students in Germany, where the author regularly lectures, and also for readers in other countries who are interested in the underlying power arrangements that make up an effective constitutional system and preserve the rule of law. The development of ideas is subtle, but the author summarises the conclusions in a direct way. The style is readable, and the approach makes what could be a dry topic, enjoyable and accessible to a wide audience.

This work was developed from the FFA program at Münster University and, consistent with the objective of that program to develop understanding of foreign legal language, the book has a useful glossary of legal terms and common words that have unusual meanings. The meanings are footnoted where they first occur.

Professor Thomas Lundmark
Münster University

September 2007

CONTENTS

Chapter 1:

THE INFLUENCES ON THE AUSTRALIAN CONSTITUTION and THE COMMON LAW METHOD

The European settlement of Australia

Aborigines first populated Australia over 50,000 years ago. There have been several immigrations of different Aboriginal groups. Their culture was oral and so little detail is known of their history. 'Terra Australis' was known to the Dutch and Portuguese traders to South East Asia but it had no obvious riches and was left undisturbed. Captain Cook was despatched by the British Navy to observe the transit of Venus across the sun in 1770 from Tahiti and afterward to explore the East coast of Australia. He landed at Botany Bay, just south of the present day Sydney and claimed the east coast of Australia for Great Britain. The early industrial revolution had brought social disruption and consequential crime to England, which was met by a policy of deportation of criminals as convicts to undertake forced labour in colonies. With the loss of the American colonies in the American War of Independence in 1783 the British cast about in its African and Canadian colonies for new destinations for convicts but there were disadvantages in all of them. Accordingly they determined to act on Cook's claim of Australia and establish a convict colony at Botany Bay. This had the advantage of pre-empting any claim by rival European powers to Australia and establishing a naval base in the South Pacific Ocean.

New South Wales was designated as a place to which convicts could be transported by an order in council[1] made under the *Transportation Act* 1784 (Imp)[2] authorising the designation of convict colonies. The first fleet of eleven ships carrying convicts under the command of Captain Phillip arrived at Botany Bay on 26 January 1788[3] to begin Australia's history as a European colony. Governor Phillip as he then became moved the fleet to the better harbour in Sydney cove where the first settlement started. The colonists recognised no legal entitlement of the Aborigines to the land, regarding Australia as legally 'terra nullius'[4], nor any legal system other than their own that they brought with them. The English Parliament on occasions passed Acts to have effect in its extensive empire and in that capacity was known as the Imperial Parliament[5]. Imperial Acts had paramount force over all other law in the colonies. Examples are the *Transportation Act* 1784 (Imp), and the *New South Wales Act* 1787 (Imp)[6] which provided for the establishment of the new colony. Subject to Imperial statutes, the statutory and common law of England was imported as the law of the colony.

1 The Queen with her council of key ministers, in Australia the Executive Council.

2 Act 24 Geo III c56, Lumb, *Australian Constitutionalism* Butterworths 1983 Sydney, at p 37

3 Celebrated each year as Australia Day, a public holiday.

4 Latin for vacant land; the principle that the Aboriginal people had no legally enforceable rights to the land they occupied in Australia.

5 the English Parliament exercising authority over its colonies and dominions, abbreviated (Imp).

6 Act 27 Geo III.

Initially the Governor was a complete autocrat exercising authority under Letters Patent[7] issued by the Crown[8] in 1786 and 1787[9]. Although he was subject to direction from the British Home Office[10] he had a high degree of autonomy, bearing in mind that the only communication was by sailing ship and it would take a return voyage of up to a year to obtain instructions on any matter. He exercised administrative and judicial power and could make local laws or ordinances[11] of more powerful effect than the common law[12]. The seeds of trouble lay in the appointment of the naval governor with autocratic power, logically enough given the major sea voyage to establish the colony, and the separate power of the marine corps who had separate responsibility for the management of the convicts. Once the colony was established their power was in practice the greater. When Phillip returned to England the Governorship fell to the commander of the NSW marine corps who established a corrupt regime based around the manufacture and sale of rum which became a de facto currency, earning them the nickname of the Rum Corps. Subsequent naval governors attempted with limited success to re-establish good government, culminating in a rebellion in 1808 against the autocratic rule of Governor William Bligh[13] who was arrested by the Rum Corps troops hiding and confined to his residence for a year before he was replaced. In response the British government installed a military governor Lachlan Macquarie with his own contingent of troops to establish good government.

The original purpose of the colony was for convicts and 162,000 convicts were brought to Australia between 1787-1868[14]. Many stayed when they had served their time. Among these were people transported for political rebellion in England such as survivors of the killing of the Tolpuddle martyrs in 1834. Their 'crime' was establishing a workers association, the birth of the trade union movement in England. Colonies were established in Tasmania, to forestall a possible French settlement, Brisbane, Melbourne, Perth and Adelaide in 1836, which was established as a land development scheme, without convicts. Australia had by then opened up to free settlers and they quickly outnumbered the convicts, which led to the need for a form of government other than a military autocracy. Notable among the free immigrants at this time were Lutheran migrants from central and eastern Germany who came to South Australia from the 1840s to 1850s to seek a place where they might practice their old-style Lutheran religion freely. They settled at Hahndorf and in the Barossa Valley, which they made famous as a centre of viniculture.

---

7 An open letter of appointment by the Crown.

8 An impersonal way to describe the Queen or King. The Head of State.

9 Lumb, op. cit. p. 38

10 The British Department of the Secretary of State for Home Affairs that had responsibility for administering colonies.

11 Legislation by an authority lesser than a State, such as a Territory or a local council.

12 *Cooper v Steward* (1889) 14 AC 286 is authority for the paramountcy of Imperial Statutes and local ordinances and later Acts of the colonial legislatures over the common law.

13 This was the second mutiny that Bligh had in his career. The first was on a voyage on HMS Bounty in 1789 to collect breadfruit plants in the Pacific. He was set adrift by the mutineers led by Fletcher Christian and his voyage in an open boat to Batavia, now Timor was one of the epic voyages of survival. This incident formed the basis of the Hollywood movie, *Mutiny on the Bounty* with Marlon Brando as Fletcher Christian.

14 *Webster's History of Australia.* CD Published by Webster Publishing, 1995. Jonathan King was a major contributor.

Meanwhile the colonists began to explore the continent led by the notable German explorer Ludwig Leichhardt[15]. In his second expedition in 1844 to 1846, he covered more than 5000 kilometres from Brisbane via the Gulf of Carpentaria to the small settlement of Port Essington near the present day Darwin. He was quickly followed by pastoralists grazing cattle and the newly bred Australian merino sheep, well adapted to hot landscapes and with the fine long staple in its fleece, that founded the very valuable Australian wool industry. For years it was said that economically Australia rode on a sheep's back. Leichhardt saw none of this. He disappeared without trace on an attempt to cross Australia from East to West in 1847.

Free migration was boosted by a period of goldrush fever, especially in the Victorian goldfields of Ballarat and Bendigo in the 1850s and later in Kalgoorlie in Western Australia and other mining areas in NSW, South Australia and Queensland. This brought a large population of free thinking people to Australia. They refused to pay the exorbitant miners' right fees of 30 shillings (£1.5) per month (in the value of that day) and objected to the corrupt and oppressive military police and repressive colonial government. On 3 December 1854 in Ballarat, a group of miners led by Peter Lalor armed themselves and built the Eureka Stockade and under their own flag of the Southern Cross[16], defied the government forces. This flag has been a symbol of rebellion in Australia ever since. The troopers[17] routed them but the rebellion was a clear signal of the need for increased democratic government. The goldrushes also brought a substantial Chinese migration. Attempts to prevent entry to Victoria failed as they came to little seaport Robe in South Australia where they were charged 10 shillings to row them ashore to then walk across the ninety mile desert to Victoria. There is still a watering point half way called Chinaman's Well. Cultural differences and their success aroused prejudice that laid the seeds later for the "white Australia policy" that prohibited coloured migration to Australia until it was progressively abandoned between 1968 and 1973. The population had reached 437,665 in 1851 and with gold rushes quickly doubled to 1,168,149 ten years later[18]. Business to service this expanding population thrived and the wealth from gold gave the colonies a sound financial foundation.

Thus by the time of the federation of these separate colonies in 1901, Australia had a financial and business class, a landed gentry and many smaller farmers, and a large free thinking working class, with a strong trade union movement. Its dominant culture was English, but it had large migrant groups from elsewhere in Europe and the Americas. The indigenous inhabitants were excluded from the political and economic process.

The British government kept up with these developments by progressively devolving its power to democratic institutions that it established.

---

15 Colin Roderick, *Leichhardt, the Dauntless Explorer,* Angus and Robertson, North Ryde, 1988.

16 A kite shaped star constellation, visible only in the Southern Hemisphere from which the direction due South can readily be established. This is also represented on the current Australian flag.

17 Soldiers.

18 *Webster's* (1995) op.cit.

Early constitutional arrangements in Australia

After the re-establishment of order by Governor Macquarie the British despatched Commissioner J.T. Bigge to recommend constitutional reform for the colony of Sydney. As a result of his recommendations in the 1820s a Legislative Council to make laws, made up of up to seven members nominated by the Governor and a Supreme Court[19] to apply the law, were established by enactment of the Imperial Parliament.

In England the rising middle class demanded reform of the corrupt electoral system of 'rotten' boroughs[20] through which seats in Parliament could be purchased. This led to the English *Representation of People Act of* 1832[21], which reformed the election processes for the House of Commons but leaving in place male and wealth conditions to the right to vote. The notion of representative[22] government spread to Australia with the *Australian Constitutions Act* 1842 (Imp)[23] under the authority of which the first elected Legislative Council was established in NSW. This had two thirds of its members elected, but it still had no executive power. It became a protest body, without real power. Although the ability to exercise power does not always bring responsibility with it, it is often true that lack of power is associated with irresponsibility.

The *Australian Constitutions Act (2)* 1850 (Imp)[24] empowered the Australian colonies to establish bi-cameral legislatures and to frame their own constitutions within parameters set by the Imperial Statute. The Imperial Parliament had the legal authority to assert control over the colonies with over riding legislation, even to the extent of abolishing their constitutions, but in practice it withheld its power. The *Colonial Laws Act* 1865 (Imp)[25] limited the doctrine of paramount power of the Imperial Parliament to legislation[26] expressly or by necessary implication applying to the colonies.

Each colony established its own constitution, based on the English model, with the important difference that the constitution was written. They operated as separate Crown colonies; in effect separate countries, even to the extent of having border control and tariff protection between each other, but without foreign affairs power. The British Queen, Victoria, was represented by a Governor in each State (and still is) who governed in accordance with the advice of the Executive Council[27]. Executive Council is made up of key ministers of the Cabinet[28] from the group that holds a majority in the

---

19 *Australian Courts Act* 1828 (Imp) 9 Geo. 4 c 83.

20 An older English term for a property or area that had parliamentary representation. In Australia this is now called an electorate.

21 2 and 3 William 4 c 45

22 That is elected, as in my local member of parliament is my representative.

23 Vic. 5 & 6 c 76 (Imp)

24 13 and 14 Victoria c 59 (Imp).

25 28 and 29 Victoria c 63 (Imp), section 2.

26 A law duly passed by both Houses of Parliament, assented to by the Queen and proclaimed to come into operation.

27 The Governor and key ministers of Cabinet.

28 The chief ministers of the government meeting as a governing group.

lower house of the bi-cameral[29] parliaments. To maintain power these political groupings later formed into the two major parties, now Labor and the Liberal National coalition.

A robust democracy developed in all the colonies. In 1858 NSW introduced manhood suffrage[30] without property qualifications, said to be one of the first in the world[31] and soon after Victoria introduced payment for Members of Parliament that permitted people other than the rich to enter Parliament. By the 1890s the trade union movement had organised itself to field candidates for elections. A strong women's suffrage movement in South Australia led to female suffrage in that colony in 1894, again one of the first in the world to give women the vote.

The forces of history made the colonies consider a federation. Most significant was the progressive withdrawal of British naval and military protection of the colonies. Real and imagined fears of foreign powers arose from the German annexation of North East New Guinea and French annexure of Pacific Island states and an abiding fear of Russian and Asian territorial ambitions. The colonies felt they were underpopulated English outposts and feared cultural and other invasion from their much more numerous Asian neighbours. These fears gave rise to demands for an Australian wide defence force. The progressive development of telegraph and railways improved communications that both unified the colonies and by permitting quick communication made a centralised government possible. An Australian national identity was developing with a national newspaper *The Bulletin* and national poets, authors and artists such as Banjo Paterson, Henry Lawson and Norman Lindsay gaining Australia wide fame. The Canadian colonies had gained federation in 1867. There was strong public support for federation. These forces overcame resistance from self interest and parochialism. The common English cultural and legal heritage made unification easier than it would have been to unify colonies with different cultures.

The Colonial Secretary Earl Grey proposed a general assembly for Australia to deal with customs duties, roads and railways in the *Constitution Bill* 1850 but this did not proceed[32].

In the 1880s Queensland attempted to pre-empt Germany by annexing New Guinea but this was not accepted as valid by the Secretary of State in England as one colony cannot act with extra territorial affect. This led to the *Federal Council of Australasia Act* 1885 (Imp) but it had little effect particularly as NSW would not participate.

A fiery speech by the NSW premier Henry Parkes at the town Tenterfield on 24 October 1889 is credited as a turning point for federation. It led to the first drafting

29 A Parliament with two houses, as in Australia, the lower house, the House of Representatives and the upper house, the Senate.

30 The right to vote, hence Suffragettes were the group of women campaigning for the right to vote.

31 *Websters* (1995) op. cit.

32 W Harrison Moore, *Constitution of the Commonwealth of Australia,* (1902) London, John Murray at p.20 quoted in Oliver Peter C. *The Constitution of Independence, The Development of Constitutional Theory in Australia, Canada and New Zealand,* Oxford University Press, Oxford 2005 at p. 203 footnote 5.

convention in 1891 culminating in a final form of the Constitution for a federation of the colonies to create a new Dominion[33] at the fourth convention in 1898. The Constitution was largely the work of Samuel Griffith, Edmund Barton, Charles Kingston and Alfred Deakin. It was passed in referenda in all colonies except Western Australia in 1899 and taken to England to be passed by the Imperial Parliament. After some near riots on the Western Australian gold fields it was put to the people who voted to join the federation.

The English insisted on including a right of appeal to the Privy Council[34], which is a judicial body formed from within the House of Lords in London, to ensure that the common law in all Dominions[35] kept cohesion under the same final court of appeal[36].

The Imperial Parliament passed the *Commonwealth of Australia Constitution Act* 1900 (Imp), it was assented to by Queen Victoria on 9 July 1900 and at a ceremony in Centennial Park in Sydney on 1 January 2001 Australia as a nation commenced. The first elections were held in March 1901.

The path to full independence

The creation of the new Dominion did not give it immediate legal independence. This was expressed by the fact that the Constitution, even though it had been passed by referendum in all of the States, still had to be passed as a law of the Imperial Parliament. Notionally, Australia was still legally dependant on the Imperial Parliament even though it was a self-governing Dominion. The *Colonial Laws Validity Act 1865* (Imp) remained good law and it provided that no law of a colony could over ride a law passed by the Imperial Parliament. The Imperial Parliament is a sovereign parliament so it cannot bind it successors. Later it could theoretically amend, or repeal the Australian Constitution. However, legal theory needs to keep pace with political reality. Great Britain declared war on Germany in 1914 on behalf of not only itself but also its Australia and the other Dominions. Australia fought in the first World War but at the end of the war, independently of Great Britain, Australia signed the *Treaty of Versailles* and the Treaty to establish the League of Nations. This established Australia as a sovereign nation in international law and arguably from then Great Britain was

---

33 A nation that was previously a British colony and that still has the English crown as its head of state.

34 The Queen's council of ministers and advisors. More often in the Australian context used to describe the judicial wing of the House of Lords constituted to hear appeals from colonies and Dominions.

35 A nation that was previously a British colony and that still has the English crown as its head of state.

36 This right of appeal was removed in two stages in 1968, by the *Privy Council (Limitation of Appeals Act)* 1968 (Cth) and in 1975 by the *Privy Council (Appeals from the High Court) Act* 1975 (Cth). There remains a theoretical legal avenue for appeal to the Privy Council in an inter se case under s.74 by certificate from the High Court. The High Court has made it clear *Kirmani v Captain Cook Cruises Pty Ltd (No. 2)* (1985) 159 CLR 461, that no such certificate will be given. Appeals to the Privy Council from State Courts were ended by the *Australia Acts* 1986 of the Commonwealth of Australia and United Kingdom Parliament. This was necessary because the Commonwealth Constitution did not of itself give the power to abolish these appeals and neither did any of the States have that power.

bound not to legislate in its Imperial Parliament to affect another sovereign nation. To confirm this new status, the leaders of Great Britain and the Dominions in the *Balfour Declaration* in 1926 declared that Great Britain and the Dominions are:[37]

> "... autonomous communities within the British Empire, equal in status, in no way subordinate one to another in any aspect of their domestic or external affairs, though united by a common allegiance to the Crown, and freely associated as members of the British Commonwealth of Nations."

This was a declaration of political leaders but it did not undo the legal impediments to complete legal independence. The *Statute of Westminster 1931* (Imp) set out new restrictions on how the Imperial Parliament could legislate for Dominions, that is only if they request it and repealed the effect of the *Colonial Laws Validity Act* 1865 (Imp). This was not adopted by Australia until 1942, back dated to 1939.

Despite this apparent independence, in *British Coal Corporation v King*[38] Lord Sankey argued, but only in obiter dicta[39] and in relation to Canada, that at least theoretically the Imperial Parliament could ignore the *Statute of Westminster*[40]. The argument is based on the notion that a sovereign parliament can simply repeal its own earlier legislation if it wishes. In Canada the independence problem was more acute because its Constitution did not have the power of amendment so all amendments had to be enacted by the Imperial Parliament upon request from the Canadian Parliament. Also it did not have the separate legitimacy of being adopted by referendum of the Canadian people. The Canadian Supreme Court in 1981 in the *Patriation Reference*[41] ruled that the Imperial Parliament could repeal the *Statute of Westminster*. The *Canada Act* 1982 (Imp) ended this by giving the tools of constitutional amendment and independence to Canada.

An immediate change at the time of the *Statute of Westminster* was the power in the Australian Prime Minister to nominate the Governor-General. This was put to the test by the government of Prime Minister Scullin in 1930, which nominated Sir Isaac Isaacs of the High Court to be the Governor-General. King George V was opposed to Isaacs appointment but was forced to accept him. This involved a significant transfer of power from the English Crown to the Prime Minister. The Governor-General is the nominal head of government, but if he only holds office until the Prime Minister nominates another person then the real power lies with the Prime Minister. An example of the importance of this power balance between the Governor-General, or in this instance a State Governor, and an elected government became clear in 1932 when the Governor of NSW Sir Phillip Game sacked the Premier Jack Lang because of a dispute

---

37 Cmnd 2768 (1926) quoted in Oliver (2005) op. cit.

38 [1935] AC 500 at 520 (PC).

39 Expressions of views and rulings on the law in a judgment that are not essential for the decision in the particular case. They are not binding on later cases

40 In similar vein in England, *Vauxhall Estates Ltd v Liverpool Corporation* [1932] 1 KB 733 and *Ellen Street Estates Ltd v Minister of Health* [1934] 1 KB 590 both decided that the *Acquisition of Land (Assessment and Compensation) Act* 1919 could not bind future parliaments and made obiter remarks that no parliament could bind a later parliament.

41 *Reference re Resolution to Amend the Constitution* [1981] 1 SCR 753.

when his government would not pay agreed debt payments to the Commonwealth government. The same thing happened later with the controversial sacking[42] of the federal Whitlam government in 1975, which is discussed in Chapter 2. These incidents show that although the government of the day can arrange for the replacement of the Governor-General, asserting Australia's control over its Head of State, the Governor-General is not just a figurehead as s/he can sack the government.

For Australia, full legal independence from the Imperial Parliament was finally settled by the *Australia Acts* 1986, passed both by the Imperial Parliament, at the request of Australia and all of the States, and passed by the Australian Parliament, with the agreement of the States and relying on s. 51(xxxviii) of the Constitution. The Acts removed the fetter of the *Colonial Laws Validity Act* 1865 (Imp) for the States[43]. The States now could pass laws repugnant to Imperial legislation, and it removed appeals from the States to the Privy Council and provided that no Act of the Parliament of the United Kingdom can apply to Australia, including repealing s. 4 of the *Statute of Westminster* 1931 (Imp) which had allowed Imperial legislation to apply if it was requested.

s. 51(xxxviii) empowers the Australian parliament "to make laws ... with respect to:

> the exercise within the Commonwealth, at the request or with the concurrence of the Parliaments of all the States directly concerned, of any power which can at the establishment of this Constitution be exercised only by the Parliament of the United Kingdom or by the Federal Council of Australasia;"

This combination of the exercise of power to sever Australia from any remaining imperial authority by both the Imperial Parliament and the Australian Parliament, invested with the power of the Imperial Parliament by this clause, should put at rest any future argument that the Imperial Parliament retains any residual power to legislate to have effect in Australia. In the view of the High Court of Australia it is the *Australia Act* 1986 (Cth) passed by the Australian Parliament that is important for this result, and the *Australia Act* 1986 (Imp) passed by the Imperial Parliament has effect for the English law rather than in Australia[44].

The exact time when Australia became fully independent is uncertain. Some argue that it was once it had international status as a separate nation by signing the *Treaty of Versailles,* some once the *Statute of Westminster* 1931 (Imp) was accepted into Australian law in 1939, or 1942 when it was actually adopted by the Australian Parliament with retrospective effect to 1939, and some when the *Australia Acts* 1986 were proclaimed in 1986. It was never put to the ultimate test of what the Australian courts would have accepted, so this remains a nice area for theoretical legal discussion. The fact that the Australian Constitution is complete with its own power of amendment (s. 128), explicit foreign affairs power (s. 51 (xxix)) and the inclusion of the power to act as the Imperial Parliament in s. 51(xxxviii) set out above, are clear indications that it was intended as a fully independent constitution. Its adoption by the people of

---

[42] Dismissal.

[43] It had been removed for the Commonwealth by the *Statute of Westminster 1931* (Imp).

[44] *Sue v Hill* (1999) 199 CLR 462, and A-G (WA) v Marquet (2003) 202 ALR 233 at para 70.

Australia in referenda gave it an independent legitimacy. These factors, when combined with Australia's conduct as an independent nation at the end of the first World War, indicate an early full independence, regardless of the later legislation to ensure the legal enactments accorded with the practical reality.[45]

A similar discussion of the inability of a parliament to bind its successors has arisen in relation to the States. The original intention of State Constitutions was to have the same sort of flexibility as the English Parliament, namely the ability by simple statute to change itself. This view was asserted by the Privy Council in the *McCawley v R.*[46]. However in *Trethewan's case*[47] Dixon J. ruled:

> "It is true that these constituent powers were meant to give the Constitution of New South Wales as much of the flexibility which in Great Britain arises from the supremacy of the Parliament as was thought compatible with the unity of the Empire, the authority of the Crown and the ultimate sovereignty of the Imperial Parliament. But this consideration, although generally of importance, affords small help in a question whether the constituent authority of a legislature in a Dominion suffices to enable it to impose a condition or a restraint upon the exercise of its power. The difficulty of the supreme legislature vesting its own power does not arise from the flexibility of the Constitution. On the contrary it may be said that it is precisely the point at which the flexibility of the British Constitution ceases to be absolute. Because it rests upon the supremacy over the law some changes, which detract from that supremacy, cannot be made by law effectively. The necessary limitations upon the flexibility of the Constitution of New South Wales result from a consideration of exactly an opposite character. They arise directly or indirectly from the sovereignty of the Imperial Parliament. But by virtue of its sovereignty it was open to the Imperial Parliament itself to give, or to empower the legislature of New South Wales to give to the Constitution of that State as much or as little rigidity as might be proper."

Thus limitations in State constitutions on the Parliament's power to amend the Constitution are upheld by the High Court. The usual provision in place is a referendum[48], as a procedural precondition for any Bill being put to the Crown for consent. The argument lies that this is not a fetter on the *power* of the later sovereign parliament, but merely a procedural requirement.

When Australia grasps the nettle and replaces the English Crown as the head of State of Australia, there is an interesting legal issue as to whether either or both parliaments can do that given that the theoretical font of all power comes from the Crown. There is little doubt that if a referendum of the people under s. 128 decides to do that, it will in fact occur so that the express will of the people will override the theoretical legal

---

45 However, the Imperial Parliament purported to legislate to bind Australia by the *Whaling Act* 1934 (Imp), s. 15, the *Geneva Convention Act* 1937 (Imp), s. 2, and two acts at the outset of WWII: see Oliver (2005) op.cit. footnote 40 at p. 332. This shows a view in England that it held the power to still bind the Australian legal system.

46 (1920) AC 691.

47 (1930-31) 44 CLR 394 at p. 426.

48 See for example *Constitution Act* 1934 SA s.10A & *Constitution Act Amendment Act* 1979 (NSW).

difficulties. This will then be recognition that the source of power at this point in Australia's history can be found in an expression of the will of the people, the Imperial Parliament is not longer a source of power for Australia and the power of the Crown has become an artifice.

English and American influences on the Australian Constitution

The Australian Constitution is a pragmatic document designed to carefully share power between the States and Commonwealth, and to protect the less numerous States from domination by the more powerful States of NSW and Victoria. It has served its purpose, with only eight minor amendments, for more than a hundred years. It includes elements of both the English and American constitutional arrangements.

The English notion of separating power to constrain it entered Australia through he influential writings of Blackstone's Commentaries, published in 1765. Blackstone's ideas of separation of powers mirror those of Montesquieu and his notions of the legitimacy of the power in Parliament relate to the rationalist views of Grotius, Burlamaqui and Pufendorf in limiting the power of sovereigns.

"Power tends to corrupt and absolute power corrupts absolutely"[49]. Power must be constrained by dividing it. Under the English constitutional model notional power lies with the Crown, which is the Head of State but its power is divided into an executive government that is answerable to Parliament, legislative power that is exercised by Parliament and Judicial power, which constrains the other two. Parliament is the main source of power, which is constrained by parliamentary processes and the requirement that its members face regular elections. The efficient functioning of this system depends on the central place of Cabinet. Executive and legislative powers are in fact unified in Cabinet, the meeting of all key ministers in the government. Ministers must be members of Parliament and can be questioned about their work. Cabinet's discussions are private and it speaks with one voice. The check on the exercise of their power is the fact that the money to run Government, supply[50], depends on the passing of an Appropriation Act each year and so if Government loses its majority in the House of Commons, it loses its ability to govern. This is the real power underpinning the notion that a government is brought to an end if is defeated in a vote of confidence on the floor of the lower House[51]. England does not have a written constitution and reached its delicate balance of power through the civil war and subsequent reinstatement of the Crown with understandings as to the limitations that it would accept to its power. These understandings are embodied in the Australian constitutional arrangements, as in England, by unwritten conventions[52].

---

49 Lord Acton, letter to Bishop Mandell Creighton, 5 April 1887. See also William Pitt, Case of Wilkes speech, January 9, 1770: "Unlimited power is apt to corrupt the minds of those who possess it; and this I know, my lords, that where laws end, tyranny begins."

50 The sum of money granted by Parliament by the annual *Appropriation Act* to permit the executive to govern.

51 In Australia the States insisting that the Senate could refuse supply, giving the power to the upper house, the Senate, to starve the government of money, complicated this notion.

52 Unwritten rules of political and constitutional conduct. Also a meeting to draft laws as in constitutional convention.

Underpinning efficient government was the development of the party system, which delivered a stable majority group, which could exercise executive power, and through its majority in parliament, legislative power.

The judiciary interprets legislation, and subject to the restraint of legislation, develops the law through its own precedents, the common law, and ensures executive power is exercised in accordance with the law. Blackstone as a judge himself emphasised the importance of judicial power and independence[53].

The other great influence on the Australian Constitution was the American Revolution and federation. American colonists relied on the notion of fundamental laws that could be used to justify the overthrow British legislation, and ultimately to justify rebellion. As an example, James Otis in 1761 argued for judicial review of enactments contrary to equity in a Massachusetts Court in the *Writs of Assistance Case*[54]. These ideas found firm expression in the American Declaration of Independence at the second continental congress on 4 July 1776:

> "We hold these truths to be self evident; that all men are created equal; that they are endowed by their creator with certain inalienable rights; that among these are life, liberty and the pursuit of happiness; that to secure these rights, governments are instituted among men, deriving their just powers from the consent of the governed; that whenever any form of government becomes destructive to these ends, it is the right of the people to alter or to abolish it; and to institute a new government, laying its foundation on such principles, and organising its powers in such form, as to them shall seem most likely to effect their safety and happiness."

The violation of those rights by the British was the legal justification for revolt. The federal Constitution became binding when nine states ratified it in 1788, the year when the first convict fleet arrived at Botany Bay to settle Sydney and Australians were well aware of its jurisprudence when they came to draft their own constitution a hundred years later.

The USA model was a departure from the European notion of natural law as a basis to constrain sovereign power. The emphasis on individual rights of people who constitute government to define and secure their rights gave the democratic will a central place in defining rights, which can be altered by the majority. Hence the United States Constitution includes a Bill of Rights. Australia was not borne out of revolution and so lacks the recourse to high ideals to justify its existence. It does not have a Bill of Rights in its Constitution, but there are guarantees of free trade, freedom of religion and protection of property from unfair acquisition and the High Court has implied a right to freedom of speech in political matters[55]. There can be a tension between the notion of majority rule and judicial rejection of democratically passed legislation.

---

53 English Judges received tenure under the *Act of Settlement*, 12 and 13 William III.

54 Corwin "The Higher Law. The inner "Background" of American Constitutional Law" (1928-1929) 42 Harvard Law Review 149 at p. 365.

55 See Chapter 3.

Majority rule can itself be a tyranny and a proper restraint on it by the judiciary will involve, by definition, unpopular decisions. It was interesting to see Australian judges going back to natural law as a justification for the Court's most controversial decision in relation to Aboriginal land rights[56].

In contrast to the USA, the Crown remains as the Head of State in Australia without real power, rather than an elected President with executive power and power to reject legislation and who holds office for a fixed term without being dependant on a majority in Congress. In Australia, and England, the executive government only holds office as long as it maintains a majority in the lower house. This is known as the doctrine of responsible government and the High Court noted this is a central point of difference separating the Australian system from the United States system[57]. The separate election of the President in the USA gives the President a separate elected legitimacy to Congress and it follows that s/he selects ministers from wherever s/he wants them. They need not be members of Parliament and the Parliament cannot bring the executive government down by a vote of no confidence. There is an attraction to this because a wider talent pool is available from which to select ministers,

A federal system with reliance on a written constitution to define the extent of the power of the federal government, which Australia and the USA have in common, further divides power between the States and the Commonwealth, and enhances the role of the judiciary by giving it the ability to declare legislation or executive actions invalid because they are beyond power. Consistent with this American heritage, the High Court of Australia has often turned to American judicial precedents in its work, and in the early years of federation expressed frustration at the failure of the Privy Council to recognise the importance of American experience to Australian constitutional interpretation[58]. All of the UK, USA and Australia use the common law method in developing principles of interpretation.

Common law case law method and citations

The common law judges follow the precedents (decisions) of earlier cases in accordance with formal rules. In deciding whether to follow any case the decisions on the law are separated from the decisions on the facts. A decision on fact is not binding on other courts. A case that is not popular can sometimes be distinguished as confined to its unusual facts, which are unlike any other. Decisions on the law may be separated into those that are essential to the argument, the *ratio decidendi* and those that are incidental, *obiter dictum.* It is the ratio decidendi that must be followed and the obiter dictum is only of persuasive value. A court of lower status is bound to follow the ratio decidendi of a decision of a court higher in the hierarchy of courts and courts at the same level can treat decisions of single judges as only of persuasive value, i.e. they are not bound to follow the ratio of decisions at the same level, although they usually do. These principles are known as *stare decisis*, which underpins the common law method.

---

56 See the discussion of *Mabo (No. 2)* in Chapter 6.

57 *The Amalgamated Society of Engineers v Adelaide Steamship Co Ltd* (1920) 28 CLR 129 at p. 172.

58 See for example Griffiths CJ comments in *Baxter v Commissioner for Taxation (NSW)* (1907) 4 CLR 1087. Griffiths was one of the key drafters of the Australian Constitution.

The exceptions of confining an unpopular case to its particular facts and limiting what is the ratio decidendi gives the system considerable flexibility to adapt to changing circumstances. In the common law method the judges decided cases individually and the academics make sense of their logic afterwards as opposed to the civil law system where the judges make sense of an elegant academic formulation of the law. This difference is expressed in wage structures. In Australia judges are paid much more than professors; in Germany this is not the case and a professor may be entitled to sit as a judge.

Cases are cited by the names in the reported decision, usually typed in italics and separated by a lower case 'v' for versus[59]. The name is followed by the year of the decision in brackets and the volume number, the accepted acronym for the report, e.g. CLR, or C.L.R. for Commonwealth Law Reports, the authoritative reports for the High Court of Australia[60], or AC, or A.C. for Appeal Cases, the authoritative report for the English House of Lords[61], and the page number in the report. A quotation is referred to by the page reference. Thus *John Doe v Richard Roe*, (1957) 26 FLR 267 at p. 288, would be the case of John Doe against Richard Roe decided in 1957 and reported in the Federal Law Reports volume 26 at page 267, with the particular quote at page 288. Incidentally John Doe and Richard Roe[62] are mythical legal actors whose names you may come across. In serious criminal cases the citation is *R v Jones*, with R being short for Regina, the Queen, or Head of State and Jones the family name of the defendant. In the internet age more cases are published on line and in Australia to accommodate this change, judgments[63] use paragraph numbers rather than page numbers. The case is cited by the court reference, the date and case number, if that is shown on the report, and the internet reference: e.g. *Smith v Jones* High Court 26 February 2005 no. 13 of 2005 (http://www.austlii.edu.au) and quotes are identified as 'para. 28-30'.

Higher court judges are properly described in text by their family name followed by 'J' for Justice, as in McHugh J. Their full formal address for correspondence is 'the Honourable Justice McHugh' but you would not use that full address in legal texts.

---

59 Sometimes "ats" instead of "v"is used in older reports.

60 The ultimate court of appeal and the constitutional court in Australia.

61 The upper house in the British Parliament, and also its legal part, which is the highest court of appeal in the British legal system.

62 Fictitious people sometimes used to mask the identity of a party to a legal action.

63 A judgment is the decision of a court, sometimes used to describe the reasons given and sometimes the enforceable result, or in German terms, the enforceable title.

Chapter 2:

KEY ELEMENTS IN THE AUSTRALIAN FEDERAL CONSTITUTION

There are two matters in the following discussion that German readers may find strange. The first, from the English tradition, is that much is determined by unwritten accepted practice, or conventions, rather than what is written in the Constitution. The second is that in interpreting the Constitution the development of principles is through case law in the common law tradition. It follows that most of this discussion will proceed by reference to the case law rather than the constitutional statute itself.

The Constitution was a contract between the six States[64] to create the new central power, called the Commonwealth and between the people and the new central power to manage the power to prevent abuse of it. There are careful provisions[65] to manage the balance of power between the States and the Commonwealth and other provisions to prevent the larger States dominating the new central power to the disadvantage of the smaller States. With the passage of time the new central power has increased at the expense of State power. This is not a result of constitutional amendment but of the shift of economic power to the Commonwealth. The balance of power between the States and the Commonwealth is discussed in Chapter 4.

The method of managing the new central power to prevent its abuse is by dividing the power between the legislative, executive and judicial arms of government.

Legislative power is to be exercised by the Federal Parliament (s.1). Executive power is given to the Queen in her representative, the Governor-General[66], and is formally executed by Executive Council (comprised of key members of the Cabinet who advise the Governor-General). It is by convention, and is not written, that the Governor-General must accept that advice. The power to appoint the head of the armed forces rests in the Governor-General (s.68) but again, by convention, he exercises that power on advice of the Prime Minister[67] on behalf of Cabinet. The third arm of Government is the Judiciary (s.71). The Judiciary have tenure of office and remuneration that cannot be diminished (s.72).

There is a bi-cameral Parliament (i.e. two houses). The lower house, known as the House of Representatives[68], is the house of government and has members elected from individual electorates of similar voter numbers. They sit with green upholstery. The upper house, known as the Senate, is a house of review and has equal numbers from each State. They sit with red upholstery.

---

64 The original states were New South Wales, Victoria, Queensland, Western Australia, South Australia and Tasmania in order of their present population. There are two territories, the Australian Capital Territory and the Northern Territory which have been separated from States and which have joined the Commonwealth since Federation.

65 A section of legislation.

66 The Queen of England's representative in Australia.

67 The head of government of Australia.

68 The lower house in the Australian Parliament. The upper house is the Senate.

One of the great constitutional debates was whether the Senate should have the ability to reject money bills, known as supply. Eventually the smaller States prevailed so that it could reject money bills (although not amend them). This gives the Senate power beyond just a house of review. It can starve the government of money and by that means cause a constitutional crisis. In the event of a deadlock[69] between the two houses the government can recommend a double dissolution[70] and then all members of both houses have to stand for election.

Amendment of the Constitution is difficult[71] in a way that is designed to protect the less numerous states.

The Australian constitutional arrangement is a federal system with defined powers[72] given by the States to the Commonwealth. Most of these powers are set out in Section 51, namely:

"51. The Parliament shall, subject to this Constitution, have power to make laws for the peace, order, and good government of the Commonwealth with respect to:

(i) trade and commerce with other countries, and among the States;

(ii) taxation; but so as not to discriminate between States or parts of States;

(iii) bounties on the production or export of goods, but so that such bounties shall be uniform throughout the Commonwealth;

(iv) borrowing money on the public credit of the Commonwealth;

(v) postal, telegraphic, telephonic, and other like services;

(vi) the naval and military defence of the Commonwealth and of the several States, and the control of the forces to execute and maintain the laws of the Commonwealth;

(vii) lighthouses, lightships, beacons and buoys;

(viii) astronomical and meteorological observations;

(ix) quarantine;

(x) fisheries in Australian waters beyond territorial limits;

(xi) census and statistics;

(xii) currency, coinage, and legal tender;

(xiii) banking, other than State banking; also State banking extending beyond the limits of the State concerned, the incorporation of banks, and the issue of paper money;

(xiv) insurance, other than State insurance; also State insurance extending beyond the limits of the State concerned;

(xv) weights and measures;

(xvi) bills of exchange and promissory notes;

---

69 When the two House of Parliament cannot agree on a Bill.

70 Dissolution: ending a Parliament and submitting the members to election. In Australia this involves all members of the House of Representatives and half the members of the upper house, the Senate. In a double dissolution, all the Senators submit to election.

71 See Chapter 4.

72 ss 51 and 52.

(xvii) bankruptcy and insolvency;

(xviii) copyrights, patents of inventions and designs, and trade marks;

(xix) naturalization and aliens;

(xx) foreign corporations, and trading or financial corporations formed within the limits of the Commonwealth;

(xxi) marriage;

(xxii) divorce and matrimonial causes; and in relation thereto, parental rights, and the custody and guardianship of infants;

(xxiii) invalid and old-age pensions;

(xxiiiA) the provision of maternity allowances, widows' pensions, child endowment, unemployment, pharmaceutical, sickness and hospital benefits, medical and dental services (but not so as to authorize any form of civil conscription), benefits to students and family allowances;

(xxiv) the service and execution throughout the Commonwealth of the civil and criminal process and the judgments of the courts of the States;

(xxv) the recognition throughout the Commonwealth of the laws, the public Acts and records, and the judicial proceedings of the States;

(xxvi) the people of any race for whom it is deemed necessary to make special laws;

(xxvii) immigration and emigration;

(xxviii) the influx of criminals;

(xxix) external affairs;

(xxx) the relations of the Commonwealth with the islands of the Pacific;

(xxxi) the acquisition of property on just terms from any State or person for any purpose in respect of which the Parliament has power to make laws;

(xxxii) the control of railways with respect to transport for the naval and military purposes of the Commonwealth;

(xxxiii) the acquisition, with the consent of a State, of any railways of the State on terms arranged between the Commonwealth and the State;

(xxxiv) railway construction and extension in any State with the consent of that State;

(xxxv) conciliation and arbitration for the prevention and settlement of industrial disputes extending beyond the limits of any one State;

(xxxvi) matters in respect of which this Constitution makes provision until the Parliament otherwise provides;

(xxxvii) matters referred to the Parliament of the Commonwealth by the Parliament or Parliaments of any State or States, but so that the law shall extend only to States by whose Parliaments the matter is referred, or which afterwards adopt the law;

(xxxviii) the exercise within the Commonwealth, at the request or with the concurrence of the Parliaments of all the States directly concerned, of any power which can at the establishment of this Constitution be

(xxxix) matters incidental to the execution of any power vested by this Constitution in the Parliament or in either House thereof, or in the Government of the Commonwealth, or in the Federal Judicature, or in any department or officer of the Commonwealth.

All powers not given to the Commonwealth remain with the States. In the event of inconsistency between Federal and State law the Federal Law prevails[73]. However, as we shall see, some of these powers, especially the foreign affairs and corporations powers permit an expansion of Commonwealth power through the back door, such as via international treaty obligation and by regulation of the activities of corporations in areas outside the defined powers. The interpretation of some important powers in section 51 is discussed in Chapter 6.

Protection of the smaller States

The primary protection for the smaller States is the upper house, the Senate. The Senate can amend all legislation, except appropriation (budget money bills discussed below) or reject any legislation.

The Senate originally had 6 members for each State and now has 12 members[74] for each original State and two[75] for the new Territories of the Northern Territory and the Australian Capital Territory. This theoretically gives the States with small populations some protection against the larger States. However in practice most Senators are members of the two major parties, the Liberal National coalition (right of centre) or the Labor[76] Party (left of centre), and follow party discipline rather than State interests, so the apparent protection is largely lost. Senators are elected for fixed terms of six years or twice the time of the House of Representatives with half the Senate retiring at each election of the House of Representatives. This achieves a rotation of members to provide longer-term stability than in the House of Representatives. The senators are elected on a proportional vote basis rather than from electorates. The only exception to the six year rotational cycle is in the event of a double dissolution when everyone is up for election. The fact that the Senate is a States' house is demonstrated by the fact that the States call the election for Senators[77] not the Prime Minister. However in practice the Senate elections are synchronized with the House of Representatives election.

73 Covering clause 5 and s.109.

74 The reason for the increase has been to permit more members in the House of Representatives whose size is linked to the size of the Senate.

75 *Commonwealth Electoral Act 1918* s. 40. This might appear to be against the opening words in s. 7, but the High Court held that this could be achieved under s.122 which allows for laws to permit representation of territories in Parliament.

76 Labour with the 'u' is the correct spelling of manual work (except in the USA where it is labor). The Australian Labor Party, the party whose origins lie in the trade union movement, have dropped the 'u' from the spelling.

77 s. 12.

Another demonstration is the fact that if a Senator leaves office before the end of her or his term the replacement is chosen by the State[78].

In 1949 proportional representation was put in place so that the number of Senators is divided into the number of electors in the State to give a quota and representation is in accordance with the number of quotas that each party achieves. This system of voting permits minority parties to achieve one or more quotas so the Senate usually is not dominated by either of the large parties who have to compromise with minority parties such as the Democrats, a party to the left of the Liberal Party, and two rising forces, the Greens tending in their general policies to the left wing and Family First, a Protestant religious party tending to the right wing.

The number of members of the House of Representatives must be as nearly practicable twice the number of senators[79]. This is to protect the State's house, the Senate from having its votes swamped in the event of a joint sitting[80] of both Houses. A joint sitting occurs when there is a deadlock between the two Houses (see below). Once the number of members of the House of Representatives is determined by this method, this number is divided into the number of people in the Commonwealth to give a quota for each electorate and these quotas are allocated to the States on a population basis.

Resolution of disputes between the Senate and the House of Representatives

The procedure to resolve disputes between the two Houses of Parliament is set out in s.57. If a Bill[81] is rejected by the Senate, or amended in a way that the House of Representatives will not accept, the House of Representatives, after an interval of three months can pass the Bill again and send it to the Senate. If the Senate rejects it the second time, then this gives a trigger to the Government to ask for dissolution of the whole of the Senate and the House of Representatives (known as a double dissolution). This dissolution is a substantial threat to minor parties in the Senate because for the same percentage of vote they are likely to achieve less seats on an election of all Senators than they will on an election of half the Senators, so there is pressure on them not to provoke a double dissolution. If after a double dissolution, the Senate still will not pass the Bill then there can be a joint sitting of both Houses of Parliament and the Bill can pass by an absolute majority of the total number of members of both the House of Representatives and the Senate.

Since federation there have been six double dissolutions but only one joint sitting. In 1914 and 1983 the Government lost the election following the dissolution so the Bills were left because the incoming government did not like the Bills of the previous government. In 1951 the Government won the election with a majority in the Senate so it was able to pass the Bill in the Senate. In 1974 the Whitlam Labor Government won the election without a majority in the Senate. This was an occasion for a joint sitting. A

[78] s. 15.
[79] s. 24.
[80] The House of Representatives and the Senate sitting together.
[81] Legislation that has been presented to Parliament but not yet passed.

majority of both houses combined to pass the six deadlocked bills in the joint sitting. This was the only joint sitting so far in Australia's constitutional history. The new legislation was controversial so much of it was tested in the High Court, leading to interesting cases. Many of the cases discussed below occurred in the mid 1970s from this Labor government that changed a great deal in a short space of time.

Representative democracy

The influx of sometimes rebellious, free thinking migrants from Europe and America to the gold rushes in the 1850s resulted in strong movements for democratic reform in Australia. Although the Eureka stockade rebellion against excessive fees and corrupt troopers was crushed, they won the longer term struggle to change the culture of government from an elitist colonial authority over a convict colony to a representative democracy.

Manhood suffrage, the vote for all men, regardless of wealth or other factors, was achieved in South Australia, Victoria and New South Wales before 1860. They were world leaders in establishing this democratic right. Some other colonies took longer and property owners retained additional voting rights particularly in the upper houses of state Parliaments.

There was also a strong women's movement in Australia. Catherine Helen Spence (1825-1910) of the South Australian Women's Suffrage League was a leader of this movement. As a result of their efforts women received the vote in South Australia in 1894, one of the first places in the world to have women's suffrage. She continued the struggle for equality for women in other states, founding the influential Effective Voting league and the National Council of Women. National adult suffrage (except for Aborigines) was agreed in the new Australian Constitution[82]. However, Aborigines did not receive the right to vote until 1967. Women were also permitted to stand for the national Parliament.

Some States were slower to adopt these reforms. Western Australian women won the vote in 1899 and the right to stand for Parliament in 1920. Edith Cowan (1861-1932) the leader of the movement in that State was the first Australian woman to enter Parliament. NSW granted women's suffrage (right to stand in 1918), Tasmania 1902 (right to stand in 1921), Queensland, 1905 (right to stand in 1923) and last Victorian women were given the vote in 1908 and the right to enter state Parliament in1923[83]. The leader of the suffragettes in Victoria, Vida Goldstein (1869-1949), wanted women to actually enter parliaments. She was the first woman to stand for Parliament, the Senate, in 1903, and other elections, unsuccessfully. She was defeated largely because she refused to join a mainstream political party. She represented Australian women at the Women's peace conference in Zurich in 1919. The first woman did not succeed in entering the national Parliament until Dame Enid Lyons (1987-1981) won a Tasmanian seat to the House of Representatives in 1943. Party machines were male dominated so the winnable seats went to men. It was not until the 1960s that women entered

---

[82] Now it is in s 93 *Commonwealth Electoral Act* 1918 (Cth).

[83] Webster's, op.cit.

Parliaments in Australia in significant numbers and with the women's liberation movement of the 1970s much greater equality was achieved. Rosemary Follett became the first leader of a Territory government, the ACT, followed by Dr Carmen Lawrence, the Premier[84] of Western Australia in 1990 and Joan Kirner, the Premier of Victoria. There has been no female Australian Prime Minister, but a minor party, the Australian Democrats was led by Janine Haines in 1986.

As a result of this strong democratic tradition representative democracy has been part of the Australian Constitution since its adoption in 1901. The members of the Senate, who theoretically represent the States, stand as a team and are elected by the States as a whole. In contrast the members of the House of Representatives stand individually for election in geographical electorates. The Constitution provides[85] that the country is divided into areas of about equal population and each elects its own local member. It has been held[86] by the High Court that this section does not impose a requirement of equality of voters of electorates. In *McKinlay's* case[87] the Court upheld[88] a provision in the *Commonwealth Electoral Act* 1918 (Cth), which allowed a variation from a quota of up to 10%. However, the High Court would almost certainly find gross variations in electorates to be unconstitutional.

Voting is by a preferential voting system. The voter must indicate a preference by numbering each candidate from one to the last one. The votes for the candidates with least first preference votes are then distributed to their second preference and candidates are eliminated until only 2 remain with the winner being the one with the most votes. This means candidates with small support are progressively eliminated leaving the major parties in control of the House of Representative seats with virtually no independents or small parties. Independents are only elected when the major parties so offend the members of an electorate by bad preselection choices that a local identity in the electorate who has left the party in disgust may be elected for a term or two.

In Australia in effect voting is compulsory. Technically it is attending to vote at elections that is compulsory and in the privacy of the ballot box, the elector can deface or not place the ballot in the box. A small fine is imposed on citizens who fail to attend to vote. There is of course a secret ballot.

The government is answerable to parliament and the electorate. Parliament must sit every year[89] and the government must face an election every three years[90]. The government can dictate the timing of the election so it attempts to manipulate the economic conditions to suit its electoral chances, although the effect of the world economy can thwart such local attempts, particularly in a relatively small and open economy like Australia.

---

84 The head of government of a State.

85 s.24.

86 The decision of a court. *Found* is used in the same way, as " the court found".

87 *A-G(Cth) ex parte McKinlay v Commonwealth* (1975-6) 135 CLR 1.

88 Uphold, to: to confirm a decision, particularly a higher court upholds the decision of a lower court (past tense "upheld").

89 s. 6.

90 s. 28.

Key conventions of responsible government

The structures of power in the Australian Constitution follows the English Westminster system. This relies heavily on conventions, which every one accepts should govern their behaviour, even though they are not written in any Statute. A good example of the importance of conventions is Chapter II of the Constitution, which deals with executive government. The words of the Constitution are misleading without the explanation of conventions. Here are the key sections of the Constitution.

61 *Executive power*
The executive power of the Commonwealth is vested in the Queen and is exercisable by the Governor-General as the Queen's representative, and extends to the execution and maintenance of this Constitution, and of the laws of the Commonwealth.

62 *Federal Executive Council*
There shall be a Federal Executive Council to advise the Governor- General in the government of the Commonwealth, and the members of the Council shall be chosen and summoned by the Governor- General and sworn as Executive Councillors, and shall hold office during his pleasure.

63 *Provisions referring to Governor-General*
The provisions of this Constitution referring to the Governor- General in Council shall be construed as referring to the Governor- General acting with the advice of the Federal Executive Council.

64 *Ministers of State*
The Governor-General may appoint officers to administer such departments of State of the Commonwealth as the Governor-General in Council may establish.

Such officers shall hold office during the pleasure of the Governor- General. They shall be members of the Federal Executive Council, and shall be the Queen's Ministers of State for the Commonwealth.

Ministers to sit in Parliament
After the first general election no Minister of State shall hold office for a longer period than three months unless he is or becomes a Senator or a member of the House of Representatives.

66 *Salaries of Ministers*
There shall be payable to the Queen, out of the Consolidated Revenue Fund of the Commonwealth, for the salaries of the Ministers of State, an annual sum which, until the Parliament otherwise provides, shall not exceed twelve thousand pounds a year.

67 *Appointment of civil servants*
Until the Parliament otherwise provides, the appointment and removal of all other officers of the Executive Government of the Commonwealth shall be vested in the Governor-General in Council, unless the appointment is delegated by the Governor-General in Council or by a law of the Commonwealth to some other authority.

68 *Command of naval and military forces*

The Commander in Chief of the naval and military forces of the Commonwealth is vested in the Governor-General as the Queen's representative.

These sections make it sound as if Queen Elizabeth of Great Britain is represented by the Governor-General who governs with advice from an Executive Council. However, in fact power is focussed on the Prime Minister and neither the Queen nor the Governor-General have any effective power. Conventions bind the Queen to appoint or dismiss the Governor-General on the wish of the Prime Minister. The Governor-General is bound by convention to appoint the leader of the party that has the confidence[91] of the lower house, the House of Representatives, to form a government and it continues to govern until the next election, as long as it retains the confidence of the House of Representatives.

The Government is supposed to speak with one voice and by convention a vote of no confidence brings down all the Ministers. They stand and fall together. This doctrine of collective responsibility requires the unity of Cabinet and the control of Cabinet by the Prime Minister. The government is responsible to parliament and ministers can be questioned in a special session of parliament called simply, Question Time[92], and if caught lying the minister is expected to resign. Catching a politician lying is of course not easy. This is the English system and contrasts to the USA where the executive power lies with the elected President, who holds office for a fixed term and is not answerable to Congress[93] (impeachment aside). In Australia the unelected Governor-General has the power of executive government but by conventions s/he must exercise it on advice of the Government of the day through Executive Council. However, it has been noted that the Governor-General retains the practical power to dismiss the Government without advice to do so. This is not just on advice as the events in 1975 show, when the Whitlam government was dismissed by the Governor-General even though it retained control of the lower house. It seems to follow that Australia has a new convention that if the government cannot assure supply by passing the appropriation bill through the Senate then the Governor-General can dismiss the government.

The Governor-General rules on the advice of the Executive Council, which is comprised of the Prime Minister and key ministers. The role of Executive Council was discussed in *FAI Insurances v Winneke*[94]. In that case an insurance company had lost its business with the government as a result of a decision by Executive Council. The Court decided it could review executive power exercised by the Executive Council. However, the usual way that the Court criticises an exercise of power is to say there was a denial of natural justice in its deliberations. The Court held that this was not a problem here because the Executive Council was not a deliberative body but an authenticating body. It is like a rubber stamp rather than exercising real discretionary power, which happens in Cabinet. Thus the Court asserted it had the power to review

---

91 Commanding the majority vote in the lower House of Parliament, as 'a vote of confidence'.

92 A special session of Parliament when the members can question Ministers.

93 The legislative House of Parliament of the USA.

94 (1982) 151-CLR 342. see also *R v Toohey: ex parte Northen land Council* (1981) 151 CLR 170.

Executive Council but characterised its role so that it did not. They also observed that the Governor-General could refer advice back to the ministry but in the final analysis s/he must act on advice.

The key conventions of responsible Government in Australia are as follows:[95]

> "1. A Government defeated at an election must resign. The Premier should ordinarily return his commission to the Governor when the counting of the votes has been completed and a clear electoral result know.
>
> 2. A new (Prime Minister) will be asked to form a Government. That person will be the leader of the party which has won a majority of the seats of the Lower House or the person who has the support of a coalition of parties who have won such a majority. In rare circumstances a minority party which has won a plurality of seats may be commissioned.
>
> 3. A Government defeated on a vote of no confidence in the Lower House or which has been refused supply by Parliament must advise a dissolution or resign.
>
> 4. The Government's responsibility to Parliament is collective. This means that Ministers must not publicly criticise decisions of the Cabinet or reveal the nature of statements made or divisions of opinion occurring in the Cabinet room. The latter principle of Cabinet secrecy is subject to certain qualifications such as a release of Cabinet documents after 30 years for archival purposes or subject to limitations for the purposes of litigation.
>
> 5. Under administrative arrangement orders individual Ministers have responsibility for areas of allocated responsibility ... they are responsible individually to Parliament for matters falling within these areas including acts of public servants in their departments. A motion of censure passed by the Lower House entails their resignation."

These English conventions are central to Australia's constitutional arrangements for all the States and the Commonwealth but nowhere will you find them written in a constitution Act.

A noted Australian Chief Justice Sir Owen Dixon said this:[96]

> "I believe that the central point of Australian political beliefs has been faith in the soundness in the opinion of the majority of electors as a means of solving any large political question, and the need of providing constitutional machinery to ensure that, when occasion demands, the opinion of the people is ascertained, and when ascertained is carried into effect. When an American speaks of democracy, I do not believe that this is his predominant conception. The American tradition, founded upon, and developed by, a long course of history, has concentrated much more on the position of the individual, upon the protection of his natural rights from the abuse of power, and upon the

---

95 Lumb op. cit. p. 68.

96 Dixon, 0 *Jesting Pilot* Lawbook Co, Sydney, 1965 p106-7.

formulation of guarantees against the encroachment of one organ of Government upon the domains of another, or of the States or of the Union upon the liberty of the citizen. ...

Dean Roscoe Pound told an audience in Chicago that it is not the American idea of government that democracy must be the absolute rule of those chosen by popular election, and of their subordinates. He proceeded to treat as living instruments of democracy the constitutional guarantees of the liberties of the individual contained in the Bill of Rights. ...

He laid particular stress on the separation of the Executive Government and its power from the Legislature and from the Judiciary. We, under our conception of democracy, so far from separating the Executive and the Legislature, insist on the dependence of the Cabinet upon Parliament. We insist too, that if a difficulty arises between the Executive Government and the Parliament, it shall be resolved by an appeal to the people, and we place on the representative of the Sovereign, the responsibility of the saying whether the case is one for the dissolution of Parliament and a general election. This we can do because we have proudly preserved the Monarchy as the apex of our Constitutional system. In the United States the President is elected for four years – a fixed period. Congress cannot be dissolved."

This was a speech in 1944. The current view of the Monarchy may be different but it correctly identifies a key point of departure between the Australian approach and the American.

It is worth noting that although the Queen's powers are nearly all delegated to her local representative, the Governor-General, she still retains the power of appointment of the Governor-General, and some signing of documents relating to the appointment of ambassadors, but again by convention these residual[97] powers in the British Monarch are exercised on advice from the Australian Prime Minister.

Money Bills

Except in relation to money Bills the Senate has the same powers in relation to legislation as does the House of Representatives. The Senate has the power to reject a money bill although it cannot originate nor amend money bills. This is as result of s.53, which provides:

"The Senate may not amend proposed laws imposing taxation, or proposed laws appropriating revenue or moneys for the ordinary annual services of the Government."

The last sentence of s.53 provides

[97] What is left after a specified list.

"except as provided in this section the Senate shall have equal powers with the House of Representatives in respect of all proposed laws."

This has been interpreted to permit the rejection of the monetary bills since that is not an exception provided in the section[98]. It follows also that apart from money bills the Senate has full power to introduce Legislation, amend it and reject it. What are money bills for the purpose of the sections has of course been a matter of considerable interpretation. Under an agreement known as the compact of 1965 between the Houses is was agreed that one-off projects such as major construction of buildings and infrastructure and grants to States are not ordinary supply for the purposes of s.53, that is the Senate can amend them. Thus, when the Commonwealth Budget is considered, there are always two Appropriation Bills, one dealing with ordinary annual supply which cannot be amended and the second giving the authority for spending for other purposes.

Requests for dissolution of Parliament

There are clear conventions for the circumstances in which the Prime Minister can ask for Parliament to be dissolved. These are: [99]

- "The Governor-General (or a State Governor[100]) would normally follow the advice of the Prime Minister as to whether to dissolve Parliament or to accept the resignation of the Government and find an alternative with the confidence of the House. Some exceptions however might be that the Governor must ensure that supply is secured to allow the Government to continue until after the election.
- A Prime Minister defeated at an election cannot ask for a dissolution before Parliament meets.
- A Government with support in the Lower House should not ask for a dissolution early in its office unless there is some serious political issue to take to the people.
- A Government defeated in the House might in some circumstances be refused a dissolution and the alternative majority in the House be allowed to form a Government.
- Where a majority Government loses a vote of confidence and Government is handed to a minority Government which then loses a vote of confidence the request for dissolution by the minority Government might be refused and Government returned to the majority Government as long as it retains the confidence of the House."

Dissolution means the ending of the government and a new election. There have been occasions when the leader of government has not been willing to go.

---

98 There is a rule of statutory interpretation that if a list is particularised in a Statute it is presumed to be comprehensive, sometimes described in the Latin maxim *Expressio unius est exclusio alterius:* the expression of one thing excludes the other. See the English cases *Burgin v Forbes* 293 KY. 456, and 169 SW2d321 and *Newblock v Bowles* 170 OKL. 487 and 40 P.2d 1097. in H.K. Black, *Black's Law Dictionary,* (5th edition 1979) West Publishing Co., St. Paul.

99 Lumb op. cit. pp. 76-77.

100 The Queen of England's representative in a State in Australia.

Dismissal or forced dissolution

This would occur where a Government had lost a vote in the lower House, or supply, but refused to resign. There have been examples of this. In New South Wales in 1932 Premier Lang was dismissed in effect for failing to honour the financial agreements between the States and the Commonwealth. It was at this time that NSW built its Harbour Bridge to relieve unemployment. There was a conflict here between Federal Government policy in the depression, which was fiscally prudent and New South Wales Government policy, which was expansionist. Lang refused to resign after losing a vote of confidence but was dismissed by the State Governor Sir Phillip Game. Here the Governor had a clear reason because of the loss of the vote of confidence, which under conventions should have caused the Lang government to resign.

Greatest difficulty occurs where the Upper House refuses supply but the Government retains the confidence of the Lower House. This can arise in several States and under the Commonwealth Constitution. It did with great controversy with the Whitlam Labor government. This government was elected in December 1972 after a long period of conservative rule. It brought an end to Australia's involvement in the Vietnam War where conscripted troops had been involved. On the international scene it distanced itself from the American alliance[101]. It recognised communist China, and protested against French nuclear tests on Muruoa Atoll in the Pacific. At home it began an adventurous period of legal and social reform. It increased welfare benefits, abolished university fees[102], lowered the voting age from 21 to 18 years, introduced no fault divorce and a new Family Court, took responsibility for environmental protection, Trade Practices legislation to regulate company conduct and many other changes. The Whitlam government was re-elected in a double dissolution election in May 1974. The reform program was of course controversial and in addition the government had many scandals. It had a sex scandal, although nothing more serious than a minister having an affair with his secretary, but also there were allegations of mismanagement of money and an attempt to borrow funds secretly from a shadowy Middle Eastern financial intermediary to nationalise large mineral and energy projects. Just over a year after the Whitlam government's re-election, in October 1995, the Senate, which was controlled by the Liberal opposition party, refused to pass the annual budget supply bills, starving the government of money. This was a time of high drama. There was dark talk of CIA involvement because Whitlam had offended America over the Vietnam War, recognising China and antagonism to US spy satellite bases in Australia, and a serious whiff of a military coup as the government struggled on with its money supply drying up.

---

101 In contrast an earlier conservative Prime Minister Harold Holt when committing more troops to the long running Vietnam war had said: "All the way with LBJ!" referring to the American President, Lyndon Baines Johnson.

102 Introduced again by a subsequent Labor government on an optional loan basis known as the Higher Education Contribution Scheme (HECS).

The Governor-General, Sir John Kerr, who had been appointed by the Queen in England on the request of Gough Whitlam, on 11th November 1975[103] dismissed the Whitlam Government and asked the Leader of the Opposition Malcolm Fraser to take over as a caretaker Prime Minister on condition that he would advise him, the Governor-General, to dissolve both Houses of Parliament. The real issue here was the deadlock over the money Bills but the constitutional trigger to dissolve both Houses of Parliament was the backlog of twenty double dissolution Bills that the Senate would not pass. The Whitlam Government lost the election and on 13th December 1975 the Fraser Government, a Liberal National Government was returned with a large majority in both Houses. It had no interest in the twenty Bills, so they lapsed. This demonstrated problems with the Constitution. The first is that the ability of the Senate to reject supply can conflict with the convention that the party with a majority in the House of Representatives is entitled to govern. Another problem is the type of election that results from this circumstance. Had there not been the rejected Bills, which provided the trigger, a double dissolution could not have been ordered. Arguably the Governor-General could still have sacked the government based on its lack of supply and called a normal election, rather than a double dissolution. There are two schools of thought to resolve these problems. One is to remove the power of the Senate to reject money Bills. The other is to allow the Governor-General to call a double dissolution upon rejection of a money Bill.

At the practical level it is worth noting that if Whitlam had seen the action of the Governor-General coming he could have rung the Queen in London and had her dismiss Kerr and install a lackey[104]. Whitlam was doubly out manoeuvred. Not only did he fail to anticipate the Governor-General withdrawing his commission to govern, but he then failed to end the sitting of Parliament so that the opposition leader Fraser had the Appropriation Bill resubmitted to the Senate, his party changed its vote and passed it and then his interim Government had supply to govern until the election. After his dismissal Gough Whitlam called the opposition leader, Malcolm Fraser, 'Kerr's cur'[105], but in the ensuing election the Fraser Government was swept into power with a substantial majority. The majority would say this vindicated the Governor-General's decision, although Whitlam supporters regard it as an unprincipled coup. This polarised opinions and the controversy continued in recent debates about Australia becoming a republic as it has made controversial what powers the Head of State, who replaces the Queen, should have to dismiss the government.

Separation of powers

Although the doctrine of separation of powers is important in the Constitution, the separation between executive and the legislative function in practice is not strict. Both rely on support in parliament and because government has a majority in parliament effectively Cabinet can ensure the exercise of both executive and legislative power.

---

[103] Ironically this is Remembrance Day, to remember at 11am the time when the guns fell silent on the Western front to end World War I.

[104] A follower of a leader who tries to seek the favours of the leader.

[105] An oral pun: the two words sound the same and a cur is a worthless mongrel dog.

Consistent with this practical mixing some legislative function can by exercised by the executive. In contrast there is a strict separation of judicial power.

Legislative powers may be exercised by the executive

There is a power in the executive to make subordinate legislation, called regulations[106], which have to lie[107] before Parliament which can disallow them. The judiciary have tolerated this[108]. The justification is that Parliament provides a delegation of the power to make regulations for defined purposes in the main legislation and can disallow any regulations that are made. An example of the type of matters that might be covered in regulations would be detail of office sizes and conditions made under an *Occupational Health and Safety Act* 1991 (Cth).

In the *Boilermakers' Case*[109] the Privy Council drew the distinction between this delegation or mixing of power, which can be tolerated, in contrast to judicial power that cannot be mixed:[110]

> "The delegation of legislative power by the legislature to any executive body does not mean that the legislature has abdicated a power constitutionally vested in it. For the executive body is at all times subject to the control of the legislature. On the other hand in the Federal system the absolute independence of the judiciary is the bulwark of the Constitution against encroachment whether by the legislature or the executive. To vest in the same body executive and judicial power is to remove a vital constitutional safeguard."

The separation of judicial power

The Australian Constitution has accepted the American notion that the separation of powers is subject to checks and balances and in particular that the judiciary are the final arbiter on constitutional issues and also can review the proper exercise of executive power through administrative law review. The concept of judicial review in Australia had its origins in the colonial constitutions. Here the judiciary not only had power to rule that legislation was not constitutional but it also could review legislation because it did not comply with superior Imperial legislation from the English Parliament acting as an Imperial Parliament over its Dominions. Some early colonial judges were so adventurous they suggested that legislation could be reviewed as contravening common law principles but this was over ruled by the *Colonial Laws Validity Act* 1865 (Imp). Under the Federal Constitution the High Court is the arbiter of the division between the power of the Federal Government and the residual power of State Governments. This role of review is different from that in America, where the

---

106 Subordinate legislation as to detail authorised by an Act of Parliament.

107 To place before.

108 In *Victorian Stevedoring and General Contracting Co Pty Ltd v Dingin* (1931-32) 46 CLR 73 the Court permitted the executive to enact subordinate legislation as long as it remained under Parliamentary control.

109 *AG(Cth) v R* (1956-7) 95 CLR 529.

110 Ibid. pp. 540-541.

Supreme Court also has the Bill of Rights, which can be used to strike down legislative and administrative acts.

The High Court has jealously guarded the separation of judicial power. The first hint of this came in the *Wheat Case*[111]. Section 101 of the Constitution required an interstate commission entrusted with "such powers of adjudication and administration as the Parliament deems necessary" to deal with trade and commerce issues. This led to the establishment of the interstate commission. The High Court held that many of its powers were of a judicial nature and as such were invalid because it was not a court that complied with Chapter III of the Constitution, which has special provisions for the establishment of courts that must be complied with[112]. The Court drew a distinction between adjudication, authorised under section 101 and judicial power, which is discussed in Chapter 7.

The same strict approach was taken to the Commonwealth Court of Conciliation & Arbitration established under s. 51 (xxxv) of the Constitution. This court was constituted of a judge who also served as a High Court judge. The judge held tenure in the Conciliation Court for seven years. The Waterside Workers Federation alleged a breach of award[113] by an employer. On an appeal to the High Court it was held that the president's seven-year term was incompatible with section 72 of the Constitution, which at that time gave life tenure to judges[114]. The arbitration function of the Court was held to be valid, but its enforcement powers were not[115]. In response to this decision the enforcement powers of the commission were conferred on a state court. Later the Conciliation & Arbitration Court was re-established and staffed by judges holding office for life. This did not solve the problem. There was still a mixture of judicial power & arbitration, which is not a judicial power. A Chapter III court cannot have non judicial functions and judicial power cannot be given to anything other than a Chapter III court.

This was made clear in 1956 in the *Boilermakers Case* where an employer organisation tried to enforce a no bans clause[116] in an award. The arbitration court fined the union for contempt[117] of court. The High Court held that the fine was unenforceable[118].

> "... in a Federal form of government a part is necessarily assigned to the judicature which places it in the position unknown in a unitary system or under a flexible Constitution where the Parliament is supreme. A Federal Constitution must be rigid. The government it establishes must be one of defined powers; within those powers it must be paramount, but it must be incompetent to go beyond them. It is beyond the competence of the Parliament to invest with any

---

111 *NSW v Commonwealth (Wheat Case)* (1915) 20 CLR 54.

112 Ibid.

113 A fixing of minimum wages and conditions for a class of workers.

114 Now until age 70 years of age.

115 *The Waterside Workers' Federation of Australia v JW Alexander Ltd* (1918) 25 CLR 434.

116 A requirement in an award for workers that prevents the union from putting bans on any type of work or overtime.

117 Disrespect for a court that can be punished with a fine or imprisonment.

118 *R v Kirby: Ex parte Boilermakers' Society of Australia* (1956) 94 CLR 254, at p.267.

part of the judicial power any body or person except a court created pursuant to section 71 and constituted in accordance with section 72 or a court brought into existence by a state. It is a proposition that has been repeatedly affirmed and acted upon by this Court …"

This case was upheld by the Privy Council, which was quoted above.

This strict separation of judicial power does not apply to State constitutions, but because the Commonwealth Constitution anticipates conferral of federal jurisdiction on State Supreme Courts[119], the States are obliged to maintain a Supreme Court that has integrity, independence and impartiality so that it is fit to exercise federal jurisdiction[120]. A consequence from the strict separation of judicial power is the need to define what is an exercise of judicial power. This is discussed in Chapter 7.

Free trade between the States - Section 92

A central plank of the constitutional arrangement was that there would be free trade between the States. Section 92 provides that "trade, commerce and intercourse among the states shall be absolutely free." Of course what may be free for one purpose may be a restriction for another purpose. The High Court has held that 'absolutely free' requires a balance that permits States to protect local conditions but not in a way that discriminates against commerce from interstate. After many tests in many cases, some of which were irreconcilable in principle, the current test was enunciated in *Cole v Whitfield*[121], a case about crayfish[122]. These were once so abundant that during the gold rush days of the 1850s there was a regulation making it illegal to feed crayfish to domestic workers more than 5 days a week. These days they are an expensive luxury mostly exported to Asia.

This case concerned the *Sea Fisheries Regulations* 1962 (Tas) made under the *Fisheries Act* 1959 (Tas). These set the minimum carapace[123] length of a crayfish that are permitted to be caught or sold in Tasmania at a larger size than for South Australia. It is believed that crayfish mature and breed earlier in warmer waters in South Australia so that fish stocks can be preserved with smaller and younger fish stock. David Whitfield had 97 crayfish in Tasmania he said were imported from South Australia. They were a legal catch in South Australia but under the legal size in Tasmania. When prosecuted for having undersize crayfish he sought to impugn the regulation as invalid under s.92 of the Constitution. In this case the High Court overturned 86 years of its prior approach to s.92.

---

119 s. 73.

120 *Kable v DPP (NSW)* (1996) 189 CLR 51. Note the DPP is the Director of Public Prosecutions, the officer in charge of prosecuting services for the government.

121 (1988) 165 CLR 360.

122 A large edible saltwater lobster, without claws, which are common in Australian waters.

123 The body shell.

The Court said this:[124]

> "No provision of the constitution has been the source of greater judicial concern or the subject of greater judicial effort than s.92. That notwithstanding, judicial exegesis[125] of the section has yielded neither clarity nor meaning or certainty of operation. Over the years the Court has moved uneasily between one interpretation and another in its endeavours to solve the problems thrown up by the necessity to apply the very general language of this section to a wide variety of legislative and factual situations. Indeed these shifts have been such as to make it difficult to speak of the section as having achieved a settled or accepted interpretation at any time since Federation."

The Court then embarked on a fresh interpretation of the section.

The Court held that the Tasmanian law did not discriminate between crayfish from any State. It applied equally to crayfish regardless of their State of origin. It did not infringe s.92. The basis of the decision was that the regulations did not 'discriminate in a protectionist sense'. The Court also noted the impossibility of distinguishing Tasmanian crayfish from South Australian crayfish, which gave a practical imperative to uphold the law. The Court said this:[126]

> "If (a State law) applies to all trade and commerce, interstate and intrastate alike, it is less likely to be protectionist than if there is discrimination appearing on the face of the law, but where the law in effect, if not in form, discriminates in favour of intrastate trade, it will nevertheless offend against s.92 if the discrimination is of a protectionist character. A law which has as its real object the prescription of a standard for a product or a service or a norm of commercial conduct will not ordinarily be grounded in protectionism and will not be prohibited by s.92. But if a law which may be otherwise justified by reference to an object which is not protectionist, discriminates against interstate trade or commerce in pursuit of that object in a way or to an extent which warrants characterisation of the law as protectionist, a court will be justified in concluding that it nonetheless offends s.92."

Although this is accepted as the key statement in the judgment, it is in later cases that the new doctrine was expanded and explained. *Cole v Whitfield* was a unanimous decision but the judges did not hold their unanimity later in the same year in the case of *Barth v Alston Holdings Pty Ltd*[127]. In this case the Victorian Government were seeking to impose a substantial fee on the sale of tobacco, as a licence fee on wholesalers and retailers[128]. Where a Victorian wholesaler of tobacco products had already paid the fee, if the tobacco products were sold to a Victorian retailer the fee

---

124 Ibid. p. 383.
125 An obscure word meaning explanation.
126 Ibid. p. 408.
127 (1988) 165 CLR 411.
128 The State government could not impose it as a tax which would have been an excise which can only be imposed by the Commonwealth under section 90 of the Constitution.

was not payable again. This had the effect that when Alston bought tobacco products from outside Victoria it paid the fee but it did not on product bought in Victoria. The majority held that it was discriminatory to impose a higher tax on imported goods to neutralise a wholesaling impost on locally produced goods.

The next clarification of the test arose over the important issue of beer. In 1975 in South Australia a small refundable deposit was introduced on all beverage containers except refillable beer bottles. This favoured local beer suppliers who sold their beer in refillable bottles. Time passed and this was not contested because the benefit was small. However, in 1986 the South Australian government sought to increase the deposit for non-refillable containers to 15 cents with a 4 cents deposit on refillable bottles creating now a differential of 11 cents. The majority held that s.92 was infringed because it gave the local brewers a competitive or market advantage, which amounted to discriminatory protectionism.

Protectionism that is saved from the operation of s.92 must be for an appropriate and non-protectionist object and the impact on interstate trade must be incidental and not disproportionate to the non-protectionist object[129]. In understanding this case it is important to note that the agreed facts were that the different deposits would have resulted in the same rate of return to recycling depots of refillable and non-refillable bottles. It followed that the differential deposit had no effect on return rates, the non protectionist objective, and it was discriminatory against interstate trade.

Another case involving beer arose in *Barley Marketing Board (NSW) v. Norman*[130]. New South Wales barley growers were prevented from selling their barley direct to a Victorian maltster, but had to sell it through the marketing board. The previous interpretation of s.92 before *Cole v. Whitfield* would have prohibited this scheme. However, under the new test the Court found[131] it was not discrimination in a protectionist sense because the Victorian maltsters were treated equally to New South Wales and other maltsters. They could buy New South Wales barley from the board equally to New South Wales maltsters. The scheme was intended to ensure a better overall return for New South Wales growers and did not do so by discriminating against interstate maltsters in the process.

From the cases it emerges that[132]:

> "The essence of the idea is the conferring of a local economic advantage through discriminatory treatment of interstate trade. The discriminatory protectionism will more likely come about through the disparate impact of a law upon interstate trade than be evident from the terms of the law. Difficulties may be expected in areas such as price fixing and product standards. ... (I)f the law leaves undisturbed the relative competitive positions of interstate and intrastate trade as

---

129 Michael Coper, "s.92 of the Australian Constitution since Cole v. Whitfield" Chapter 5 in Lee & Winterton *Australian Constitutional Prospectus* Law Book Co. Sydney 1992 at pp 467-468.

130 (1990) 171 CLR 182.

131 The decision of a court, viz: "the High Court *found*". *Held* is used in the same way.

132 Coper s.92 op.cit. p.138.

determined by factors such as geography then it should not be regarded as discriminatory in a protectionist sense."

What is clear from this is that a simple general principle is unlikely to emerge. Each case will depend upon a balance of the purpose of the legislation and its sometimes incidental effect on restricting interstate trade.

Chapter 3:

RESTRAINTS ON ABUSE OF POWER

Rule by the majority can be tyranny and to protect against abuses of power many constitutional arrangements guarantee basic rights as in the Bill of Rights in the USA. There is no Bill of Rights under the Australian Constitution, although there are some protections such as freedom of religion and protection of property from compulsory acquisition. The main protection of rights in Australia lies with the common law. In Australia an appeal lies from all the State courts to the High Court of Australia with a unified common law applying throughout the country. This contrasts to America where the common law resides in the States. Collateral consequences in America are some difficulties of notional legal differences between the common law in different States[133]. In contrast in Australia the common law inherited from England was the foundation law of the colonies and although it was subject to idiosyncratic decisions in each colony notionally it was pervasive in one form in all of them. Appeals from the colonies to the Privy Council in England, and after federation, the High Court, provided cohesion. There is one common law throughout Australia, not different versions in each State. At a practical level, an example of the difference to the USA is that the High Court in Australia has used the common law to prevent double jeopardy[134] for criminal offences under Commonwealth Law and State Law. A citizen cannot be tried twice for the same substantive crime even if one offence is against State and one against Commonwealth law. However, in America people can be separately tried for the same offence under State and Federal Law[135]. A well known case involved Los Angeles Police caught on video beating Rodney King after a high speed car chase. A State jury acquitted the police in April 1992 resulting in wide spread rioting. Federal charges of violating King's civil rights in relation to the same incident resulted in conviction of the police in April 1993[136]. Another example was the conviction of preacher Ray Killen in Mississippi in 2005 under State law for manslaughter for Ku Klux Klan murders committed in 1964 for which a jury had failed to convict him on similar Federal charges[137].

An eminent Australian Chief Justice, Sir Owen Dixon CJ discussed the fundamental importance of common law: [138]

> "At the bottom it is because of this fact that in the working of our Australian system of government we are able to avail ourselves of the common law as a jurisprudence antecedently existing into which our system came and in which it

---

[133] *Erie Railroad Co v Tompkins* (1938) 304 US 64.

[134] Being prosecuted twice for the same criminal offence.

[135] *US v Lanza* (1922) 260 US 37.

[136] Famous trials home page: http:// www.law.umkc.edu/faculty/project/ftrials/lapd/lapd.html

[137] This is strictly not an example of double jeopardy as at the first trial one juror only refused to convict because she could not convict a preacher. A jury that cannot reach a verdict is known as a hung jury and it does not count as an acquittal so the case can be retried.

[138] Owen Dixon *Jesting Pilate* (1965) Law Book Company Ltd, Sydney, at p.204:

operates. When a Judge of the High Court of Australia sits exercising the original jurisdiction of his Court[139] in a matter between residents of different States, his attitude to the substantive law, indeed, to the law of evidence[140] is very different to that of the Judge of a District Court in the United States. …

The Australian Judge knows that he must give effect to the relevant statutory law of the appropriate State. If he is in doubt, which is the appropriate State he turns for the purpose of resolving his doubts to that part of the common law called private international law[141]. But, if there be no statutory law in the case, or subject to such statutory provisions as are material[142], he proceeds to administer the common law as an entire system. He ascertains its contents as best he may among the judicial decisions to which he may turn. Those of the State whose law he finds that he must apply will have no higher authority than the decisions of any other State and the authority of the decisions will be persuasive only and not imperative. In the protest, famous in America, which Justice Holmes made against the view that the Federal Courts in his country might proceed in this way, he wrote:[143]

> 'Books written about any branch of the common law treat it as a unit, cite cases from this Court, from the Circuit Courts of Appeal, from the State Courts, from England and the colonies of England indiscriminately, and criticise them as right or wrong according to the writer's notions of a single theory. It is very hard to resist the impression that there is one august *corpus*, to understand which clearly is the only task of any court concerned.'

An Australian Judge is not bound to resist this impression. He may have other notions but at least he may declare the common law, *nullius addictus iurare in verba magistri.*"

Common Law proudly proclaims *Magna Carta*[144] as a statement of basic human rights and notions of natural law, which led to basic rights recognized in common law of personal liberty, property and protection of the person. The High Court has built on this notion of the common law as a protector of individual rights against the State to enhance the few rights guaranteed in the Constitution.

---

139 They were all male then.

140 Information that can be admitted at a trial to prove a fact in issue. In the common law the rules of evidence emphasise oral evidence, having grown up around the jury trial method, and are very complicated.

141 An area of law that resolves which law applies between competing laws, eg if a contract made in one State for the export of goods is breached in another State which has different contract law. Described by Kirby J as 'a swamp'.

142 Relevant.

143 *Black and White Taxi cab and Transfer Co v Brown and Yellow Taxi Cab and Transfer Co* (1927) 276 US 518 p.533.

144 In fact *Magna Carta* was a pact between the English King and his feudal nobles to protect the nobles against regal excess. It has nothing to do with the ideas of general personal liberties of the citizen, nor the democratic legitimacy of Governments today. The general citizens were serfs.

In *Street v QLD Bar Association*[145] Deane J had this to say about rights in the Constitution:

> "It is often said that the Australian Constitution contains no Bill of Rights. Statements to that effect, while literally true, are superficial and potentially misleading. The Constitution contains a significant number of express or implied guarantees of rights and immunities. The most important of them is the guarantee that the citizen can be subject to the exercise of Commonwealth judicial power only by 'courts' designated by Chapter III (s.71). Others include: the guarantee that the trial on indictment[146] of any offence against any law, shall be by jury[147] (s.80); guarantees against discrimination between persons in different parts of the country in relation to Customs and excise duties, and other, taxes and bounties (ss 51 (ii), (iii), 86, 88 and 90); the guarantee of freedom of interstate trade, commerce and intercourse (s. 92); the guarantee of direct suffrage and of the equality of voting rights among those qualified to vote (ss24, 25); the guarantee of the free exercise of religion (S116); and the guarantee against being subject to inconsistent demands by contemporaneously valid laws (ss 109 and 118). All these guarantees of rights or immunities are of fundamental importance in that they serve the function of advancing or protecting the liberty, the dignity or the quality of the citizen under the Constitution."

However, some of these rights are quite circumscribed. For example the right to trial by jury provided by s. 80 depends on the offence being commenced by a procedure known as an indictment.

> *" 80 Trial by jury*
> The trial on indictment of any offence against any law of the Commonwealth shall be by jury ..."

Parliament can circumvent this by allowing the offence to be charged on a complaint[148], as most are and then it is triable by a judge alone in lower courts. The High Court has not prevented this although one strand[149] of judgments says that any 'serious' offence must be commenced on indictment. Deane J in *Kingswell v The Queen*[150] said that any offence with had a maximum penalty of twelve months or more should be prosecuted on an indictment. Kirby J (in a minority judgment) approved this in *White v Director of Military Prosecutions* in these strong terms[151]:

> "However, a persistent minority has rejected this view as inconsistent with the function of s. 80 as providing a guarantee of jury trial which could not so easily be circumvented. With respect, I favour what is presently the minority view. It is

---

145 (1989) 168 CLR 461 at pp.521-2.

146 The written statement of charges for serious criminal matters (known as indictable offences). Lesser charges (known as summary offences) are commenced on a complaint.

147 A group of lay people, usually twelve in number who decide a case.

148 A process to start a criminal prosecution in a lower court.

149 A thread of argument or a line of cases.

150 (1985) 159 CLR 264.

151 HCA (2007) 29 delivered 19th June 2007 at para 167, http://www.austlii.edu.au.

> more harmonious with the language, constitutional context, purpose and function of the section. The contrary view renders trial by jury for the applicable federal offences optional in the hands of the very governmental agencies against whom jury trials can be a precious protection for the individual. That cannot be the meaning of the Constitution. When Australian judges and lawyers become more accustomed to reasoning by reference to fundamental rights, they will see the truth of this proposition more clearly."

The guarantee of freedom of religion is likewise circumscribed.

Freedom of religion

Freedom of religion is guaranteed by s. 116 of the Constitution:

> *"116 Commonwealth not to legislate in respect of religion*
> The Commonwealth shall not make any law for establishing[152] any religion, or for imposing any religious observance, or for prohibiting the free exercise of any religion, and no religious test shall be required as a qualification for any office or public trust under the Commonwealth."

This has been given a narrow interpretation. Not long after federation Mr Krygger refused to undertake compulsory military training because he said it was against his religion. The High Court held that the *Defence Act* 1903 (Cth) which required him to undertake the training did not offend section 116 of the Constitution[153]:

> "It may be that the law requiring a man to do an act which his religion forbids would be objectionable on moral grounds, but does not come within the prohibition of section 116 ..."

During the Second World War the government formed an adverse view of the Jehovah's Witness Church due to its opposition to the war and the refusal of its members to swear an oath of allegiance to the King, rather recognising only the authority of God. Under the authority of the *National Security (Subversive Associations) Regulations* the Governor-General dissolved the Adelaide Company of Jehovah's Witnesses Incorporated and took possession of its meeting hall. The Jehovah's Witnesses complained to the Court[154], relying on s.116. The High Court found that the regulations did not offend s.116. Chief Justice Latham found that a corporation couldn't exercise religion, only individuals so the corporation was not protected. The Court did find that the regulations permitting the seizing of property were not linked to the purpose of protection against subversive organisations so they were beyond the defence power. This protection of property even in wartime is consistent with a strong approach to protecting property rights in peace time, as

---

[152] Establish, to: in normal use to set up but it has a particular meaning of the adoption by the State of a religion in preference to others.

[153] *Krygger v Williams* (1912) 15 CLR 336, at p. 369.

[154] *Adelaide Company of Jehovah's Witnesses Inc. v the Commonwealth* (1943) 67 CLR 116.

exemplified by the Bank Nationalisation Case mentioned below, but in contrast the Court has taken at times a narrow view of protecting religious freedom under s.116.

Consistent with this the High Court has taken a tolerant view of government funding of religious schools. In Australia there is a strong private school system, much of it run by churches. In 1981 by majority of 6:1 the Court held that government funding of church schools did not amount to the establishment of religion[155]. The minority Justice, Murphy J, of whom we shall hear more later, relied heavily on the United States Supreme Court decisions taking restrictive view of attempts to establish religion when interpreting the first Amendment. The majority of five judges held those cases not to be relevant because the US Constitution says, "Congress shall make no law *respecting* the establishment of religion" compared to the Australian provision which says, "the Commonwealth shall not make any law for *establishing* any religion" (author's emphasis). Murphy described this distinction as:[156] "hairsplitting, and not consistent with the broad approach that should be taken to constitutional guarantees of freedom." It will be interesting to see if this view holds for schools proselytising a fundamentalist religious view.

Acquisition of property on just terms (s.51(xxxi))

The Court has taken a strict view in protecting property rights. In World War II taking of possession of land for an indefinite period was held to be an acquisition of the land, and contrary to the expansive attitude given to the defence power in other cases[157] it was not used to over ride the protection built into this head of power[158]. In peace time the Court would not support an attempt by a Labor government to nationalise the banks, despite the power to make laws with respect to banking (s.51(xiii)) and financial corporations (s.51(xx)[159]). In the *Bank of NSW v Commonwealth* (the *Bank Nationalisation case*) the Court held that a power by government to appoint directors to the board of a private bank instead of those elected by the shareholders amounted to acquisition of property and it was not permitted, as the terms were not just. This finding was made even though the legislation gave access to an independent tribunal to fix the compensation[160].

An implied Bill of Rights

After a long period of conservative government, in 1972 a Labor government, headed by Prime Minister Gough Whitlam came to power and some more radical judges were appointed to the High Court, and more under a later Labor Government in the 1980s. A more adventurous court for a while flirted with the idea of establishing rights by common law. They later drew back from this judicial adventure but found other ways

---

155 *AG Vic; Ex rel Black v Commonwealth* (1981) 148 CLR 559.

156 bid. p. 632.

157 See *The Jehovah's Witnesses* above and Chapter 6.

158 *Minister of State for the Army v Dalziel* (1944) 68 CLR 26.

159 The corporations power. This has now been given such a wide interpretation as to threaten the federal nature of the Constitution: see Chapter 6.

160 *Bank of NSW v Commonwealth* (1948) 76 CLR 1 per Dixon at p. 349 Chapter 5 under the heading Characterisation..

to protect the important rights. This flood and ebb of judicial activism can be best seen in the way the Court has protected the right of free speech in political matters.

An implied freedom of political communication

A national paper, *The Australian*, was prosecuted under the *Industrial Relations Act* 1988 (Cth), which prohibited articles bringing the commission into disrepute. The article referred to:

> "a vast bureaucracy in the Ministry of Labour and enforced by a corrupt and compliant 'judiciary' in the official Soviet style Arbitration Commission."

Four judges held that even if the prohibition was within power it was invalid as infringing an implied guarantee of freedom of political discussion[161].

> "To sustain a representative democracy embodying the principles prescribed by Constitution, freedom of public discussion of political and economic matters is essential: it would be a parody of democracy to confer on the people power to choose their Parliament but to deny the freedom of public discussion from which the people derive their political judgments."

This case was reinforced when the High Court struck down legislation that banned political advertisements on radio or television in the last three days leading up to an election and established a scheme that restricting the way in which the advertisements could be constructed. The legislation seemed to be within the constitutional power dealing with elections. Five judges implied a guarantee of freedom of political discussion into the common law and struck the legislation down as infringing the guarantee: [162]

> "Only by exercising (freedom of communication) can the citizen communicate his or her views on the wide range of matters that may call for, or are relevant to, political action or decision. Only by exercising that freedom can the citizen criticise government decisions and actions, seek to bring about change, call for action where none has been taken and in this way influence the elected representatives. By these means the elected representatives are equipped to discharge their role so that they may take account of and respond to the will of the people. … Absent such a freedom of communication, representative government would fail to achieve its purpose, namely, government by the people through their elected representatives; government would cease to be responsive to the needs and wishes of the people and, in that sense, would cease to be truly representative.

---

161 *Nationwide News Pty Ltd v Wills* (1992) 177 CLR at p. 44 (Brennan, Deane, Toohey and Gaudron JJ).

162 *Australian Capital Television Pty Ltd v Commonwealth* (1992) 177 CLR 106 per Mason CJ p. 138.

… and the Court must scrutinise with scrupulous care restrictions affecting free communication in the conduct of elections for political office for it is in that area that the guarantee fulfils its primary purpose."[163]

It is important to understand that there is no wording in the Constitution to support this implied right. It was constructed as an invention of the common law. There is much resistance in Australia to a Bill of Rights so for the High Court to imply one was controversial.

This led to a series of cases involving defamation[164] law. In Australia defamation law provides large awards of damages for loss of reputation caused by defamatory speech (slander) or written words (libel). This is the litigation of the rich and so it is very complicated[165]. It is the nature of politicians' work that they are often defamed. Suing for defamation has been a lucrative pastime for many politicians. The High Court turned this around in the case *Theophanous v Herald and Weekly Times Ltd*[166] and later in *Lange v Australian Broadcasting Commission*[167]. Here politicians lost defamation cases on the new principle of the implied right of freedom of political discourse, but in the latter the basis of the defence moved to a less controversial basis than the implied Bill of Rights. In *Lange* the High Court expanded an existing defence to defamation, known as qualified privilege, to achieve its objective of protecting political comment, but without the controversial approach of implying a Bill of Rights.

In 1999 the I had a case involving a political figure who was spokesperson for a party known as National Action. The party is against immigration, puts out a great deal of racist propaganda, and perpetrates the Auschwitz Lie: they deny the Holocaust. In that case I found that the plaintiff had been defamed but I awarded him no damages. For my purpose I had to look at the *Theophanous* and *Lange* to understand and apply the changing views of the High Court. At this point in time the High Court was stepping back from the notion of implied rights in the Constitution but had now arrived at a similar result by expanding any other defence to defamation known as the defence of qualified privilege[168]. This defence is normally limited to occasions of appropriate private discussion such as when employees discuss one of their colleague's performance for promotion purposes. Forgive me the arrogance of quoting my own judgment but it is a useful example of how a judge at first instance[169] refers to and uses the case law[170] from higher courts.

---

163 Ibid. p.143.

164 A right to recover damages for harm to character caused by published unfair statements. If the publication is oral it is called slander. If the words are written it is called libel.

165 The complexity of the common law tends to expand to utilise the budget available: see Cost Shifting Policies in Chapter 7.

166 (1994) 182 CLR 104.

167 (1997) 189 CLR 520.

168 A defence to an action in defamation available for statements published to a small group to serve a legitimate purpose of the group, e.g. commenting to a selection panel about an employee's suitability for promotion. The defence is lost if the statement can be shown to have been made with malice.

169 The first trial in a case, in Australia generally the facts are decided at the first level and the appeal is only as to procedural faults and the law.

170 Legal principles established from cases under the common law method.

"The present position is that the defence of qualified privilege which previously depended upon a narrow circumstance of reciprocity has now been expanded in circumstances of political discussion to be available to the defendant in this case notwithstanding no reciprocity, in the narrow common law sense, with its readers. There are limitations. Political discussion is not an open season for defamation. I note the recent authority of *Lange v Australian Broadcasting Commission* (1997) 145 ALR 96, or (1997) 189 CLR 520. I have for my convenience used the ALR report. At page 113 the Full Court of the High Court said this:

> 'The purpose of the law of defamation is to strike a balance between the right to reputation and freedom of speech. ... The protection of the reputations of those who take part in the government of political life of this country from false and defamatory statements is conducive to the public good. The constitutionally prescribed system of government does not require - to the contrary it would be adversely affected by - an unqualified freedom to publish defamatory matter damaging the reputations of individuals involved in government or politics.'
> (Their Honours' footnote references from *Theophanous* (1994) 182 CLR 104 which I have not individually set out in this quote).

At page 116 their Honours say:

> 'Similarly discussion of government or politics at State or Territory level and even at local government level is amenable to protection by the extended category of qualified privilege, whether or not it bears on matters at the federal level ... The real question is as to the conditions upon which this extended category of common law qualified privilege should depend.'

I assume that the approach in *Lange* at page 117 should in general terms be applied to this case. That is:

> ' ... reasonableness of conduct seems the appropriate criterion to apply when the occasion of the publication of defamatory matter is said to be an occasion of qualified privilege solely by reason of the relevance of the matter published to the discussion of government or political matters. ... The defendant must establish that its conduct in making the publication was reasonable in all the circumstances of the case. In all but exceptional cases the proof of reasonableness will fail as a matter of fact unless the publisher establishes that it was not aware of the falsity of the matter and did not act recklessly in making the publication. ... Having regard to the interest of the members of the Australian community have in receiving information on government and political matters that affect them the reputations of those defamed by widespread publications will be adequately protected by requiring the publisher to prove reasonableness of conduct. The protection of those reputations will be further enhanced by the requirement that the defence will be defeated if the person defamed

proves that the publication was actuated by common law malice[171] to the extent that the elements of malice are not covered under the rubric of reasonableness. In the context of the extended defence of qualified privilege and its application to communications with respect to political matters, 'actuated by malice' is to be understood as signifying a publication made not for the purpose of communicating government or political information or ideas but for some improper purpose.'

Their Honours go on to suggest that as a general rule the publisher should take reasonable steps to verify the accuracy of material prior to publication and give the person defamed an opportunity to respond.

This is one of those cases that test the boundaries of established principles. There is some change in language in the development of these cases from political discussion to discussion of government and political matters. Nothing can hang[172] on that. In this case Mr Brander is clearly in the political arena. My factual findings establish that he has stood for positions in Parliament and was standing for local government[173] office at the time of the article about which he complains. The very activity of himself and Australian National Action in pursuing his and its agenda[174] in the immigration debate is political discussion and is the discussion of a government and of a political matter. What is at issue here is the expanded defence of qualified privilege striking the proper balance between right to reputation and freedom of speech. If the test of the defendant's access to qualified privilege is reasonableness then the fact that Mr Brander and Australian National Action have pursued their objectives by the incitement of racial hatred and the use of Nazi symbolism, aggression and threats to intimidate those who oppose them, must go on one side of the scales of reasonableness. They balance the defamatory imputations of Mr Brander being childish, not to be taken seriously and the calculated separation of him in physical and other attributes from the male macho aggressive elements typical of Australian National Action. I weigh those factors and say the article was reasonable and comes under the expanded umbrella of qualified privilege which is available for political discussion.

Fair comment

The plaintiff and his associates in Australian National Action are racists in the worst sense. They are willing to pursue their objectives by the incitement of racial hatred and the use of Nazi symbolism, aggression and threats to intimidate those who oppose them. SG Tallentyre's oft quoted 1906 paraphrase from Voltaire 'I disapprove of what you say, but I will defend to the death your right to say it' has been called into play during this case. Nothing in my decision

---

171 In defamation a deliberate intention to harm someone's reputation that invalidates the defence of qualified privilege.

172 Follow from, as in "nothing hangs on that proposition".

173 The lowest level of government for the town or suburb of a city. Also known as the local council or municipal council.

174 Program, often used to describe the outline of issues to be discussed at a meeting.

> deprives Mr Brander and Australian National Action of the right to pursue their views on the immigration debate. However the need for boundaries to freedom of speech was well expressed by Oliver Wendell Holmes Jr. In *Schenk v United States* 249 U.S. 47(1919): 'The most stringent protection of free speech would not protect a man in falsely shouting 'fire' in a theatre and causing a panic. ... The question in every case is whether the words are used in such circumstances and are of such nature as to create a clear and present danger that they will bring about the substantial evils that Congress has a right to prevent.'
>
> In the context of the plaintiff and Australian National Action exploiting instincts of tribalism by inciting racial hatred, using Nazi symbolism, aggression and threats to intimidate those who oppose them it is my finding that this robust lampooning and satirical article is fair comment. In a democratic, tolerant society such as ours to deprive opponents of people who use tactics like Mr Brander of the right to mount the word attack in this article is to put at risk the very fabric of society.

This case went on appeal to a single judge in our Supreme Court and then to the Full Court of our Supreme Court[175]. Then went on appeal to the High Court and was withdrawn as having no chance of success. This was a pity in a way because the case had many aspects which would have given the High Court is a chance to expand their view of the law.

Later they had a further chance to comment on this area in a case that arose from a political pamphlet defaming a candidate by falsely implying he had abused travel rights by spending too much time overseas. Now the Court has settled on the common law defence of qualified privilege as its method to defend free speech in political matters this case demonstrates how they qualify and define this new area of law. This is a good example of the development of law by the common law method.

The present Chief Justice of the High Court, Gleeson CJ said this:[176]

> "One difference between what was described in *Lange* as the extended category of qualified privilege, and the pre-existing category of common law privilege, is that a requirement of reasonableness of conduct applies to the former, but not to the latter. Because of the way in which the present proceedings were conducted, it will be necessary to return to the subject of malice in relation to the pre-existing category. Neither irrationality, nor prejudice, constitute or establish malice. In *Lange*, it was said that the interest that members of the Australian community have in receiving information on government and political matters would be met sufficiently, in the case of widespread publication which would have failed to attract a common law defence of qualified privilege, by requiring the publisher to prove reasonableness of conduct. In the case of this 'extended defence of qualified privilege in its application to communications with respect

---

175 The court structure in Australia is discussed in Chapter 7.

176 *Roberts v Bass* (2002) 212 CLR 1.

to political matters' the defence would also be defeated if the person defamed proves that the publication was actuated by common law malice.

12 At the same time, a motive of injuring a candidate's prospects of election by damaging his or her reputation is not a defence. It would be wrong to think that, because such a motive does not constitute malice, it negates malice. If it were so, electoral contests would for practical purposes constitute a defamation-free zone. The privilege would be virtually absolute, not qualified. And 'the extended defence of qualified privilege' recognised in *Lange*, which was held to conform to the requirements of the Australian Constitution, would be but a pale reflection of the common law defence. The freedom of political speech inherent in the Constitution's concept of representative democracy would be much more limited than the freedom given by the common law in relation to the distribution of material to thousands of voters in an electorate. …

18 The trial judge described the 'Free Travel Times Pamphlet' as 'an inflammatory document which clearly reflected on the integrity of the plaintiff ... and contained [a] forged purported copy of his Frequent Flyer Activity Statement'. As to the frontispiece, he said the reasonable and ordinary reader would take it that the respondent had been on holiday in Nauru at government expense and was the most travelled parliamentarian for the year and that, rather than attending to his electoral duties, he was content to lie in the sun in Nauru eating and drinking. The second page contained the forged mock-up of a frequent flyer points statement. The respondent had never been involved in a frequent flyer programme. As to the third page, it was held that the ordinary and reasonable reader would take it to mean that the respondent, in an underhanded way, had used his position as a Member of Parliament to accrue frequent flyer points for his own use and for the use of members of his family. The final page portrayed the respondent as among the politicians who had blatantly misused parliamentary entitlements. …

21 The trial judge found that the respondent was a man of the utmost integrity; that he adopted a highly ethical approach to his parliamentary activities; that he had not misused his travel or other entitlements; that his attendance at the Nauru conference was for parliamentary purposes; that there was no basis for any criticism of his travel; that he was not a member of any frequent flyer scheme; and that his conduct in relation to the Modbury Hospital and firearms control provided no basis for criticism. He decided that Roberts had no defence having acted with malice and that Case had a defence having acted reasonably. Case was just handing out pamphlets at a polling booth. …

64 In *Lange*, the Court unanimously held that freedom of communication on matters of government and politics is an indispensable incident of the system of representative government created by the Constitution. The Court emphasised that 'communications concerning political or government matters between the electors and the elected representatives, between the electors and the candidates for election and between the electors themselves were central to the system of

representative government, as it was understood at federation.' Hence, this litigation is concerned with matters at the heart of the constitutional freedom of communication respecting political or government matters. …

68 Three points in particular should be noted concerning the development of the defence of qualified privilege in *Lange*. First, in extending the law of qualified privilege to protect publications concerning governmental and political matters to mass audiences, the Court imposed as a condition of the extended privilege that the publisher's conduct be reasonable. But the Court emphasised:

'reasonableness of conduct is imported as an element only when the extended category of qualified privilege is invoked to protect a publication that would otherwise be held to have been made to too wide an audience. For example, reasonableness of conduct is not an element of that qualified privilege which protects a member of the public who makes a complaint to a Minister concerning the administration of his or her department. Reasonableness of conduct is an element for the judge to consider only when a publication concerning a government or political matter is made in circumstances that, under the English common law, would have failed to attract a defence of qualified privilege.'

Second, in *Lange*, the Court held that, having regard to the subject matters of government and politics, the motive of causing political damage to the plaintiff or his or her party is not an improper motive that would destroy a defence of qualified privilege. The Court also held that the vigour of an attack or the pungency of a defamatory statement concerning such matters cannot, without more, discharge the plaintiff's onus on the issue of malice. Third, in some respects the Court's development of the law of qualified privilege extended beyond what was required for conformity with the constitutional norm. …

74 Roberts and Case, if held to their cases in the Full Court, will retain the advantage of a finding of qualified privilege. And they are entitled to rely on the impact that the constitutional freedom of communication has on the law of malice in respect of publications concerning political matters that are protected by conventional qualified privilege. As we have pointed out, intentionally causing political damage to the plaintiff or his or her party is not an improper motive where a statement on political matters is protected by conventional qualified privilege. Nor can the vigour of an attack or the pungency of a defamatory statement, without more, be evidence of improper motive in respect of such a statement. …

83 In our opinion, neither lack of honest belief nor knowledge of falsity *ipso facto* destroys a defence of qualified privilege. But knowledge of falsity is 'almost conclusive evidence' of improper motive, except where the defendant is under a legal duty to publish the defamation. …

103 Carelessness of expression or carelessness in making a defamatory statement never provides a ground for inferring malice. The law of qualified

privilege requires the defendant to use the occasion honestly in the sense of using it for a proper purpose; but it imposes no requirement that the defendant use the occasion carefully. Even irrationality, stupidity or refusal to face facts concerning the plaintiff is not conclusive proof of malice although in 'an extreme' case it may be evidence of it. And mere failure to make inquiries or apologise or correct the untruth when discovered is not evidence of malice. …

110 When the law concerning malice is properly understood, no basis exists for finding that Roberts published the defamatory material in the Nauru postcard or the Orange pamphlet without 'considering or caring whether it be true or not'. None of the matters referred to by counsel for Bass come close to establishing recklessness in the sense of wilful blindness. They show, for example, that Roberts concluded that Bass' trip to Nauru 'was a holiday' and that his constituents were not going to benefit from him attending the Nauru Speakers' Conference. Having formed that view, Roberts made no 'attempt to find out in more detail what was going to occur at the conference and what role Mr Bass would play at the conference'. Nor did he 'particularly care because it was typical of somebody who'd gone over the top in relation to their role and it was just yet another abrogation of responsibility to the constituents who were paying him'. This evidence indicates that Roberts, having formed an adverse view about the nature of Bass' trip and representation of his constituents, leapt to a conclusion on inadequate evidence and thought that the details of what Bass was going to do on this 'junket' were immaterial. Roberts' reasoning process is open to serious criticism and led him to an unfair conclusion concerning the nature of Bass' trip to Nauru. But no matter how irrational his reasoning might seem to a judge, it is unfortunately typical of 'reasoning' that is often found in political discussions. If Roberts' conduct on this matter was held to constitute malice sufficient to destroy the privilege of communicating electoral material to voters, the freedom of communication protected by the Constitution would be little more than a grand idea of no practical importance."

He went on to conclude that no malice existed for Case but for Roberts it was open in relation to the *Free Travel Times* pamphlet and this point had to go to retrial because the evidence as to the issue of malice by Roberts was insufficient. In appeals in Australia at all levels the appeal court rarely decides factual matters and if it has the view that the factual findings are inadequate, or wrong, the case is sent back, or remitted[177] to the lower court for further hearing[178], or a retrial[179].

Another point can be made here. In many cases each judge gives separate reasons. This was such a case. Contrary to the Chief Justice, Kirby J decided the present evidence supported malice by Roberts in relation to the *Free Travel Times*, but the whole issue of malice needed to be retried. He found that there was no malice established against Case. Hayne J agreed with the effect of the Chief Justice but for separate reasons. However, Callinan J held that it was not an occasion for *Lange* and malice was

177 Remit, to: to send back to a lower court from a higher court.

178 The trial, or other formal attendance, in a court.

179 A rehearing of trial due to error or other reasons.

established and would have dismissed the appeal. So the majority supported Gleeson CJ but in detail their reasons subtly differ, leaving much room for later argument, and flexibility.

This topic was further developed in case arising from a relatively minor incident when a man insulted a policeman in a shopping mall in Townsville, a provincial city in Queensland[180]. He stood in front of a placard reading: "Get to know your local corrupt type coppers, please take one" and distributed pamphlets alleging four police officers, including a Constable Power, were corrupt. When Constable Power approached, the appellant loudly accused him of being a corrupt police officer. The appellant was convicted[181] of an offence pursuant to[182] section 7(1)(d) of the *Vagrants, Gaming & Other Offences Act 1931* (Qld). Section 7(1)(d) stated that:

> "Any person who in any public place or so near to any public place that any person who might be therein, and whether any person is therein or not, could view or hear – uses any threatening, abusive or insulting words to any person; shall be liable to a penalty of $100 or to imprisonment for 6 months."

The High Court split 4:3 in favour of allowing the appeal against the section 7(1)(d) conviction. At issue was whether s. 7(1)(d) infringed the implied freedom of political communication. All Justices applied the two-limb test formulated in *Lange v Australian Broadcasting Corporation*[183] (no party argued that this unanimous decision should be reconsidered):

(1) does the law effectively burden freedom of communication about government or political matters either in its terms operation or effects?

(2) (i) does the law serve a legitimate end, the fulfilment of which is compatible with the system of representative and responsible government prescribed in the Constitution? and,
(ii) is the law reasonably appropriately and adapted to serve that end?

If the answer is 'yes' to (1) and 'no' to (2) the law breaches the implied freedom of political communication and is invalid.

In this case the defence conceded the first limb of the *Lange* test. This decision was questioned by two minority Justices, Callinan and Heydon JJ, but they accepted the concession.

The second limb was at issue. There was a preliminary question as to the construction of s. 7(1)(d). The construction issue centred on the phrase 'insulting words' and whether this is this limited to words intended to or reasonably likely to provoke unlawful physical retaliation or does it have a broader meaning?

---

180 *Coleman v Power & Ors* (2004) 220 CLR 1.

181 The formal recording of guilt of a criminal charge. Sometimes in view of a defendant's prior good character, even where a charge is proved it might be dealt with without a conviction.

182 In reliance upon, as in "pursuant to the *Motor Vehicles Act* ..." .

183 op cit. (1997) 189 CLR 520.

Three of the majority (Gummow, Hayne & Kirby JJ) said that the operation of s. 7(1)(d) was limited to words intended to or reasonably likely to provoke unlawful physical retaliation. In support of this conclusion Gummow and Hayne JJ cited the principle of statutory construction that fundamental rights (such as freedom of speech) are not to be eroded or curtailed save by clear words. Thus the ambiguous 'insulting words' was construed narrowly.

Kirby J agreed with this point but cited another principle of statutory construction in support of this view. Where a statute is susceptible to an interpretation consistent with international law, that construction should prevail. Kirby J cited Article 19 of the *International Covenant on Civil and Political Rights* 1966 (ICCPR), concerning freedom of expression, as relevant here. Kirby J maintains that this principle of statutory construction operates here even though the ICCPR has not been enacted in domestic Australian law and s. 7(1)(d) pre-dates the ICCPR. Australia is a party to the ICCPR and is also a party to the subsequent *First Optional Protocol* that permits communications to be made to the United Nations Human Rights Committee when it is alleged that Australian law does not conform to the requirements of the ICCPR. Here the judge was using the foreign affairs power to introduce freedom of speech into Australian law.

Gummow and Hayne JJ, in their joint judgment, and Kirby J identified keeping public places free from violence as a legitimate purpose of s. 7(1)(d) compatible with representative and responsible government. They said that s. 7(1)(d) was appropriate and adapted to this end. Thus section 7(1)(d) was constitutionally valid, however the appeal was allowed as the appellant was not guilty of an offence against s. 7(1)(d), narrowly construed.

The other member of the majority, McHugh J, saw no reason to give the phrase 'insulting words' any other than its natural and ordinary (dictionary) meaning. The words merely need to be insulting, rather than likely to provoke a physical reaction. Having given s. 7(1)(d) a broad interpretation, McHugh ruled that the section fails the second limb of the *Lange* test and is thus constitutionally invalid. McHugh identified two legitimate ends compatible with the prescribed system of representative government, namely: preventing breaches of the peace and removing insults from the arena of public discussion so people would not be intimidated into silence. However, the broadly construed s. 7(1)(d) amounted to an unqualified prohibition on insulting words, which is beyond anything that could be considered reasonably appropriate and adapted to serve these legitimate ends.

In separate judgments the three minority Justices, Gleeson CJ, Callinan & Heydon JJ dismissed the appeal. Each gave s. 7(1)(d) a similarly broad construction to McHugh J, again relying on a literal, dictionary definition of the phrase 'insulting words'. However the minority Justices each found that even broadly construed, s. 7(1)(d) passed the second limb of the *Lange* test and so was constitutionally valid. Each Justice found that s. 7(1)(d) was reasonably appropriate and adapted to serve the legitimate end of preserving public order.

Here then all the judges preserved the *Lange* implied right to political discourse. Kirby J has found alternative support for it in international treaty obligations. However, the preferred method to strike down this legislation was by giving it a narrow interpretation rather than declaring it invalid. Only McHugh J, a member of the *Lange* bench[184], relied on the implied freedom of political discourse to invalidate the legislation. The minority, who have since emerged as a conservative majority have indicated a reluctance to invoke the implied freedom, even though they have left it in place.

These cases show that the High Court has stepped back from its adventure into implying its own Bill of Rights into Australian law, if indeed that is where it was headed. The High Court of the late 1980s and early 1990s was quite radical in its outlook as a result of appointments made by Labor governments. A subsequent period of Conservative party rule, known in Australia as the Liberal National Coalition government has resulted in the High Court now having judges with a more conservative legal view.

The common law is generally regarded as residual, that is it can be modified by clear legislative amendment. Thus implied rights may be taken away by legislative enactment in contrast to a Bill of Rights in statute or even more deeply enshrined as a constitutional right. However, by implying rights as part of the constitutional arrangement, which can be used to declare legislation invalid, the High Court has set itself above Parliament in that respect, and the extent that such rights might later be circumscribed by express legislation is unfinished business. It is likely to remain so whilst the present bench remain, as they appear to have made it clear that they will avoid the issue.

Restraints on executive power

The executive authority is answerable to Parliament. Parliaments in Australia have a system of committees, most developed in the Senate (and Upper Houses of State Parliaments) where proportional voting systems mean the government of the day often does not control the upper house. Senate committees may investigate proposed legislation before it is passed, and suggest amendments. When the Senate is not in the hands of the government of the day this may force compromise on the government for new legislation.

Senate select committees[185] can be convened to investigate acts of the executive on topical issues. This is usually for a political purpose but forms a useful method of exploring controversial issues. Proceedings in Parliament are privileged, that is no one can be sued for what they say, so they are a useful way to ventilate discussion. A topical example occurred after immigration became an election issue in 2002. In Australia immigration can be controversial. Australia permits substantial immigration by lawful methods. In 2004 this policy permitted 120,000 lawful migrants who can

---

184 The judge or group of judges or magistrates. The seat in the court room where the judge(s) sit.

185 A committed formed by the Senate, to enquire into a particular topic or specially consider legislation that is before it.

obtain permanent residence and citizenship each year. This is against the population of about 20 million[186]. The current government has aggressively discouraged unauthorised migration by people using boats. Most of these migrants are displaced people from Afghanistan, Pakistanis pretending to be Afghanis, Iranians, Iraqis (before the American invasion) and people from other Middle Eastern countries. They use the services of people smugglers and make the last part of the journey in leaky boats from Indonesia. Prior to the election in 2002 their numbers were increasing. At that time the Indonesian government did little to prevent this traffic. To avoid international treaty obligations the government declared that Australia's small island possession between Indonesia and Australia, called Christmas Island[187] was not part of Australia for migration purposes. Thus although the navy intercepted these boats of refugees and took them to Christmas Island the government maintained the legal sophistry that Australia had no obligation to the boat refugees because they had not reached Australia. There were too many for Christmas Island so it paid Pacific countries such as Papua New Guinea and Nauru to look after them in secure camps whilst the United Nations assessed their refugee status. In fairness to the government hindsight has shown that many of them did not qualify as having refugee status.

In the lead up to an election this became a matter of excited controversy. In no small part the government's tough stance on this issue contributed to the government winning the election. In the middle of this a Norwegian freighter, the '*Tampa*' rescued a group of refugees from a sinking fishing boat and took them to Christmas Island. The government ordered the *Tampa* to go back to Indonesia but the captain refused. The government sent commando type troops to board the *Tampa* and take control of it, a controversial act. The end result was that the refugees were taken off the *Tampa* and transported mainly to Nauru but also some to Papua New Guinea and New Zealand. As can happen in the heat of such matters the unfortunate refugees were demonised and the government published photos purporting to show another group of refugees who had thrown their own children into the sea to force a naval patrol boat to take them on board. After the election a Senate select committee investigated the children overboard incident. It established with little doubt that the reason the refugees had put their children in the sea, wearing lifejackets, was that their boat was sinking. The allegations made just before the election that these were terrible people who would risk the welfare of their children to gain an advantage was discredited. Here then is an example of the Senate exercising a review function over the executive power of government, although its only sanction lies in public opinion not in any actual legal authority. However, if the government controls the Senate the protection is largely lost because the government will scarcely permit a committee against its own interest.

The Commonwealth government has a system of Administrative Appeals Tribunals with responsibility to hear appeals and review administrative decision making, typically disputes over pension and tax issues and the busy migration area. These tribunals are not courts constituted under Chapter III of the Constitution so the tribunal members lack the protection of tenure. There are also concerns whether they have sufficient administrative independence from the departments they review to ensure that

---

186 http://www.abs.gov.au.

187 Named Christmas Island by Captain Cook who discovered it on Christmas Day.

they can make difficult decisions. At the State level there is also a system of ombudsmen who are statutorily created authorities with the power to investigate administrative decisions by Government and local councils. This model has also been copied in a way by private enterprise dispute resolution schemes discussed in Chapter 7.

The Constitution provides direct jurisdiction to the High Court for judicial oversight of administrative decisions in s. 75(v). This provides for injunctions[188] to be granted on a writ[189] of mandamus[190], which in the common law is an order that government or its officers do something, a writ of prohibition[191], or cease from doing something and certiorari[192] to cancel a previous decision or action. This is a very broad jurisdiction but the great expense in having a case heard in the High Court does not encourage its use. This jurisdiction is in the Constitution so the Parliament cannot limit it.

Conclusion

In the final analysis the effective restraints on abuses of power lie in the political process, exposure by the press and the independent judicial system. Under the Constitution the executive government is accountable to Parliament whose members are in turn accountable to the people through the electoral process, which gives the capacity to the people to end the reign of a government. The Constitution guarantees the electoral process by prescribing the nature of electorates and the requirement that Parliament must sit so that the government is subject to questioning and must submit to an election every three years. To be effective this depends on a free press that can bring bad government and abuses of power to the attention of the voting public. In the Australian Constitution there is no guarantee of the freedom of the press although it has been noted that the High Court has been vigilant in protecting the ability of the press and others to engage in frank political discussion. This points to the key role of the judiciary in protecting a civil political process. In the USA this central role of the judiciary was recognised by President Roosevelt in his message to Congress on 8 December 1908:[193]

> "The chief lawmakers in our country may be and often are the judges because they are the final seat of authority. Every time they interpret contract, property, vested rights, due process of law, liberty, they necessarily enact into law parts of a system of social philosophy; and as such interpretation is fundamental, they give direction to all lawmaking. The decisions of the courts on economic and social questions depends on their economic and social philosophy; and for the peaceful progress of our people during the 20th century we shall owe most to

[188] A court order forbidding or requiring something being done.

[189] A document that commences a civil case in a higher court. The document in a lower court is called a claim or a summons.

[190] An order of a court requiring an action to be taken.

[191] A court order to prohibit an action being taken.

[192] An order of a court overturning, or quashing an executive decision.

[193] 43 Congressional Record Part 1, p 21, quoted in B.M. Cardozo, *The Nature of the Judicial Process* Yale University Press, New Haven, 1921, 30th edition, 1971, at p. 171.

> those judges who hold a 20th century economic and social perspective and not to a long outgrown philosophy, which was itself the product of primitive economic conditions."

This is demonstrated in the Australian decisions. The Constitution protects freedom of religion but the High Court permitted worship of the Jehovah's Witness Church to be stopped and the Constitution prevents the establishing of a religion but the High Court permits the government to subsidise schools that teach a particular religion. On the other hand the Constitution is silent on any right to free speech in political matters but the High Court has protected it. The mere words in the Constitution give no protection; it is in the meaning given to them by the High Court that gives protection from abuse of power. The judiciary, and the press, are guardians of the liberty in a constitutional arrangement.

Chapter 4:

THE BALANCE OF POWER BETWEEN THE STATES AND THE COMMONWEALTH

Constitutional amendment

The Constitution was a negotiated outcome between independent colonies and they were of course keen to ensure that the extent of power given to the Commonwealth was not later increased by sleight of hand or amendment. The Constitution gives specified powers to the Commonwealth and the residual powers remain with the States. The importance given to protection of the States is expressed in the manner in which the Constitution can be amended. Amendments to the Constitution are provided for in s.128. The proposal must by passed by both Houses of Parliament (subject to special provisions in the event of a deadlock between the Houses) and approval at a referendum two to six months later by all the electors in Australia by absolute majority. There also must be a majority of electors in a majority of States in favour of the amendment[194]. Any proposal to affect the representation of a State in either House of Parliament or otherwise particularly effecting a State, in addition must be approved by a majority of the electors in the State affected.

If one of the major political parties is opposed to an amendment then it is almost certainly doomed to fail one of these requirements. If both of the major parties are in favour of an amendment then there is still a problem because the electors are suspicious of anything that all the politicians support and nearly all will express their opinion because voting is effectively compulsory in Australia. The effect of this is that the success rate of amendments has been less than one-quarter. In Chapter 1 it was conclude that there is no power remaining in the Imperial Parliament to amend the Australian Constitution. The founding draftsmen locked in the protection of State power at the constitutional level. However, the reality of power can defeat the written word.

The changing policy of the High Court

The final arbiter of where the legal balance lies is the High Court. The original High Court judges were Griffiths CJ, Barton J and O'Connor J, all of whom had participated in the drawing up of the constitution. They followed the lead of the US doctrine enunciated by Marshall CJ in *McCulloch v Maryland*[195] to the effect that State laws could not fetter the exercise of constitutionally authorised Commonwealth powers. In practical terms this meant that Commonwealth bodies did not have to pay State government taxes and Commonwealth employees did not have to pay State

---

194 S. 128. This idea of requiring the assent of the people in the States to amend the Constitution was drawn from Switzerland.

195 (1819) 4 Wheat. 316, 4 L. Ed. 579.

Government income tax[196]. This was later over-ruled in the Privy Council by a ploy of fresh litigation through the State Courts and an appeal to the Privy Council that by passed the High Court[197]. The High Court took the view that in this matter the Privy Council had no jurisdiction and ignored the decision.

However, contrary to this early interpretation of large Commonwealth power came an application by state railway workers to have their wages determined under the federal arbitration system. The Court balanced its earlier decision by saying that just as the Commonwealth could not be interfered with in the exercise of its power, where the States were exercising their powers, the Commonwealth could not interfere with them[198].

The First World War saw a substantial increase in Commonwealth power through the defence power. Australia as part of the British Commonwealth[199] joined the battles in Europe and formed a military tradition with its near neighbour New Zealand. The joint units known as the Australian and New Zealand Army Corp, ANZACs, have entered Australian history in annual commemoration of the wars, on what is called ANZAC day. The necessities of war led to a practical expansion of Commonwealth power, a presage of a much more fundamental shift in WWII. An example of the increase of power was the use of the defence power to authorize such matters as price fixing of bread in the suburbs of Melbourne. The High Court upheld this[200].

The Engineers Case

Two further judges, Isaacs J and Higgins J had been appointed to the Bench and they tended to favour Federal power particularly in industrial matters. By 1920 the three original judges had retired and there was a shift of sentiment in favour of the power of the now well established Commonwealth government. In 1920 in a landmark case the *Amalgamated Society of Engineers v Adelaide Steamship Co Ltd*[201] (commonly known as *the Engineers Case*) the Court reviewed all the cases on the immunity of States from the exercise of Commonwealth power and established the principle that in any field of Commonwealth legislative power the Commonwealth laws are paramount over State laws. Thus, contrary to the earlier decision, Commonwealth awards for wages and conditions of workers could apply to employees in a State, Commonwealth taxes would apply to the States and State employees, but the Commonwealth remained exempt from State laws in its activities. From then, as long as a Commonwealth law was within power, it applied without State instrumentalities being immune nor any notions of implied protection of State reserve powers. This upset the States who always

---

196 *Deakin v Webb* (1904) 1 CLR 585.

197 *Webb v Outtrim* (1907) AC 214.

198 *Federated Amalgamated Government Railway and Tramways Service Association v New South Wales Railway Traffic Employees Association* (1906) 4 CLR 488.

199 A loose grouping of nations that were formerly British colonies.

200 Owen Dixon *Jesting Pilate* op. cit. p116.

201 (1920) 28 CLR 129.

tried to take litigation to the Privy Council when they could, but of course the Constitution gave control over constitutional appeals to the High Court[202].

Also in 1920 the High Court ruled that although the prohibition on restraints of trade in s. 92 bound the States, the Commonwealth could regulate and control such trade[203]. This had a significant practical effect in vesting in the Commonwealth power over marketing and regulatory schemes dealing with primary produce, which was the major economic activity in Australia at that time. This involved a substantial economic and psychological shift of power to the Commonwealth[204].

In the second World War the High Court upheld a substantial shift of economic and practical power to the Commonwealth, which is discussed below. More recently broad interpretation of the external affairs power and the corporations power[205] has given the Commonwealth powers in areas not intended in the Constitution. The way that power can be shifted to the Commonwealth by these other powers is seen graphically in the *Industrial Relations Case.*

The Industrial Relations Case

Australia had a powerful trade union movement at the time of federation which ensured the inclusion in s. 51 of the Constitution of the industrial relations power:

> "(xxxv) conciliation and arbitration for the prevention and settlement of industrial disputes extending beyond the limits of any one State;"

In Australia there is a history of centralised wage fixing and awards set by a national specialist commission dealing with industrial matters and flowing on to similar bodies in the States. In recent times a competing system of individual work contracts has been established to provide greater flexibility and to break down the power of the trade unions, which is founded on the collective bargaining implicit in an award system that fixes wages and conditions across an industry. It can be seen that the constitutional conciliation and arbitration power is limited to industrial disputes that extend beyond any one State. The Commonwealth has no power under this head to regulate industrial issues that are not related to the prevention and settlement of disputes nor to disputes that remain within the limits of any one State. However, the Commonwealth government decided to do just that relying on the Corporations power, establishing a new approach to industrial relations and the negotiation of wages and conditions nationwide. In *New South Wales v Commonwealth (the Industrial Relations Case)*[206] a

---

202 S. 75 gives the High Court jurisdiction in matters involving the Commonwealth or between States, and by their nature constitutional cases fall into these categories. An appeal in these from the High Court to the Privy Council in England only lies if the High Court gives a certificate under s.74, which it will not give.

203 *W. & A. McArthur Ltd v. State of Queensland* (1920) 28 CLR 530.

204 Owen Dixon *Jesting Pilate*, op cit p.118. Note this decision was overturned by the Privy Council 16 years later but by then the psychological and actual shift in power to the Commonwealth was well in place.

205 See Chapter 6.

206 (2006) HCA 52 (14 November 2006), http://www.austlii.edu.au.

majority of five justices of the High Court published a joint judgment upholding the Commonwealth Law. Two minority judges disagreed for separate reasons.

The majority of Gleeson CJ and Gummow, Hayne, Heydon and Crennan JJ upheld the new laws. They noted that the new laws would affect 85% of the Australian workforce[207] because employers overwhelmingly are companies or other corporate entities. Their judgment systematically rejected all contrary arguments, in a way that will leave little room for later courts to step back. In relation to concerns about the balance of power of between the Commonwealth and the States they said:[208]

> "In the present matters, the appeals made to notions of federal balance, no matter whether the appeal was explicit or only implicit, were propositions about a "balance" of legislative power between the Commonwealth and the States. Two points must be made about those propositions. First, as Dixon J said[209] in *Melbourne Corporation*:
>
> > "The position of the federal government is necessarily stronger than that of the States. The Commonwealth is a government to which enumerated powers have been affirmatively granted. The grant carries all that is proper for its full effectuation. Then supremacy is given to the legislative powers of the Commonwealth."
>
> > Secondly, again as Dixon J pointed out[210] in *Melbourne Corporation*, the framers "appear ... to have conceived the States as bodies politic *whose existence and nature are independent of the powers allocated to them*" (emphasis added). Thus when it is said that there is a point at which the legislative powers of the federal Parliament and the legislative powers of the States are to be divided lest the federal balance be disturbed, how is that point to be identified? It cannot be identified from any of the considerations mentioned thus far in these reasons, and no other basis for its identification was advanced in argument."

The significance of the shift can be gauged by quoting the minority opinion of Kirby J:[211]

> "In effect, the risk to which I refer is presented by a shift in constitutional realities from the present mixed federal arrangements to a kind of optional or "opportunistic" federalism in which the Federal Parliament may enact laws in almost every sphere of what has hitherto been a State field of lawmaking by the simple expedient (as in this case) of enacting a law on the chosen subject matter whilst applying it to corporations, their officers, agents, representatives,

207 Ibid, para 45.
208 Ibid, para 195.
209 (1947) 74 CLR 31 at 82-83.
210 Ibid, page 82.
211 Ibid, para 543 and following.

employees, consumers, contractors, providers and others having some postulated connection with the corporation.

...

608 To insist on this resolution of the intersecting principles fulfils this Court's role as the guardian of the Constitution. It preserves decisions of this Court, delivered over more than a century, that have either held, or impliedly accepted, that the corporations power has to be read as subject to the industrial disputes power. The view now endorsed by the majority of this Court effectively discards a century of constitutional doctrine. It ignores the express structure of the Constitution and the language of the two heads of constitutional power in question in this case, each of equal validity and effect. I refuse to accept that our predecessors in this Court were so blind to the true meaning of the Constitution that their decisions, in such number and detail over the past hundred years, were pointless exercises in constitutional futility. Yet that is the hypothesis inherent in the decision now reached by the majority.

...

614 ... I accept that the corporations power in the Constitution, when viewed as a functional document, expands and enlarges so as to permit federal laws on a wide range of activities of trading and financial corporations in keeping with their expanding role in the nation's affairs and economic life. But there are limits. Those limits are found in the express provisions and structure of the Constitution and in its implications. This Court's duty is to uphold the limits. Once a constitutional Rubicon such as this is crossed, there is rarely a going back.

615 That is why this is such an important case for the content of constitutional power in Australia. The majority concludes that not a single one of the myriad constitutional arguments of the States succeeds. Truly, this reveals the apogee of federal constitutional power and a profound weakness in the legal checks and balances which the founders sought to provide to the Australian Commonwealth."

The precedent permits a single power in the Constitution to be used to legislate in areas that are collateral to that power and beyond specific heads of power that might seem to be the head of power being exercised. In this instance the Corporations power has been used to exercise a far greater industrial relations power than the grant of that power in the Constitution. It is judicial high point of enabling greater exercise of power by the Commonwealth that no doubt future Commonwealth governments will seek to exercise. It has the potential to sweep away the federal division of powers in the Constitutional arrangement in Australia and concentrate power in the Commonwealth government. Other practical factors have been to the same effect.

The financial agreement

The practical economic power founded on the power of taxation has been a greater influence over the division of powers between the Commonwealth and the States than the words in the Constitution.

In money lies real power and this has been proven in Australia's federation. At the time of federation state debts were large and although it was agreed that the newly formed Commonwealth would take over these debts the agreement foundered on arguments about future borrowing arrangements. These were not agreed until 1927. Section 105A of the Constitution resulted from the financial agreement. This was one of the few Constitutional amendments that passed, by a referendum in 1928. The Commonwealth took over existing State debts and agreed to fund interest payments on future debt to an agreed level. The State governments in return agreed to make payments into a sinking fund. A loan council was established at which each State and the Commonwealth is a member to co-ordinate future borrowings. The agreement remains in place and has evolved substantially with time.

When the Great Depression came, the Lang Government in New South Wales sought to take a Keynesian[212] or spending approach to dealing with the depression contrary to the Federal Government policy, which was fiscally[213] restrained. For example New South Wales built Sydney's famous 'coat hanger' Harbour Bridge, but it refused to make its payments to the sinking fund. New South Wales was the most populous and wealthy State. The Commonwealth passed special legislation authorising the Commonwealth to intercept State revenue to recover its debt to the sinking fund. Needless to say this was a great political and legal battle, which culminated in the High Court decision in *New South Wales v Commonwealth*[214]. The majority of the Court upheld the legislation, maintaining Commonwealth financial power over NSW, the most populous State. It has been noted earlier that this led to the Lang government being dismissed by the NSW Governor.

Meanwhile Western Australia was so discontent with these arrangements that it sought secession[215]. Its Parliament passed a statute prescribing a referendum, or plebiscite[216] of its people to leave the Commonwealth. There were suggestions of obtaining an injunction in the High Court to prevent the referendum but the Federal Government did nothing and a two to one majority passed the referendum for secession[217]. The Commonwealth just ignored the plebiscite. Western Australia appealed to the British Parliament to secede from Australia. A committee of the British Parliament recommended the rejection of the State's petition on the basis that it was a matter of Australian constitutional concern. There the matter has rested since 1935.

An emerging power in practice lies in the Commonwealth financial grants to the States. When the Commonwealth make grants to States under s. 96 of the constitution it can attach conditions to how those grants are spent. These conditions are not limited to the constitutional powers of the Commonwealth. This was a sleeping power, which became of great significance during the World War II and after it. The Commonwealth now often achieves its objectives by making grants to the States conditional on them

---

212 An economic policy for government to fund projects from borrowings to take an economy out of depression; after the English economist John Maynard Keynes.

213 Financially

214 (1932) 46 CLR 155.

215 Withdrawal from the federation.

216 A vote of all electors.

217 Owen Dixon, *Jesting Pilot* op cit p.120.

undertaking reforms according to the Commonwealth agenda. An example was to link funding to repair roads to a requirement that the States adopt uniform traffic laws such as speed limits.

The shift of power in WWII

On these foundations of a strong Federal Government were built a substantial edifice of Commonwealth power during World War II. For reasons of loyalty to England, Australia was initially involved in that war in European theatres. For example, Australia still honours the exploits of Australian troops known as the rats of Tobruk who at Tobruk and Alamein fought against Axis troops under the leadership of Field Marshal Rommel. But then the Japanese intervention in the war threatened the very existence of Australia by the rapid advance down the Malaysian Peninsula to defeat the British fortress island of Singapore whose defences were all designed for a sea invasion not one from the land behind them. The best of Australia's remaining army was captured there. The British ordered Australian troops returning from the Middle East to go to Burma, a directive countermanded by the Australian Prime Minister Curtin. This left several brigades of ill trained and equipped reservists to fight a bitter campaign on the Kokoda trail over the Owen Stanley ranges in Papua New Guinea against the Japanese. Papua was a German Colony taken over by Australia after the First World War. Poor supply lines caused by American naval dominance over Japan after the Battle of the Coral Sea turned the tide in Australia's favour. The purpose of this is not jingoistic[218]. It is to explain Australia's independent existence was under threat. At times of such threats long held beliefs may be abandoned for survival. It was put this way at the time in a speech by the then Chief Justice Owen Dixon on 18 March 1943 to the School of Law at the University of Toronto[219].

> "When the present war broke out it became necessary for the Commonwealth Government to assume very wide powers. The total nature of this war was driven home to everybody whose duties involved the consideration of the measures proposed for the prosecution of the war and who understood the reasons for their adoption. Many things which might on their face appear to have little connection with the prosecution of war, on closer examination were found to be intimately bound up with it. For instance, the Court held that regulations controlling the collection and marketing of apples and pears were within the defence power, because the export of apples and pears depended upon shipping, and it was for the Government to take any measures thought desirable for the purpose of making it easier to divert ships to other purposes. The consequence has been that many of the things otherwise falling within the province of the States have passed into the province[220] of the Federal Government for the duration of the war. A still further step was taken. The Australian constitution does not divide the field of taxation between State and Commonwealth in any such manner as that which you are familiar with under your sections 91 and 92. Each

[218] Excessively patriotic or chauvinistic.

[219] Ibid. p.120.

[220] Area of responsibility. This word can also mean a political region much the same as a State, especially in Canada.

Government has a full power of taxation. Australians therefore enjoy the privilege of paying a State income tax and a Federal income tax assessed on the same income. During the war the Federal Parliament decided that only one income tax should be levied and by only one authority, viz.[221], the Federal Government. A calculation was made of the total sum produced by aggregating Federal and State taxation then in force. A plan was then adopted by means of four acts of Parliament for the purpose of eliminating the States from the field of income tax. The first step was to impose by one statute[222] a Federal tax, which would produce the aggregate sum found to result from all the income taxes at that time in force. The next step was to provide in another statute passed in the exercise of the power to give financial assistance to the States, that a State which repealed its income tax laws should receive from the treasury of the Commonwealth the sum which, according to calculations already made, those income tax laws produced at that time. The third step was in still another statute to provide that every taxpayer should pay his full Federal income tax before he paid any of his State tax. The fourth step was to enact that, by a notice in writing addressed to the State treasurer, the Federal Treasurer[223] might cause any persons employed by a State in its income tax department to be transferred, without mores[224], into the employment of the Federal Government to serve in its taxation department.

The last provision was justified under the defence power, which, it was claimed, gave full authority to require the employment of men in the services of the Federal Government. The majority of the High Court upheld all four measures[225]. The first was upheld under the power to make laws with respect to taxation; the next under the power to give financial assistance to the States and to impose conditions; the third as an incidental to the taxation power, and the fourth under the defence power."

The Constitution does not define the powers of taxation that lie with the States and the Commonwealth. This omission has made the shift of taxation power relatively easy. Of course the Commonwealth never gave back the power of income tax, which was then the main revenue base of governments.

Another consequence of the war experience was to shift Australia's dependence on Britain in external affairs and replace it with a similar relationship with the USA.

In 2002 the Commonwealth adopted a 10% tax on goods and services (GST), which it returns to the States instead of previous grants of revenue. Now the Commonwealth has both income tax and goods and services taxation in its hands the States are increasingly starved of independent revenue and this has resulted in an increasing shift of practical power to the Commonwealth.

---

221 Namely, from the Latin videlicet.
222 An Act of Parliament, or legislation.
223 The minister with responsibility for government finances.
224 Deductions (obscure), also morals.
225 *South Australia v Commonwealth* (1942) 65 CLR 373.

Territories and the balance protecting the States

The siting of the capital Canberra in NSW was a condition that NSW attached to joining the federation. The fact that it is nearly as close to Melbourne, the capital of Victoria, as it is to Sydney, the capital of NSW, reflects the balance of power between the two most populous and rich States, NSW and Victoria. Around the Federal Capital in Canberra is a small independent area of land known as the Australian Capital Territory. Also in the middle of the North of Australia is a Territory known as the Northern Territory. Neither of these were part of the original federation. They have since been given a form of statehood and in the 1970s were given representation to the Senate of two Senators. This has the potential to upset the delicate constitutional balance between the respective States equal representation in the Senate, regardless of population, and the limiting of the numbers in the lower House of Representatives to no more that double the Senate to protect the Senate's relative numbers in the event of a joint sitting to consider a deadlocked Bill. In *Western Australia v Commonwealth*[226] and *Queensland v Commonwealth* [227] the High Court held that s.122 allowed the Legislature to admit territories to the federation on terms different to those applicable to the States. However, Gibbs J in the *Queensland Case* did note that an increase in the number of Senators for a Territory could be grounds for reconsideration, as it would potentially upset the delicate balance in Chapter I, Part 2 of the Constitution protecting the States.

Conclusion

It can be seen that even with so few substantive amendments to the constitutional arrangements there has been a substantial shift of power from the States to the Commonwealth. This is largely a result of the growth of national cohesion through war and the power of taxation shifting to the Commonwealth. This transfer of effective power has been supported by the High Court as it adapted its decisions to the changing circumstances. The decision in the *Industrial Relations Case* permits the Commonwealth to legislate in areas far beyond the powers listed in the original Constitution to which the States agreed. Here is a clear example that constitutional draftsmen cannot impose their view on the future. The events of history and the interpretation of the Constitution by judges can change the balance they established. The draftsmen can do no more than establish a structure that will preserve a civil society as it meets often unpredictable challenges.

---

[226] (1975-76) 134 CLR 201.

[227] (1976-77) 139 CLR 585.

Chapter 5:

INTERPRETATION OF THE CONSTITUTION

At the core of this discussion of interpretation is the extent that the High Court is adventurous in its interpretation of the Constitution. The inclusion of an implied right of freedom of speech discussed in the last chapter is a demonstration of how the Court can find constitutional principles from the ether of the common law and put itself outside the written words of the constitution. The extent it is willing to do so has been, and will remain, a matter of debate by the Court, and sometimes heated comment by others. Underlying this is the extent that the judges are affected by their subjective beliefs and the trends and pressures of the society in which they work. These underlying issues usually are cloaked in legal terminology.

The present Chief Justice Gleeson expresses sympathy with what he describes[228] as the orthodox view of Australia's longest serving Chief Justice, Sir Owen Dixon that rejects "the abrupt change of conceptions according to personal standards or theories of justice and convenience, which the judge sets up."[229]

A recent Chief Justice Sir Anthony Mason was more willing to identify policy issues implicit in judicial decision making and to make decision for those policy reasons. He wrote of Sir Owen Dixon's view:

> "Yet in some respects his Honour's outline resembles an elegantly constructed mansion in which some of the windows have been deliberately left open."[230]
>
> "If applied too rigidly, the doctrine of precedent produces both injustice and lack of rationality - the very flaws whose purpose it is to expel. Thus adherence to a past decision which reflects either a principle undermined by subsequent legal development or the values of a bygone era, will produce an unjust result, judged by the standards of today."[231]

These contrasting views inform the law on this topic.

---

228 The Hon Justice Murray Gleeson, *THE CENTENARY OF THE HIGH COURT: LESSONS FROM HISTORY*, (October 2003) AIJA, Melbourne. His speech can be found at http://www.aija.org.au/onlinepub.htm.

229 Page 9 quoting "Concerning Judicial Method" in Owen Dixon, *Jesting Pilate* (2nd ed. 1977) William J Hein and Co Inc., at p. 152.

230 A Mason, 'Future Directions in Australian Law' *Monash University Law Review* 13 (1987): pp. 149-63 at pp. 155, 159.

231 A. Mason, 'The use and abuse of precedent', *Australian Bar Review*, 4 (1988): pp 93-111, at p. 94: also A. Mason 'Courts and community values', *Eureka Street* 6 (9) (November 1996) pp.32-4; Lionel Murphy's view in G Sturgess & P. Chubb, *Judging the World*, (Sydney 1988) p.362 and cf pp. 346, 351.

Literalism v Realism

Sir Owen Dixon on his swearing in as Chief Justice said this:[232]

> "...the Court's sole function is to interpret a constitutional description of power or restraint upon power and say whether a given measure falls on one side of the line consequentially drawn or on the other and that it has nothing whatever to do with the merits or demerits of the measure.
>
> Such a function has led us all I think to believe that close adherence to legal reasoning is the only way to maintain the confidence of all parties in Federal conflict. It may be that the Court is thought to be excessively legalistic. I should be sorry to think that it is anything else. There is no other safe guide to judicial decisions in great conflicts than a strict and complete legalism."

For the first fifty years of its existence judges of the High Court suggested that interpretation of laws could be made without political judgments. For example Rich J. said in 1945:[233]

> "Now, it cannot be too clearly understood that this Court is not in the smallest degree concerned to consider whether such a project is politically, economically, or socially desirable or undesirable."

The next long serving Chief Justice after Sir Own Dixon, Sir Garfield Barwick also put emphasis on a literal interpretation of the constitution[234] but a more recent view is that any interpretation has a political and practical effect and it is more honest to admit that effect and to tease out the legal and policy arguments lying behind the mere words to arrive at a judgment that fits the current needs of the community. Words of 1900 have different nuances in 2005 and circumstances have arisen that were not envisaged in the words written more than one hundred years earlier. It has been expressed this way:[235]

> "The practice of legal interpretation is mired in a deep and persistent crisis ... In the broadest terms, the crisis reflects a loss of faith concerning the availability of objective criteria permitting the ascription of distinct and transparent meanings to legal texts. Moreover, this loss of faith manifests itself in the intensification of the conflict among the community of legal actors, a dissolution of any genuine consensus over important values, the seemingly inescapable indeterminacy of legal rules, and the belief that all dispositions of legal issues are ultimately political and subjective. The roots of the crisis affecting legal interpretation can be traced back to the legal realists' critique of legal formalism. ..."

---

232 (1952) 85 CLR xi at xiii-xiv.

233 *Australian National Airways Pty Ltd v Commonwealth (ANA case)* (1945) 71 CLR 29 at p. 70.

234 Retirement of Sir Garfield Barwick as Chief Justice (1981) 148 CLR v.

235 M Rosenfeld "Deconstruction and legal interpretation..." in Cornell Rosenfeld and Carlson (editors) *Deconstruction and the possibility of justice* Routledge 1992, in Blackshield and Williams (1998) op. cit. at p.152.

"The substantive values of the community of legal actors do not directly figure in legal decisions but they are not simply severed from the process of legal interpretation. Traces of those substantive values are imbedded in the legal precedents that confront the legal interpreter and must therefore be implicitly taken into account by the latter in his or her formulation of an interpretation that is compatible with precedent while preserving the integrity of the legal process. Stripped of its intellectual sophistry constitutional decisions are made in an arena of lively and sometimes passionate opinion and media pressure. The judges are not immune from that but bring to the dispute the historical perspective of precedent and intellectual rigor in interpreting the constitution in the context of that current pressure."[236]

The 1980s was a time of a more open approach by the High Court to its work. Sir Anthony Mason, the Chief Justice at that time developed his approach under a principal known as proportionality. This arose in the context of the incidental power in s. 51(xxxix). The *Industrial Relations Act* 1988 (Cth) gave very strong protection to the Industrial Relations Commission against criticism. This was held to be invalid, partly because it infringed the implied constitutional right to freedom of political discussion. Mason CJ also held it was not authorised by the head of power, nor the associated incidental power:[237]

"(A law) will not fall within the scope of what is incidental to the substantive power unless it is reasonably and appropriately adapted to the pursuit of an end within power, ie, unless it is capable of being considered to be reasonably proportionate to the pursuit of the end. Secondly, in determining whether that requirement of reasonable proportionality is satisfied, it is material to ascertain whether, and to what extent, the law goes beyond what is reasonably necessary or conceivably desirable for the achievement of the legitimate object sought to be attained and, in so doing, causes adverse consequences unrelated to the achievement of that object. In particular, it is material to ascertain whether those adverse consequences result in any infringement of fundamental values traditionally protected by the common-law, such as freedom of expression."

Implicit in this is an approach that involves the Court in political judgments. This was explicitly recognised by Dawson J in the same case:[238]

"When the power is not purposive (and most of the powers in case s. 51 are not) the old question is not whether the law is reasonably adapted to the achievement of the purpose, but whether it has sufficient operation upon -- a sufficient connection with -- something forming part of the subject matter of the power. For that reason, the concept of reasonable proportionality is of limited assistance where purposive powers are not involved and the danger in employing it, is that it invites the Court to act upon its view of the desirability of the impugned[239]

[236] Ibid. p. 154.

[237] *Nationwide News Pty Ltd v Wills* (1992) 177 CLR at p. 30.

[238] Ibid p.89.

[239] Under attack, as in criticising legislation as invalid under the Constitution.

legislation rather than on the connection of the legislation with the subject matter of the legislative power."

Undeterred, in a later case Mason CJ said this:[240]

"... (I)n cases of this kind, in considering whether there is a substantial or sufficient connection between the impugned provision and the relevant law, it may be material to inquire whether the provision is capable of being reasonably considered to be appropriate and adapted to the end in view. ...

And, in determining whether the means selected by the law for achieving that object or purpose are disproportionate it is material to ascertain not only whether the provision goes beyond what is reasonably necessary for the achievement of the legitimate end sought to be obtained but also whether the provision causes adverse consequences, including infringement of fundamental values, unrelated to the achievement of that object or purpose. ...

Accordingly, the test of reasonable proportionality has an important role to play when the validity of a law hinges upon the proposition that it seeks to protect or enhance a subject matter or legitimate end within power. There is a need to ensure that such a law does not unnecessarily or disproportionately regulate matters beyond power under the guise of protecting the enhancing the legitimate end in view."

This was a period of an adventurous bench. This culminated in a decision when the High Court in a case known as *Mabo (No. 2)*[241] overturned two hundred years of land law and recognised for Aboriginal inhabitants a new form of land tenure, 'native title' that exists until extinguished by imposed titles or until "the tide of history has washed away any real acknowledgement of traditional law and any real observance of traditional customs."[242]

Chief Justice Brennan, the successor to Sir Anthony Mason, was part of the *Mabo (No. 2)* majority. After he retired he expressed his view of the principled basis to depart from precedent this way:[243]

---

240 *Cunnicliff v the Commonwealth of Australia* (1994) 182 CLR 272.

241 This is discussed in Chapter 6.

242 Brennan J, *Mabo & Ors v The State of Queensland* [No.2] (1991) 175 CLR 1 at 60. This turn of phrase was picked up by Olney J in the Federal Court when rejecting a major native claim in Victoria: "The tide of history has indeed washed away any real acknowledgement their traditional laws and any real observance of their traditional customs." *The Members of the Yorta Yorta Aboriginal Community v The State of Victoria & Ors* Unreported Judgment No.1606, 1998, Federal Court of Australia at para.129: See appeal judgments Full Court of Federal Court *Members of the Yorta Yorta Aboriginal Community v Victoria* (2001) 110 FCR 244 and High Court *Members of the Yorta Yorta Aboriginal Community v Victoria* (2002) 214 CLR 422.

243 G. Brennan, 'A critique of criticisms', *Monash University Law Review* 19 (1993), pp 213-6, Quoted in James Franklin, *Corrupting the Youth, A History of Philosophy in Australia*, Macleay Press, Sydney 2003 at p.397.

> "The existing body of law may yield no relevant legal rule, or, in rare cases, may yield a legal rule which is offensive to basic contemporary conceptions of justice." In overturning it, however, the judge does not simply impose his private morality. "The reasons for judgment in the higher appellate courts increasingly look behind the legal rule to discover the informing legal principle and behind the informing legal principle to discover the basic value."

Sir William Deane, also part of the *Mabo (No. 2)* majority, looked explicitly to guidance from natural law philosophy:[244]

> "The basis of natural law, is the belief that some things are innately right and some innately wrong, flowing from the nature of things, including our nature as human beings. That approach provides a philosophical basis for seeing such things as human rights as going deeper than any particular Act of Parliament or what have you. That is not exclusively Catholic. It runs through Christian belief."

More conservative judges have also allowed political necessity to influence their judgments. The High Court has used the defence power flexibly in time of need to increase the power of the Federal government to pursue the war effort[245]. The same Rich J who above is quoted for the proposition the Court pays no attention to political, economic or social desirability of a law, in the context of the Second World War said a country with a federal form of government:[246]

> "... cannot hope to survive unless it submits itself for the time being to what is in effect a dictatorship with power to do anything which can contribute to its defence."

There is no argument with the cause but once the necessity of war was a basis to overturn precedent, and to greater and lesser degree as the danger waxed and waned, then the principle that matters external to the elegant mansion of precedent, can override it, was established. The later approach of admitting the occasional need to seek outside guidance, and to be responsive to changing community values, is more frank. Then at least the basis of decision making is in the open. Cultural, political and legal values moulded the Constitution, legislation and precedent. Courts have a high responsibility to preserve the fragile civility of our community by interpreting them wisely and neither being the agents of fashion nor reaction. The need for a cautious approach has been emphasised by the current Chief Justice Gleeson:[247]

> "The less predictable the decision-making of a final court of appeal, the less influential its decisions will be, because it is the predictability of its conduct that constrains the decision-making of lower courts. The High Court hears only about 70 appeals a year. It has no capacity to seek out and correct judicial error in the

---

244 Ibid. quoted in Franklin 2003 at p.397: Deane to author, 14/5/1996; Stephens, *Sir William Deane: The Things that Matter*, (Sydney 2002), p. 100.

245 This is discussed in Chapter 6.

246 *Dawson v Commonwealth* (1946) 73 CLR 157 at p. 177.

247 Gleeson (2003), op cit.p. 9.

great mass of cases heard by other courts. It is only to the extent to which it states, and itself adheres to, general principle, and settles the common law, that it controls the decisions of other courts. It is only to the extent to which other courts believe they know how the High Court would resolve an issue that those courts can subject themselves to its authority."

Gleeson CJ led the majority in the *Industrial Relations Case*[248] that argued its way to use the Corporations power to ignore the limitations on the Industrial Relations power in the Constitution to the result that the federal structure of the Constitution is now at risk. This may or may not have been predictable, but it demonstrates that a conservative approach can result in radical change.

Two extremes views of the proper role of the judiciary were expressed in the European context. On the one hand Montesquieu said:[249]

> "The judges of the nation are only the mouths that pronounce the words of the law. Inanimate beings who can moderate neither its force nor its rigour."

At the opposite extreme is the view of the French jurist Saleiles:[250]

> "One wills at the beginning the result; one finds the principle afterwards; such is the genesis of all juridical construction. Once accepted a construction presents itself, doubtless in the ensemble of legal doctrine, under the opposite aspect. The factors are inverted. The principle appears as an initial cause, from which one has drawn the result which is found adduced from it."

The desirable view must lie between these extremes. There must be sufficient certainty to fulfil the needs of predictability and impartiality yet sufficient flexibility to provide compassion and adjustment of law to change. This appropriate balance between the application of established principle tempered by subjective views of justice is the very definition of the judicial method.

The eminent American jurist Benjamin Cardozo rationalised the dichotomy of judicial opinion this way:[251]

> "The eccentricities of judges balance one another. One judge looks at problems from the point of view of history, another from that of philosophy, another from that of social utility, one is a formalist, another a latitudinarian, one is timorous of change, another dissatisfied with the present; out of the attrition of diverse minds there is beaten something which has constancy and uniformity and average value greater than its component element. ... The pebble on the beach talking loudly to its neighbour does not define the shoreline."

---

248 (2006) HCA 52 (14 November 2006), discussed in Chapter 4.

249 "Esprit des Lois" LIV, XI, Chapter VI quoted in B.M. Cardozo, *The Nature of the Judicial Process* (Yale University Press, New Haven, 1921) (30th edition, 1971) at p.169.

250 "De la Personnalité Juridique" quoted in Cardozo ibid. p. 170.

251 Ibid. Cardozo at pp. 176-177.

Judicial independence is an essential part of the careful division of power that preserves a civil society by protecting against an unbridled abuse of power by the executive or the legislature. The rule of the majority can be tyranny. The judiciary are the guardians of constitutional compliance and acceptance of their rulings in matters of high controversy preserves civil order. The executive and legislature rely for their legitimacy on the electoral process. They must submit their performance for review by the electorate every three years. The judiciary in Australia are not elected and hold office until they retire by choice[252] or when they reach seventy years of age. Their legitimacy depends upon the acceptance by the community of their performance over a longer time scale. This requires that they be people of the highest calibre and that their judgments fall between the low and high watermark of long term community values. A conservative bench such as Australia had for many years can repress change and leave the law so out of step with community values that it risks being irrelevant, and may do injustice, by the prevailing standards. This is likely to be followed by a judicial rebellion, that itself will bring the Court into controversy by the sudden change it brings as the judiciary pushes beyond its usual role as a bulwark of deeply held community standards and leads change.

The Australian community is experiencing profound social and economic change and it is safer for the judicial method to be open to incremental change to ensure that the courts express legal values that remain in touch with the developing standards but not be captive to sudden fashions. They need to test modern ideas against the accumulated wisdom of the past. The judiciary should be prepared to paddle in the shallows of the sea of change but if they go surfing with the politicians they may attract a degree of controversy that undermines public confidence in them and puts their role at risk.

Inconsistency between State and Commonwealth laws

The powers of the Commonwealth are not exclusive. Hence there may be parallel Commonwealth and State legislation and in the event of inconsistency s.109 provides that the Commonwealth legislation prevails. Whether there is inconsistency can be a matter of some controversy.

The general view of invalidity is that the true analysis is that the law is ineffective only to the extent of the invalidity and not invalid per se. That is, theoretically if the Commonwealth law were subsequently repealed the State law might resume its affect. This of course is only a nice intellectual point. The Commonwealth having taken power over something never gives it away.

Tests of inconsistency

There have been three broad tests of inconsistency:[253]

---

[252] There is a limited power of dismissal for misconduct discussed in Chapter 7.

[253] Blackshield and Williams (1998) op. cit. at p. 302. K Booker, A Glass, R Watt, *Federal Constitutional Law, an Introduction,* (2nd edition) Butterworths, Sydney 1998 at 13.5.

1. If it is impossible to obey both laws there is inconsistency (the impossibility of concurrent obedience test). An example of this was in *R v. Brisbane Licensing Court; ex parte Daniel*[254]. Here there was a Commonwealth election and the Commonwealth law provided that a State referendum could not be held at the same time. There was a State referendum to be held on the same day. This was a complete and impossible inconsistency and the Commonwealth law prevailed.

2. One law confers an entitlement and the other law prohibits it (the denial or qualification of rights test). In *Colvin v Bradley Bros Pty Ltd*[255] Commonwealth legislation allowed women to work on certain classes of machines whereas State legislation prohibited it. This is not an impossibility of obeying both laws. The Commonwealth law did not require the employment of women. However, this has been held to be a clear inconsistency.

3. The cover the field test. This is the test of most practical importance. Where the Commonwealth shows a clear intention to cover the field then provided the legislation is within power then State legislation within the field is invalid. This test received its first judicial pronouncement in *Clyde Engineering v Cowburn*[256]. In this case, the Commonwealth law provided for a 48 hour week whereas the State law provided for a 44 hour week. The employer deducted a proportionate amount from his wages. Isaacs J gave this rather dated example:[257]

> "If an Act of Parliament, for instance, prescribed 25 lashes for robbery under arms and a later Act prescribed that such an offender should be punished with 20 lashes, it could, of course, with equal truth be said that both provisions *could* be obeyed, and therefore applying the suggested test, the offender must receive 45 lashes[258].
>
> But surely the vital question would be: was the second Act on its true construction intended to cover the whole ground and therefore to supersede the first? If it was so intended, then the inconsistency would consist in giving any operative effect at all to the first Act, because the second Act was intended entirely to exclude it... if, however, a competent legislature expressly or impliedly evinces its intention to cover the whole field, that is a conclusive test of inconsistency where another legislature assumes to enter to any extent upon the same field."

The test is simple enough but practical circumstance can still make it difficult to decide whether inconsistency exists. Take a case when a radio station was given a licence under the *Broadcasting and Television Act* 1942 (Cth) with conditions in accordance with its application, to erect two antennae 170 metres high[259]. A local green group

---

254 (1920) 28 CLR 23.
255 (1943) 68 CLR 151.
256 (1926) 37 CLR 466.
257 Ibid. p. 489.
258 An alternative view might be that 25 would comply with both!
259 *Commercial Radio Coffs Harbour v Fuller* (1986) 161 CLR 47.

known as 'Save our Scenery Committee' went to the New South Wales Land and Environment Court under NSW Legislation opposing the erection of the antennae. The High Court held that the Legislation in the Commonwealth and the State each dealt with different fields. The cover the field test showed no inconsistency. The requirement to erect two antennae was not authority to do so and under the first test, although failure to comply with the condition of the licence could result in its cancellation, this was not held to be a requirement not to comply with a relevant State law. Under all tests the Court held that the State environmental law survived the Commonwealth grant of licence.

Another interesting example involved the first female major commercial airline pilot in Australia. Ms Wardley was refused employment by an airline, Ansett, because of her sex and an order was made for her reinstatement under the Victorian *Equal Opportunities Act* 1977 (Vic). Pilots were employed under a Commonwealth award, which entitled an airline to dismiss pilots of less than six months service by giving seven days notice without reason. Ansett sought to interpret this to give it that right to dismiss Ms Wardley regardless of the State legislation. The High Court, by a majority, held there was no inconsistency and the State legislation was valid. Ansett could not discriminate against female pilots[260]. The general right of dismissal must be exercised in accordance with the State law. Again the basis of this decision is that the laws occupy different fields. This contrasts with a case involving a Mr Goulden who was born blind. Mr Goulden had a life insurance policy. He later tried to take out an extension to pay an additional premium to be relieved from paying further premiums if he suffered total disablement *after* the policy extension (that is a total disablement other than his blindness). The insurance company refused claiming that it had no information on the risk of totally blind people suffering disablement so it could not set a premium in accordance with s.78 of the *Life Insurance Act* 1945 (Cth) which provided that:

> "(1) A company shall not issue any policy unless the rate of premium chargeable under the policy is a rate which has been approved by an actuary as suitable for the class of policy to which that policy belongs."

Mr Goulden went to the NSW Equal Opportunity Tribunal. The *Anti-Discrimination Act* 1977(NSW) provided that it was unlawful to discriminate against a person in relation to the provision of services on the basis of a physical impairment. There was an exception for an insurer that could establish an actuarial basis for discrimination. The Court held that:[261]

> "The Act should be understood as giving expression to a legislative policy that the protection of the interests of policy holders is to be achieved by allowing a registered life insurance company to classify risks and fix rates of premium in its life insurance business in accordance with its own judgment and founded on the advice of actuaries and the practice of prudent insurers. ... State legislation which, either absolutely or subject to qualifications and exceptions, made it

---

[260] *Ansett Transport Industries (Operations) Pty Ltd v Wardley* (1980) 142 CLR 237.

[261] *Australian Mutual Providence Society v Goulden* (1986) 160 CLR 330, at p. 337.

generally unlawful for a life insurance company to take account of physical impairment in determining whether it would or would not accept a particular proposal or the terms upon which it would grant insurance cover would be inconsistent with the essential scheme of the provisions of the Act regulating the issue of policies and the fixing of premiums."

The State legislation was to that extent held invalid under s.109. One might think the High Court could have found the two Acts occupied different fields, and that the insurer had to undertake research to establish an actuarial risk for blind people, thus establishing a premium rate for the purpose of the Commonwealth Act, which, under the State Act could be a higher than normal rate, if that was justified by the actuary. However, in its unanimous decision the Court seemed to be more concerned to protect the community's life insurance funds.

In areas within its power the Commonwealth can achieve a policy objective by manufacturing an inconsistency and its law will then prevail. Although there were some early cases suggesting that 'manufactured' inconsistency might be an invalid exercise of Commonwealth power, a case involving the Sydney Airport seems to have put this argument to rest. In the lead up to the Sydney Olympics there was a big controversy in Sydney about the proposed construction of a third runway at Sydney Airport. This caused considerable political and legal controversy due to the sound imposition on residents in a highly populated area with many marginal political seats. Residents sought to prevent the runway by going to the New South Wales Land and Environment Court arguing that dredging the bay where the runway extension would occur would require further environmental impact assessment beyond the Commonwealth assessment that had already occurred. The Commonwealth passed regulations under Commonwealth Law clearly intending to cover the field. The regulations specifically overrode the relevant New South Wales Legislation, making a deliberate inconsistency. The High Court held the Commonwealth Regulations were valid.[262]

The logic of the covering the field test has been extended to Human Rights Legislation. The Commonwealth power to legislate in this area lies not directly under the Constitution but under the external affairs power[263]. In one case a publican in a hotel in Kempsey, New South Wales refused to serve three Aboriginals on the grounds of their race. A complaint was made under the *Anti Discrimination Act* 1977 (NSW). A parallel complaint was made under the *Commonwealth Racial Discrimination Act* 1975 (Cth). The High Court held that the New South Wales Act was inoperative because the Commonwealth Act had covered the field[264]. After this decision the Commonwealth Act was amended to make it clear that the Commonwealth Law would operate concurrently with the State law and this amendment purported to have retrospective[265] effect. Meanwhile an Egyptian postgraduate student at Wollongong University, again in NSW, Mr Metwally, lodged complaints against the University under the *Anti-*

262 *Botany Municipal Council v Federal Airports Corporation* (1992) 175 CLR 453.

263 s.51(xxix): see Chapter 6.

264 *Viskauskas v Nyland* (1983) 153 CLR 280.

265 Legislation which backdates changes to the law.

Discrimination Act 1977 (NSW). These complaints were lodged under the NSW Act before the amendment to the Commonwealth Act but during its purported retrospective operation. The majority held that the retrospective effect was invalid so that Mr Metwally lost because the NSW legislation was invalid for that period[266]. This decision reflects a strong tradition in Australian law against retrospective legislation, especially in relation to criminal or taxation statutes. The majority of the Court followed that approach even though this was discrimination legislation and the NSW Act had been in place and was believed to be valid. Mason J (later CJ) in a minority opinion said in relation to s.109 (which is the section making commonwealth law paramount in the event of inconsistency):[267]

> "Nor is the section a source of protection to the individual against the unfairness or injustice of a retrospective law. That is a matter, which lies quite outside the focus of the provision. In these circumstances, to distil from s.109 an unexpressed fetter upon Commonwealth legislative power is to twist the section from its true meaning and stand it upon its head."

Characterisation

Most of the Commonwealth powers lie in s. 51 which provides:

> "The Parliament shall, subject to this Constitution, have power to make laws for the peace, order, and good government of the Commonwealth with respect to: (and then thirty nine heads of power and an incidental power are listed.)

The phrase "The Parliament shall … have power to make laws for the peace, order and good government" is a standard phrase used to describe the power of Parliament in a common law system and provides no limitation on the power. The phrase "with respect to" has been used by the Court as an 'incidental power' to allow an expansive view of the enumerated powers. This is in addition to the specific incidental power in s. 51(xxxix), which has been held to further extend powers to achieve administrative matters:[268]

> "Legislative power carries with it authority to legislate in relation to acts, matters and things the control of which is found necessary to effectuate its main purpose, and thus carries with it power to make laws governing or affecting many matters that are incidental or ancillary to the subject matter."

To decide whether legislation is within power it must be 'characterised' as to its actual operation and purpose and then it can be decided if that is within a specified constitutional power.

---

266 *University of Wollongong v Metwally* (1984) 158 CLR 447.
267 Ibid. p 463.
268 *Grannall v Marrickville Margarine Pty Ltd* (1955) 93 CLR 55 at p. 77.

A starting point for this process is the US formulation by Roberts J:[269]

> "When an act of Congress is appropriately challenged in the courts as not conforming to the constitutional mandate the judicial branch of the government has only one duty -- to lay the article of the Constitution which is invoked beside the statute which is challenged and the decide whether the latter squares with the former."

Early High Court decisions followed this legalistic approach. To invoke this approach reference was sometimes had to the 'pith and substance' test of the purpose of the Act being impugned to decide whether it is a matter of Commonwealth or State power. However, one judge's pith may not appeal to another judge's view of the substance.

In practice the process of comparing the characterised legislation against constitutional power becomes intertwined, because the constitutional powers are only baldly stated. Their definition is in the cases so the new legislation is characterised by the court in relation to its own earlier decisions.

The 'pith and substance' test ended in the *Bank Nationalisation* cases. After the Second World War the Labor government decided to nationalise the banking industry. The *Banking Act* 1947 (Cth) empowered the Commonwealth to acquire the shares, dismiss the directors and nominate government representatives to the boards of private banks and prohibited the carrying on of banking business by private banks. The Act provided for a method to process claims for compensation. This acquisition was very controversial. The banking power (s. 51(xiii)), the corporation power (s. .51(xx)) and the acquisition power (s. 51(xxx)) were all potential heads of power to authorise this. The legislation was challenged and the case found its way both to the Privy Council and the High Court. In the High Court, Rich and Williams JJ used the pith and substance approach to find that banning private banking was a law about ownership, not a law about banking under s. 51 (xiii). Latham CJ rejected the pith and substance test, saying, "there is no rule that will settle all cases"[270] but arrived at the same result by finding that because the banks to be acquired had business that were not banking, and business outside Australia the acquisition was beyond power. Dixon J. reformulated the approach in these terms:[271]

> "The purpose of the enumerated powers in s. 51 is not to define or delimit the description of law that the Parliament may make upon any of the subjects assigned to it. Speaking generally, the legislative power so given is plenary in its quality. The purpose of the enumeration is to name a subject for the purpose of assigning it to that power. The names or descriptions employed are usually of the briefest kind. …

[269] *US v Butler* (1936) 297 US 1 at p.62, quoted in Blackshield & Williams, op cit at p.558.
[270] *Bank of NSW v Commonwealth (Bank Nationalisation Case)* (1948) 76 CLR 1, at p. 186.
[271] Ibid.

The power with respect to banking seems to me a plain example of the designation of a broad subject without any indication of the means by which it is to be dealt with or of the existence of limits upon the description of the laws to be made with respect thereto. …

For the reasons I have indicated, I am unable to accept the view that the word 'banking' should have ascribed to it anything but the wide meaning and flexible application of a general expression designating, as a subject of legislative power, a matter forming part of the commercial economic and social organisation of the community."

He, with the majority, found that the compensation was not just compensation in accordance with s. 51(xxxi). This case also found its way to the Privy Council in London. The Privy Council could not consider whether the Act was within power because that is the type of matter that required a certificate under section 74 of the Constitution to hear an appeal on this type of case, and the High Court did not issue one (it never does). The Privy Council found that the legislation offended section 92, which protects free trade between the States[272]. Both courts were determined to protect the private ownership of the banks.

As an alternative measure the government established its own bank known as the Commonwealth Bank. It was ironic that after this huge controversy that led to the Labor government establishing its own bank, a later Labor government in the 1990s privatised this bank.

The upshot of this is that the test is now whether a particular law can be characterised as related to the broad topic set out in the Constitution. This wide test is consistent with the growth of Commonwealth power permitted by the High Court. The wider the test of what is within enumerated powers the greater the actual power that is conferred. The present position has been summarised by the respected commentators Tony Blackshield and George Williams in these terms:[273]

"This is another reason why the simple model of characterisation in *United States v Butler* is inadequate. That model would be plausible only if the question were whether or not a law could be characterised as being 'on' the permitted subject. But the question posed by the opening words of s. 51 is whether the law is one 'with respect to' the specified topic- a broader and looser question. Moreover, in answering this question as it arises in relation to any particular law, the Court does not demand to be satisfied that it *is* a law 'with respect to' the relevant topic, but only that it can *fairly be described* as a law 'with respect to' that topic. It is this question -- whether the constitutionally supportive description of the law is a fair description -- that is answered by 'characterisation'."

---

272 *Commonwealth v Bank of NSW (Bank Nationalisation case)* (1950) AC 235.
273 Blackshield and Williams (1998), op. cit. at p.563.

The High Court has interpreted its powers to preclude giving advisory opinions so that the legislation must be passed and in place before it can be tested in the High Court and even then its validity will be tested in the context of a particular fact situation. It will be characterised and then held up to the test of whether it can be fairly described as a law in respect of the power in section 51. It then falls on scholars to undertake the sometimes difficult task of drawing those decisions into a cohesive whole. This contrasts with the civil code method where the scholars have carefully drawn a cohesive whole and the judges work within it.

An example of a broad approach taken by the High Court is in relation to s. 51(xxi) which gives the Commonwealth power over 'marriage' alone in contrast to s. 51(xxii) which gives it power over 'divorce and matrimonial causes; and in relation thereto, parental rights and the custody and guardianship of infants'. Common law rules of interpretation suggest that the express inclusion of a matter in one clause implies that its omission in another is significant.[274] Hence it would follow that the express extension of the divorce power to include parental rights of custody and guardianship of infants implies that the power over marriage, which has no express extension, should be read down to not include parental rights of custody and guardianship in relation to marriage itself. Although some judges took this narrow view, which is consistent with normal principles of interpretation, the majority view of the High Court is that the power in relation to marriage is extensive and includes parental rights.[275]

In the recent *Industrial Relations Case* the majority of the High Court summarised the principles of interpretation in these terms:[276]

> "142 The general principles to be applied in determining whether a law is with respect to a head of legislative power are well settled. It is necessary, always, to construe the constitutional text and to do that "with all the generality which the words used admit".[277] The character of the law must then be determined by reference to the rights, powers, liabilities, duties and privileges which it creates[278]. The practical as well as the legal operation of the law must be examined[279]. If a law fairly answers the description of being a law with respect to two subject-matters, one a subject-matter within s 51 and the other not, it is valid notwithstanding there is no independent connection between the two subject-matters[280]. Finally, as remarked in *Grain Pool of Western Australia v The Commonwealth*[281], "if a sufficient connection with the head of power does exist,

274 A principle sometimes described in the Latin maxim *Expressio unius est exclusio alterius:* the expression of one thing excludes the other. See footnote 98.

275 *Russell v Russell* (1976) 134 CLR 495.

276 *NSW and others v Commonwealth*, (2006) High Court 52, (14 November 2006) at para 142.

277 *R v Public Vehicles Licensing Appeal Tribunal (Tas); Ex parte Australian National Airways Pty Ltd* (1964) 113 CLR 207 at 225-226; *Grain Pool of Western Australia v The Commonwealth* (2000) 202 CLR 479 at 492 [16].

278 *Kartinyeri v The Commonwealth* (1998) 195 CLR 337 at 352-353 [7], 372 [58]; *Grain Pool* (2000) 202 CLR 479 at 492 [16].

279 *Re Dingjan* (1995) 183 CLR 323 at 369; *Grain Pool* (2000) 202 CLR 479 at 492 [16].

280 *Re F; Ex parte F* (1986) 161 CLR 376 at 388; *Grain Pool* (2000) 202 CLR 479 at 492 [16].

281 (2000) 202 CLR 479 at 492 [16].

the justice and wisdom of the law, and the degree to which the means it adopts are necessary or desirable, are matters of legislative choice[282]"."

In the same case Kirby J in commenting on the formulation of Kitto J in *Fairfax v Federal Commissioner of Taxation*[283] referring to the "true nature and character" and "real substance" of legislation said:[284]

> "Any decision-maker, approaching criteria expressed by reference to adjectival expressions such as "true", "real" or "in truth", will understand that he or she has reached the point where further verbal explanation is impossible. An opinion, in the nature of a judgment, must be provided. Legal analysis, expressed in words, can only go so far. To pretend otherwise is to succumb to the mesmerising effect of verbal formulae. It is to deny the inescapably personal judgment of the decision-maker in an illusory quest for an entirely scientific objectivity that does not exist in the task of legal characterisation."

Collateral purposes

The power of the Commonwealth has extended beyond the obvious meaning of the Constitution by the Commonwealth attaching conditions to money grants and by making the granting of licences within power the subject of conditions in fields outside its constitutional ambit. The High Court has usually upheld this. An example occurred in relation to S.51 (i), the trade and commerce power which gives the Commonwealth the power to regulate exports. The Commonwealth government refused to give an export licence for the export of sand from Fraser Island, without a prior investigation into environmental issues. Fraser Island is an environmentally sensitive sand island in Queensland at the south end of the Great Barrier Reef. It is the largest sand island in the world. In reality this was not an export issue, rather the Commonwealth government did not want mining on the island, but the Queensland state government did. The mining company took the case to the High Court on the basis that the environmental conditions were not an appropriate exercise of the export power. In *Murphyores Incorporated Pty Ltd v. Commonwealth*[285] the High Court upheld these conditions, even though they were for the collateral purpose to prevent sand mining from proceeding on Fraser Island, which is now much valued as a tourist destination. Part of the logic of this decision is that the trade and commerce power is not a purposive power. The constitutional issue is simply a matter of whether the legislation is in respect of trade and commerce. The fact that an action by the Commonwealth government has an ulterior, or collateral, purpose is not relevant to its validity. This was consistent with much older cases that permitted the Commonwealth to require preference to unionised waterside workers, again under the guise of the trade and commerce power. This was held to be a valid use of the power[286].

---

[282] *Leask* (1996) 187 CLR 579 at 602.

[283] (1965) 114 CLR 1 at 7.

[284] The *Industrial Relations Case*, op. cit at para 494.

[285] (1976-7) 136 CLR 1.

[286] *Huddart Parker v Commonwealth* (1931) 44 CLR 492.

Conclusion

These are examples of how judging involves the weighing of competing community interests and evolving standards. No doubt the mining community in QLD was deeply angered by the Fraser Island decision but in the southern States a stronger concern for environmental issues made it popular. The Court is not subject to populism because it does not need to face election, but neither is it, nor should it be, immune from community interests. The High Court has become more sophisticated in the tests it uses to interpret the Constitution, but these cloak the underlying disagreement over the extent that the judiciary should be adventurous in its interpretations and more fundamentally the extent to which it should be open and honest in disclosing the underlying policy reasons which influence the interpretations the judges make. The wartime decisions are one clear example how policy issues can lead to changes in interpretation. Here the Court admitted their decisions were influenced by the necessity of war. In decisions such as the *Bank Nationalisation Case* and the *Goulden Case* over life insurance the Court seemed to be concerned to protect fundamental financial institutions in a private enterprise structure. The Court showed a greater concern for the protection of property rather than religion in the *Jehovah's Witnesses Case* discussed in Chapter 3. In these cases and in the *Communist Party Case*, discussed in Chapter 6, where it limited the defence power to protect basic civil liberties without spelling that out, the Court has arrived at its decision, without making explicit, the implicit policy reasons that have influenced it. On the other hand it has implied a right of free speech in political matters for disclosed policy reasons. In the *Industrial Relations Case* it has taken a giant stride towards undoing the basic federal nature of the division of powers under the guise of a conservative literal interpretation of the Constitution. It appears as if some underlying policies are more readily articulated than others.

Chapter 6:

SPECIFIC POWERS

The main source of the power of the Commonwealth government is in s. 51 of the Commonwealth Constitution. The powers are subject to limitations elsewhere in the Constitution, thus for example the exercise of a power should not interfere with the freedom of religion protected by s.116. Six of these powers are discussed in this Chapter to describe how the High Court has developed them. It will quickly become clear that the present day extent of these powers might surprise the draftsmen of the Constitution.

The industrial relations power

51. The Parliament shall, subject to this Constitution, have power to make laws for the peace, order, and good government of the Commonwealth with respect to:

    (xxxv) conciliation and arbitration for the prevention and settlement of industrial disputes extending beyond the limits of any one State.

At the time of federation Australia had a strong trade union movement which led to the inclusion of the industrial relations power and a strong tradition of central fixing of wage rates and award conditions. The Commonwealth power is limited to conciliation & arbitration of industrial disputes and must have an interstate component. However, in combination with other powers such as the trade and commerce power and corporations power this power is extensive. Until now industrial law has been coincident work of both the Commonwealth and the States. There have been various incarnations of the Conciliation & Arbitration Court and Commission. It was held to be exercising judicial power without complying with the requirements of a Chapter III court in its early days[287]. This was remedied and it was split into a court and a commission to deal with conciliation and award matters. For decades on an annual basis it fixed a minimum wage and wage rates for trades, clerical and service industries, teachers and nurses and many other low to middle paid workers, which have de facto effect for the whole of Australia. Sometimes with the States in Labor party government and the Federal Government in Liberal National party or free trade hands (or vice versa) there is a competition between the policies of the two. More recently the trend has been to enterprise bargaining to achieve contracts between workers and employers, rather than industry wide awards. In The *State of Victoria v Commonwealth*[288] the High Court upheld the *Industrial Relations Reform Act* 1993 (Cth) and the *Industrial Relations Amendment Act (No. 2)* 1994 (Cth) that imposed minimum conditions, limitation on dismissal, equal pay for women and collective bargaining and limited the right to strike. This bound the States. The minimum conditions were upheld under the external affairs power[289] under conventions ratified

---

287 *Waterside Workers' Federation v JW Alexander Ltd* (1918) CLR 434, see Chapter 2.

288 (1995-6) 187 CLR 416.

289 s. 51(xxix).

by Australia under the International Labour Organisation. The collective bargaining provisions were upheld under the corporations power[290].

In 2005 the Liberal Country party gained power over the Senate and embarked on an aggressive policy to remove the award system and to allow easy dismissal of workers in an attempt to introduce a more flexible wage and conditions structure and to wind back the award system Australia has known for a hundred years. This undermines the power of the trade union movement who to a large extent finance the Labor party. This has been vigorously resisted by the unions and with the States in Labor government hands it led to a major case in the High Court contesting the new laws. In the *Industrial Relations Case*[291] a majority of five of the seven judges delivered a comprehensive victory to the Commonwealth government, upholding all the new legislation. The legislation was clearly beyond the industrial relations power but was upheld under the corporations power. They made the point that there is no reason why legislation cannot find its source of power in more than one place. Just because the new laws are beyond the industrial relations power does no prevent them finding legitimacy in another power such as the corporations power. This would seem to relegate the industrial relations power to relative unimportance.

Another recent case showed that legislative authority in this area lies in powers other than s. 51 (xxxv). The issue here was how much connection the industrial issue must have with Australia to be subject to Australian law[292]. CSL Pacific is incorporated in Barbados. One ship of its fleet operated in Australia, transporting goods between Australian ports, with a Ukrainian crew recruited in the Ukraine. This crew's employment conditions were governed by an agreement with the International Transport Federation. The Maritime Union of Australia, a powerful Australian union, applied to the Australian Industrial Relations Commission to amend the Australian award, the *Maritime Industry Seagoing Award* 1999 so as to include CSL Pacific. A sufficient connection was held to exist, despite the employer being based overseas and employees being engaged overseas, not residing in Australia and not being members of an Australian industrial organisation. They were, however, shipping goods between Australian ports and the subject matter of the law, the regulation of employment in activities forming part of trade and commerce amongst States, was deemed to be sufficiently connected to the trade and commerce power (s. 51 (i)). Here again the industrial relations power of the Commonwealth relies more on other powers. Under these powers it is now clear that the Commonwealth may exercise power over industrial issues within the States, notwithstanding the clear intention of the Constitution that this power in s. 51 (xxxv) not extend that far.

---

290 s. 51(xx).

291 *NSW and others v Commonwealth* (2006) High Court 52 (15 November 2006). This is also discussed under the corporations power and in chapter 4: The Balance of Power between the States and the Commonwealth.

292 *Re The Maritime Union of Australia & Ors; Ex parte CSL Pacific Shipping Inc* (2003) 214 CLR 397.

The corporations power

51. The Parliament shall, subject to this Constitution, have power to make laws for the peace, order, and good government of the Commonwealth with respect to:

    (xx) foreign corporations, and trading or financial corporations formed within the limits of the Commonwealth.

This power has been widely relied on to regulate the governance of corporations, their conduct and consumer protection through trade practices legislation and some aspects of the industrial legislation.

The extent of Commonwealth legal authority under the corporations power has varied over time. This power was initially given a very narrow interpretation by the High Court. Some early trade practices legislation known as the *Australian Industries Preservation Act* 1906 (Cth) prohibited unfair competition and gave power to the customs authority to require a corporation to answer questions about an allegation of such conduct. This was held to be beyond power in *Huddart Parker & Co Pty Ltd v Moorehead*[293] where the majority took a very narrow view of this power, and of the trade and commerce power. The High Court interpreted the corporations and trade and commerce power not to apply to domestic transactions within a State. This early High Court approach of protecting the reserve powers of states was overthrown in the *Engineers Case*[294]. The effect of this in relation to the corporations power was not tested until *Strickland v Rocla Concrete Pipes Ltd (Concrete Pipes Case)*[295]. The High Court in this case expressly overturned *Huddart Parker v Moorehead* but found that later the trade practices legislation still went beyond the Corporations power as it was not limited to matters within the corporations power and trade and commerce power. At this point the power was held to extend to the conduct of the corporations and in particular fair trading requirements for corporations, not to individuals dealing with them.

The High Court upheld legislation regulating the conduct of individuals dealing with corporations in *Actors and Announcers Equity Association v Fontana Films Pty Ltd*[296]. The *Trade Practices Act* 1974 (Cth) had been amended to make it an offence for a trade union to arrange for a boycott of a company. The Court held this was within power because the boycotts affected the affairs of the company.

In *The Queen v Trade Practices Tribunal; Ex parte St George County Council*[297] the Court took a narrow view of the term 'trading corporation' in finding that a municipal council body which sold electricity was not a 'trading corporation' under s. 51(xx).

293 (1909) 8 CLR 330.
294 See Chapter 4.
295 (1971) 124 CLR 468.
296 (1982) 150 CLR 169.
297 (1974) 130 CLR 533.

This was distinguished[298] in *The Queen v Federal Court of Australia; Ex parte WA National Football League*[299]. A footballer wished to change clubs from Western Australia to a club called Norwood in South Australia but his old club would not give him a clearance. The club and the league were both incorporated associations but claimed their activity of promoting and running football[300] did not make them 'trading corporations'. The Court held that *St George County Council* was decided not in relation to the nature of the activity of the corporation, but because of its origins as a municipal council. Mason J said:[301]

> "'Trading corporation' is not and never has been a term of art or one having a special legal meaning. Nor, as the Chief Justice pointed out (in *St George County Council*), was there a generally accepted definition of the expression in the nineteenth century. Essentially it is a description or label given to a corporation when its trading activities form a sufficiently significant proportion of its overall activities as to merit its description as a trading corporation."

This definition is now accepted as the best description of what constitutes a 'trading corporation' and it extends to most corporate bodies, as most of them undertake trading activities. It was accepted in the *Industrial Relations Case* (discussed below) as the definitive statement on this topic. As such most municipal corporations are now be considered to be 'trading corporations'. Thus *St George County Council* has been distinguished out of effective existence, without being over ruled, demonstrating the flexibility of the common law method.

Trade practice legislation in Australia now regulates restrictive trade practices of trading corporations such as retail price maintenance, price-cutting and monopolistic behaviour. Much of this legislation was introduced by the Labor Government of the Whitlam era.

It was assumed for many years that the expanding view of the corporations power extended to the power to regulate the formation of companies which for many years the Commonwealth regulated without challenge. However, in the *Incorporation Case*[302] the High Court threw out the national scheme, which provided a uniform set of procedures for the incorporation and regulation of companies. The Court decided that the section assumed the corporations were already formed (formed in the section is in the past tense) and control over their formation was not a matter of Commonwealth power. The States can refer (give) powers to the Commonwealth[303]. They don't like doing this but they had to in this instance to provide commercial certainty. The States have referred sufficient power to the Commonwealth to have a national Corporations Law dealing with the formation of companies[304]. In coming to this arrangement the

---

298 To distinguish, to find a case is different on the facts, or some other basis so it is not necessary to follow the ratio decidendi.

299 (1979) 143 CLR 190.

300 This is Australian Rules Football as distinct from soccer.

301 (1979) 143 CLR 190 at 233.

302 *NSW v the Commonwealth- the Incorporation case* (1990) 169 CLR 482.

303 s. 51(xxxvii).

304 *Corporations (Commonwealth Powers) Act* 2001 in each State.

States retained influence over certain key appointments in corporate regulation such as the head of the Australian Securities and Investments Commission (ASIC) which monitors breaches of the law and prosecutes where it finds them.

The potential for the corporations power to expand Commonwealth power has become explicit in the *Industrial Relations Case*[305]. In this case the High Court permitted the Commonwealth to transform Australia's industrial relations system, moving it to an individual contract basis. Since most employers are corporations in one form or another this legislation will affect some 85% of the workforce. The majority held that the corporations power is not limited to the regulation of the external affairs of corporations and it is not necessary for the nature or distinctive character of the law to be the regulation of corporations (as opposed to industrial relations as it was for these laws). Even though there is a separate industrial relations power (s. 51(xxxv)) which is limited to the prevention and settlement of disputes with an interstate component the new laws could not be solely characterised as a law under that power and read down accordingly. Previous unsuccessful referenda to expand the industrial affairs power were not relevant. Each of these arguments was considered by the majority and held no impediment to the validity of the new industrial relations laws. They held to be these laws were properly regarded as a law to regulate corporations and are enforceable. This is a precedent to permit a separate head of power to be used for a wide variety of purposes, which may be apparently inconsistent with other powers in the Constitution. Corporations conduct most commercial activity, and now what is a corporation for the purposes of s. 51(xx) includes a wide range of bodies such as municipal councils and charitable organisations.

This decision will permit the Commonwealth to radically extend its power far into areas apparently reserved to the States under the plain meaning of the Constitution. It is noteworthy that this seismic constitutional shift has attracted only muted controversy except in academic circles. This makes an interesting contrast to the strident response to the *Mabo (No.2)* decision discussed below.

The external affairs power

51. The Parliament shall, subject to this Constitution, have power to make laws for the peace, order, and good government of the Commonwealth with respect to:

    (xxix) external affairs.

The inclusion of this power in the Constitution was a clear sign of Australia's independence from the United Kingdom, and this power has clear potential to increase the power of the Commonwealth by the adoption of international obligations. This potential became clear first in a case of *R* v *Burgess: ex parte Henry*[306]. Mr Henry flew an aircraft in New South Wales without the appropriate licence under the *Air Navigation Regulations* 1920, made under the *Air Navigation Act* 1920 (Cth), which relied upon a treaty regulating air navigation matters drawn up in Paris and ratified by

[305] *NSW and others v the Commonwealth* (2006) HCA 52 (14 November 2006).

[306] (1936) 55 CLR 608. "Ex parte" means in the absence of a party.

the British Government on behalf of the British Commonwealth, including Australia[307]. The Court upheld the regulations and ruled that the external affairs power gave a broad power to the Commonwealth Government to enact into Australian law international obligations that Australia accepted.

The Executive negotiates and signs treaties. The treaty then is placed before a joint committee of both Houses of Parliament[308] for fifteen sitting days. If there is no objection it can then be ratified. Once a treaty is ratified the Commonwealth can enact legislation to give it effect and this might give the Commonwealth power over areas not specified in s. 51. A treaty obligation can also enter Australian law in areas where the Executive can adopt it without legislation, such as trade or defence, or by adoption by the High Court into the common law as with human rights obligations.

The full implications of this power did not become apparent for another fifty years. In 1973 the Commonwealth government took over sovereignty of the seabed. The States contested the transfer from their authority to the Commonwealth in *NSW v. Commonwealth.*[309] The High Court held that this was authorised because under the foreign affairs power the Commonwealth had adopted the Convention on the Territorial Sea and Contiguous Zone. A subsequent agreement between the Commonwealth and the States resolved this issue with a retransfer of authority over territorial sea to the States. In the end there was no loss of power to the States but this was an important indicator of how the Commonwealth may gain power through the adoption of treaty obligations.

In the case of *Koowarta v. Bjelke-Petersen*[310] the Court upheld the *Racial Discrimination Act* 1975 (Cth)[311] as a valid adoption of the International Convention on the Elimination of all forms of Racial Discrimination which Australia ratified on 30 September 1975[312]. In Queensland, the Minister of Lands refused to grant consent to the transfer of a pastoral lease, which the Aboriginal Land Fund Commission acquired for Mr Koowarta on behalf of the members of his tribal group. The reasons given for the refusal was that it was not Queensland Government policy to "acquire large areas of additional freehold or leasehold land for the development by Aborigines or Aboriginal groups in isolation." Section 9(1) of the *Racial Discrimination Act* 1975 (Cth), which enacted the Treaty provided:

> "It is unlawful for a person to do any act involving a distinction, exclusion, restriction or preference based on race, colour, descent or national or ethnic origin which has the purpose or effect of nullifying or impairing the recognition,

---

307 An indication of the influence the British Government still exercised over the foreign affairs matters of its former Dominions at that time. *The Statute of Westminster* 1931 (Imp) formally set this at an end when it was adopted by Australia effective as at 1939 (see Chapter 1).

308 The Standing Committee on Treaties – SCOT comprised of nine members from the House of Representatives and seven from the Senate.

309 (1975-6) 135 CLR 337.

310 (1982) 153 CLR 168.

311 This was another piece of legislation passed by the Whitlam government.

312 H. Lee and G. Winterton *Australian Constitutional Perspectives* (1992) The Law Book Co. Ltd. Sydney, p.67.

enjoyment or exercise on an equal footing, of any human right or fundamental freedom in the political, economic social, cultural or any other field of public life."

The High Court used the external affairs power to uphold the validity of the *Racial Discrimination Act* 1975 (Cth) to overturn the State Government decision. This case pointed the path to an extension of Commonwealth power through the adoption of treaty obligations. This path was then made clearer in *Commonwealth v. Tasmania*[313] known as the *Tasmanian Dam Case*. This case had as a backdrop a quite comical incident when the Federal Government ordered the Air Force to fly over a large potential hydro electro dam area in Tasmania, the island State to the south of Australia, to gather photographic evidence to support the Commonwealth legal case. Needless to say the use of the air force was seen as threatening by the Tasmanian government.

The Franklin and Gordon Rivers were in pristine wilderness in the South West of Tasmania. The Hydro Electric Commission in Tasmania excised a large area from a wilderness national park with the intention of damming the Gordon River to create a large hydroelectric scheme. This park was nominated for World Heritage Listing. To stop the construction of the dam the Commonwealth Government introduced regulations under the *National Parks Wildlife and Conservation Act* 1975 (Cth) and passed a special Act, *The World Heritage Properties Conservation Act* 1983[314]. The Court upheld the legislation under the foreign affairs power and the Franklin and Gordon Rivers remained pristine and are now substantial tourist assets.

There have been continuing battles fought between the Green movement and logging and other development lobbies and this power of the Commonwealth to intervene has been further supported in *Richards v The Forestry Commission (The Lemonthyme case)*[315] where the Commonwealth was able to protect forest areas not yet nominated for the World Heritage list.

The extent of the external affairs power can be seen in *Polyukovich v Commonwealth*[316] where the Court upheld retrospective legislation allowing prosecution of Australian residents for war crimes committed in Europe in WWII. Polyukovich was a Ukranian allegedly involved in the massacre of Jews in a village in Ukraine. A jury ultimately acquitted him. Before this the validity of the legislation was upheld in the High Court based on the external affairs power. A majority of the Court held that simply because the matter was physically external to Australia it was a valid exercise of power. Two judges in the minority, Deane and Gaudron JJ held it was a law with respect to external affairs but was invalid because it was against the fundamental implied principle against retrospective criminal culpability. These were judges who sought to imply basic rights into the constitution through the common law[317].

---

313 (1983) 158 CLR 1.

314 Winterton & Lee, op cit., p. 69.

315 (1988) 164 CLR 261.

316 (1991) 172 CLR 501.

317 See Chapter 3.

An example of the Court upholding this power in Australia's self interest involved a challenge to legislation dealing with the Timor Gap. Australia claims an extension to its normal under sea boundary in this area because Australia's continental shelf, which contains significant oil and gas reserves, extends to the Timor Gap, a deep sea trench close to the island of Timor. All of Timor, an island, was part of Indonesia at the time. Australia concluded a treaty with Indonesia agreeing the boundary and resource issues whilst a secession movement gathered strength in East Timor. Jose Ramos Horta was a representative of the resistance to Indonesian government in East Timor and, with others, sought to contest the validity of the Timor Gap arrangements between Australia and Indonesia. The Court took the view that:[318]

> "It is clear that the area of the Timor Gap and the exploration for, and exploitation of, petroleum resources within that area all fall within that phrase (external affairs). Each of those matters is geographically external to Australia. There is an obvious and substantial nexus between each of them and Australia. As the enactment of the Act demonstrates, they are all matters which the Parliament recognises as affecting or touching Australia. That being so, the enactment of the law with respect to one or all those matters is prime facie within the legislative power conferred by section 51(xxix)."

The external affairs power is controversial because of the extent to which it can extend Commonwealth power beyond it listed constitutional powers. The acceptance of treaty obligations by the executive enables the Commonwealth parliament to enact enabling legislation that would be beyond power without the treaty. Apart from the shift of power to the Commonwealth that this allows, this also confirms the worst fears of people opposed to globalisation.

The defence power

> 51. The Parliament shall, subject to this Constitution, have power to make laws for the peace, order, and good government of the Commonwealth with respect to:
>
> (vi) the naval and military defence of the Commonwealth and of the several States, and the control of the forces to execute and maintain the laws of the Commonwealth.

The High Court has taken a very pragmatic approach to the defence power and has permitted it to extend to matters far beyond the maintenance of armed forces. In the First World War, Isaacs J. argued that the limits of the defence power "are bounded only by the requirements of self-preservation" and if:[319]

---

318 *Horta and others v Commonwealth* (1994) 181 CLR 183, at para 8. Later when East Timor became independent from Indonesia, Jose Ramos Horta became a minister in the new government, and later Prime Minister, then President of East Timor. The treaty dealing with the Timor Gap was renegotiated but Horta still complained that Australia had forced an unfair settlement on the new government of East Timor.

319 *Farey v Burvett* (1916) 21 CLR 433 at pp. 453-456.

"the measure questioned may conceivably in such circumstances even incidentally aid the effectuation of the power of defence, the Court must hold its hand and leave the rest to the judgment and wisdom and discretion of the Parliament and the executive it controls - for they alone have the information, the knowledge and the experience and also, by the Constitution, the authority to judge of the situation and lead the nation to the desired end."

In the Second World War Rich J. said a country with a federal form of government:[320]

"...cannot hope to survive unless it submits itself for the time being to what is in effect a dictatorship with power to do anything which can contribute to its defence."

An example in the Second World War involved employment of women. A women's employment board was created relying on national security regulations. These were upheld by the High Court but eventually the regulations were disallowed in the Senate. This led to the *Women's Employment Act* 1942 (Cth) to validate the determination of women to be employed in jobs that were previously exclusively a male preserve and importantly after a probation period to pay them ninety percent of the male award rate. Outside wartime this legislation clearly was beyond power. The Court held that the legislation:[321]

"deals with the problem which has arisen from war, and with which it may reasonably be considered to be necessary to deal with in order to promote the successful prosecution of the war. The legislation is directed towards the efficient supply of goods and services, both for the army and the civil community, by organising the labour power of the community, insofar as it may depend upon the work of women, who in large numbers have been brought into such employment by reason of war exigencies."

The war effort involved a substantial transfer of real power from the States to the Commonwealth. The changed financial arrangements brought about to finance the war effort were discussed in Chapter 4. The expanded view of the defence power in wartime was used to justify some of these changes. These changes once made have never been reversed.

This expanded Commonwealth power under the defence power all came to an end in *The King v Foster.*[322] This was an application to declare invalid an order made by Judge Foster in relation to wages and conditions of women still employed under wartime regulations in December 1948. The High Court held:

---

320 *Dawson v Commonwealth* (1946) 73 CLR 157 at p. 177.

321 *Victorian Chamber of Manufacturers v Commonwealth* (1943) CLR 347.

322 (1949) 79 CLR 43. The Crown is a party not because it was criminal case but because it was an application for a prerogative writ which are applied for in the name of the Crown.

> "The Constitution does not confer upon the Commonwealth Parliament any power in express terms to deal with the consequences of war, but there are some consequences which undeniably fall within the scope of the legislative power with respect to defence. Repatriation and rehabilitation of soldiers is an obvious case. Rebuilding of a city, which has been destroyed or damaged by bombing, would be another case. …
>
> The effects of the past war will continue for centuries. The war has produced or contributed to changes in nearly every circumstance which affects the lives of civilised people. If it were held that the defence power would justify any legislation at any time which dealt with any matter the character of which had been changed by the war, or with any problem which had been created or aggravated by the war, then the result would be that the Commonwealth Parliament would have a general power of making laws for the peace order and good government of Australia with respect to almost every subject."

The Court noted that the wages and conditions could be dealt with under other award procedures. The time of war was over and the High Court was at that time chose to limit the power of the Commonwealth.

Another example of the narrow view of the defence power outside war time involved the *Communist Party Case.*[323] This involved an attempt by the newly elected Menzies government to ban the Australian Communist Party by the *Communist Party Dissolution Act* 1950 (Cth). This was a time of the Cold War and Australia had sent troops to Korea to fight a communist enemy. There was a heightened sense of crisis in the USA leading up to the McCarthy hearings seeking out communists in all walks of life. It was argued that this was a time requiring drastic measures to protect the free world against the communist menace. In this way parallels could be drawn to the threat of terrorist attacks in our current times. The Act declared the Communist Party to be an unlawful association, dissolved it and appointed a receiver[324] to manage its property. There was power to declare that a person was a communist with the consequence that the person could not hold office in the Commonwealth public service or in industries declared by the Governor-General to be vital to the security and defence of Australia. In making such declarations the Governor-General would of course follow the advice of the government of the day. The recitals to the Act declared that "it is necessary, for the security and defence of Australia … that the Australian Communist Party… should be dissolved." In wartime this would have most likely have been accepted by the Court.

In relation to the declaration on the recital the Court held:[325]

---

323 *Australian Communist Party v Commonwealth (Communist Party Case)* (1951) 83 CLR 1.

324 A person appointed under authority of a debenture to run the affairs of a company that defaulted on the debenture. An appointment of this sort may be made by a court to enforce orders against a debtor.

325 Ibid, per McTiernan J at p. 205.

> "The recitals are in no way decisive of the question whether the Act is valid or invalid, for that is a judicial question which only the Judicature has the power to decide finally and conclusively. If any fact stated in the recital is material to the question whether the Act is valid or invalid, the fact would need to be judicially determined or ascertained. The recitals are not judicial findings and did not bind the Judicature in any question within its own exclusive province. ... (T)he Constitution does not allow the Judicature to concede the principle that the Parliament can conclusively 'recite itself' into power."

Dixon J (as he then was)[326] identified that the powers over property and civil rights exercised in the Act were not within any head of Commonwealth power. He acknowledged the presence of Australian forces in the Korean War but distinguished this from the situation where the country was on a war footing. He treated the circumstances in effect as peacetime. He and the majority held the Act was invalid as beyond the defence power. The Commonwealth also argued it was valid as part of the inherent power to protect the Constitution. This was also rejected. Without spelling it out the High Court made a stand to protect basic political freedoms. The government tried to amend the Constitution to permit the Act to pass but the referendum failed. In a way this worked well for the Menzies government. The combination of robust economic growth through the 1950s and 60s and a fear of 'a red under the bed' as the fear of communism was sometimes styled, helped to keep it in power for the longest period of any Australian government.

In *Polyukhovich v Commonwealth (the War Crimes Case)*[327] which was mainly decided under the external affairs power Brennan J said this about the defence power:[328]

> "In times of war, laws abridging the freedoms which the law assures to the Australian people are supported in order to ensure the survival of those freedoms in times of peace. In times of peace, an abridging of those freedoms -- in this case, freedom from a retrospective criminal law -- cannot be supported unless the Court can perceive that the abridging of the freedom in question is proportionate to the defence interest to be served. What is necessary and appropriate for the defence of the Commonwealth in times of war is different from what is necessary or appropriate in times of peace."

Aborigines

51. The Parliament shall, subject to this Constitution, have power to make laws for the peace, order, and good government of the Commonwealth with respect to:

    (xxvi) the people of any race for whom it is deemed necessary to make special laws.

---

326 A politeness to acknowledge that judge who is quoted later was promoted, or elevated, to a higher judicial office.

327 Op. cit., (1991) 172 CLR 501.

328 Ibid. pp. 592-3.

Aboriginal people have been in Australia for more than 50,000 years. In that time mega-fauna have become extinct and climate has changed from lush and tropical, through harsher desert than at present, to the relatively mild coastal climate and dry pastoral to desert interior that presently prevails. Over that time sea levels fluctuated to permit several successive migrations. There was some contact between the Aborigines and Macassan islanders and later Dutch, French and Portuguese sailors as they sailed to the riches of the spice islands of South East Asia. Captain Cook claimed the East coast of Australia for England in 1770. Consequent on the loss of the American colonies, the Pitt government in England determined to settle Botany Bay as a convict colony. The first fleet arrived on 26 January 1788 and established the settlement at Sydney Cove and European contact with the Aborigines began in earnest.

This has been a chequered history. The European settlers took the best water, in a dry country, and land and when the inevitable conflicts occurred used their armed superiority of force to punish attacks by Aborigines on property and people. Much more profound harm was caused by the introduction of diseases such as small pox and influenza which devastated the Aboriginal population and cultural destruction which led to loss of dignity, disease and alcohol abuse.

At the same time official policy was to protect the Aborigines, albeit in a paternalistic way, and to introduce them to education and religion. Later paternalism gave way to assimilation and more recently a return of land rights to Aborigines in remote areas who still live in a semi tribal way. Large areas of the inland and North of Australia have been returned to Aboriginal ownership. This is a special statutory ownership conferred on the tribal group, with limitations on private development rights. This should not be confused with native title later recognised by the courts in *Mabo (No.2)* discussed below. The return of land titles has been done for the best of motives of a belated recognition of, and attempt to remedy, past wrongs. However, land rights have created new problems of statutory created councils who are a separate power group that challenge the legitimacy of traditional tribal elders, thereby resulting in fragmented authority. Linking the ownership of the land to the tribal group locks communities into a dying social arrangement and a cycle of poverty on welfare.

An icon of the recognition of Aboriginal rights and the righting of past wrongs was the return of the great red sandstone monolith near the geographic centre of Australia, Ayers Rock to Aboriginal ownership, and returning its traditional name Uluru. It was ironic, and emblematic of the difficulties in this area, that a traditional owner of that name died at that time. It is part of Aboriginal culture that a mark of respect for the dead is not to use the name of the deceased for a decent interval, often several years after the death. People of the same name are renamed Kunamurra, literally 'no-name' for that period. In the enthusiasm for the return of this great emblem this taboo was inadvertently breached as the name Uluru was on every media outlet in pride for righting previous wrongs.

In the North Queensland sugar town of Townsville they are very keen on the game known as rugby league. One of their favourite sons, who died in 1972 at the age of 74 years, has the main grandstand at the football ground named in honour of him. Hence the grandstand proudly bears the name E.S. 'Nigger' Brown. Australians have a wry sense of humour, some might even say perverse. Thus a person with bright red hair will often be nick-named Bluey. The origin of his nickname 'Nigger' is uncertain but is believed to be a reference to his blonde hair. Or perhaps it was that he had a penchant for using a brand of shoe polish that was then available called 'Nigger Brown' shoe polish[329]. Whatever its origin, the nickname stuck. It is said to even be on his gravestone. So the locals don't see it as offensive even though its origins were. The United Nations committee on the elimination of racial discrimination thinks otherwise and has said that discrimination must be measured by the standards of today and the signage should be removed. Thus our past lives with us in the present, and to evolve we must recognise this.

Here are two examples of the contrasting approaches to Aboriginal welfare in Australia's history. The first is a report from a warder[330] in Wyndam in Northwest Australia in 1901 reported in a newspaper know as the Bulletin:[331]

> "I was for some time a special warder employed by the Public Works Department to supervise native labour sent by the Gaol Department to construct a cattle road into Wyndham. Myself and another warder (armed with rifles) had charge of about 25 blacks, chained in gangs of three or four from neck to neck, about 2 foot to 2 foot 6 inches a part. Work hours 7 to 12, 2 to 5. The miserable wretches were confined at night in a galvanised iron dwelling, about 40 foot by 12 foot with no windows-only air holes about 9 foot up. They were chained by the leg at night to ring bolts in the floor, the neck chains being left on. In this black hole they had to eat their food alongside their own excrement in broken buckets in which it was impossible to put disinfectant. Their blankets were full of vermin, and the only wash they got was when, on a Saturday, they were carted down in their chains to the sea and bathed there in a batch-just to walk in and out. There was no medical officer at the time in Wyndham, and if they were sick they had to trust to their luck whether their gaoler believed them or not. When these blacks used to empty their buckets on the seashore, after incarceration-from 5.15 p.m. to 5.45 a.m. on nights when the thermometer would register 103 degrees to 105 degrees in an airy sleeping place-the stench was incredible. They were mostly cattle killers, doing from six months to two years. The local gaoler does all in his power to keep the place clean, but the Perth authorities turn a deaf ear to his repeated requisitions for better accommodation."

A contrast is this quotation from the Annual Report in 1903 of the Northern Protector of Aborigines to the Queensland Parliament:[332]

---

329 Lousie Willis, "Racist language controversy continues over the airwaves" The World Today, ABC radio, 24 April 2003.

330 A person who guards prisoners, a gaoler.

331 Evans Moore, Kay Saunders and Bryan Jamison, *Documenting Australia's Federation, 1901 Our Future's Past*, Pan Macmillan, Sydney, pp 57-59.

332 Ibid. pp.64-65.

"The Murray islanders purchased the lugger *William* from TJ Farquhar about three months ago. The purchase price was £100 payable in 12 months, bearing interest at 10%, the vendor undertaking to waive all interest if the purchase price were paid within six months. The fitting out of the boat, her insurance, and etc. cost an additional £30. The Murray Islanders have now brought in bêche-de-mer and black lip pearl shell, estimated to realise about £125; but they require new sails and other gear, and which will cost another £25 or £30. Protector Bennett, who, with Mr John Douglas, personally arranged the purchase and conducted the sale of the bêche-de-mer and shell, desired to have the boat free from debt as soon as possible, so far as the vendor and interest were concerned, and asked me if I could advance them £30 for the purpose. I have accordingly done so, and loaned them the money from the Aboriginals Protection Property account, the amount to be repaid me from the next sale of produce brought in. This deal will serve as a good object lesson, Protector Bennett thus showing the islanders what money will really buy, and teaching them how to rid themselves, not only of the middlemen, but of the exorbitant prices ordinarily charged to them by the local storekeepers. Seeing the way in which the Maubiag natives have been treated by the local European traders in dealing on the truck system (payment in goods, not cash), Protector Bennett has adopted this method of dealing a blow at it; needless to say, I was only too glad to render him the pecuniary assistance necessary."

The Murray islanders later became legally renowned. They are Torres Strait Islanders of Melanesian background. Their living tradition is to maintain gardens in a form of agriculture. One Eddie Mabo is famous for establishing a legally recognised title to his garden.

The original Constitution permitted discrimination against Aborigines in a racist way. Section 25 recognised the exclusion by two States of people from voting on the basis of race. At the time of federation Aborigines and people from Asia were prohibited from voting in Western Australia[333] and Queensland[334]. Voting by Aborigines in Commonwealth elections was discouraged by bureaucratic means, even in States where it was permitted, until the 1950s[335]. This provision is still in the Constitution, although there is no discrimination against people's right to vote in Australia today.

"25 Provision as to races disqualified from voting
For the purposes of the last section, if by the law of any State all persons of any race are disqualified from voting at elections for the more numerous House of the Parliament of the State, then, in reckoning the number of the people of the State or of the Commonwealth, persons of that race resident in that State shall not be counted."

333 *Constitution Amendment Act* 1893 (WA) s.12.

334 *Elections Act* 1885 (QLD), s.6. This also excluded South Sea islanders who were used as indentured labour on sugar plantations.

335 P. Stretton and C. Finnimore, 'Black Fellow Citizens: Aborigines and the Commonwealth Franchise" (1993) 2 *Australian Historical Studies* 521 quoted in Blackshield and Williams (1998), op cit at pp 161-162.

Section 127, now deleted, provided:

"127 Aborigines not to be included in reckoning population
In reckoning the numbers of people of the Commonwealth, or of a State or other part of the Commonwealth, aboriginal natives shall not be counted."

The use of the term 'native' in relation to Aborigines rather than the generic 'people' or 'persons' used elsewhere in the Constitution, shows a discriminatory mind set.

In 1962 the *Commonwealth Electoral Act* 1918 (Cth) was amended to clearly give Aborigines the vote and in 1967 by a referendum passed with the clearest majority ever, the Constitution was amended to delete section 127 and to delete the words "other than the Aboriginal race in any State" from section 51 (xxvi) to the effect that power to legislate for Aborigines was shifted from the States to the Commonwealth. Thus sub placitum (xxvi) had turned full circle. It was originally a racist clause to specifically permit discrimination against people on the basis of race.[336] This clause is now a basis for legislation to provide special support for Aborigines.

Stolen Children

Most States and Territories had a senior bureaucrat with responsibility for Aboriginal people, typically known, without intentional irony, as the Protector. In the Northern Territory the *Aboriginals Ordinance*[337] 1918 (NT) gave power to the Chief Protector (s. 6):[338]

> "to undertake the care, custody or control" of children if in his opinion "it was necessary or desirable in the interests of the aboriginal or half caste for him to do so."

There was genuine concern for the welfare of mixed race children on Aboriginal settlements, often conceived in casual liaisons and whose white fathers took no responsibility for them. Under a policy of assimilation these children were often seized by welfare authorities, regardless of the wishes of the parents and community, to be brought up in orphanages and adopted into the homes of white people. These homes were sometimes deeply caring and committed to the children and sometimes the adoptions were a thinly veiled opportunity for exploitation. These practices were publicly revealed in a Royal Commission[339] on a group that are now called the 'Stolen Children'. There were widespread calls for the government to say 'sorry' for these past wrongs. Australia has had national *Sorry* days where the public express regret for these past wrongs. The government has refused to say sorry on the basis that any wrongs

---

336 Sir Edmund Barton, one of the draftsmen of the Constitution, the first Prime Minister and a High Court judge said the clause was necessary "to regulate the affairs the people of coloured or inferior races who are in the Commonwealth": Blackshield and Williams (1998), op cit at p. 165. In fact Aborigines were excluded from this discriminatory provision.

337 Legislation by an authority lesser than a State, such as a Territory or a local council.

338 Blackshield and Williams (1998), op cit at p. 571.

339 A special inquiry with powers of inquisition established by the Queen on advice of the government, headed by a Royal Commissioner who is usually a judge.

were historic. Some of those taken children have made claims for compensation that have been vigorously defended by the government. On a case stated[340], the High Court upheld the validity of the Ordinance. Brennan J, a judge who is sympathetic to Aboriginal causes and whose son is a Roman Catholic priest and activist for Aboriginal rights said this:[341]

> "Moreover when a discretionary power is statutorily conferred on a repository, the power must be exercised reasonably, for the legislature is taken to intend that the discretion will be so exercised. Reasonableness can be determined only by reference to the community standards at the time of the exercise of the discretion and must be taken to be the legislative intention. Therefore, it would be erroneous in point of law to hold that a step taken in purported exercise of a discretionary power was taken unreasonably and therefore without authority if the unreasonableness arises only from a change in community standards that has occurred since the step was taken. However that may be, even if the powers conferred by s. 6 of the Ordinance and by the removal regulations were misused in the cases of the plaintiff children, the fact of misuse would not affect the validity of those provisions."

This was a preliminary ruling to clarify the law to the effect that the plaintiffs could only succeed if they could prove an abuse of the power exercised under the Ordinance at the time. Although the plaintiffs were all 'stolen children', when the case went to trial none of them could prove they were taken in circumstances that were an abuse of power and they lost the claim for damages.

Mabo (No. 2)[342]

Australia has a very high level of home ownership. Land ownership is fundamental to its culture. The law of the ownership of land is based on English medieval law. When the King gave a grant of land he usually gave it to a Baron and all his heirs and successors forever. That is called a grant[343] of an estate in fee simple[344]. It is the formal way to explain freehold[345] ownership of the land. The owner of the land can then lease[346] or mortgage[347] it to other people. To keep track of who owns the land, and who

---

340 A set of questions on law that a lower court refers to a higher court for guidance.

341 *Kruger v Commonwealth (Stolen Children Case)* (1997) 190 CLR 1. Note the difference between this approach, in a judgment in relation to a claim for damages for past wrongs compared to the United Nations view in relation to contemporary issues in relation to "Nigger" Brown and to *Mabo (No 2)* where the land law was rewritten according to contemporary standards rather than the standards that applied at the time of European settlement. Brennan J was part of the *Mabo (No 2)* majority that recognised native title, discussed below.

342 *Mabo v State of QLD (No. 2)* (1992) 175 CLR 1.

343 A grant of land is the creation of the freehold title to land by the Crown, which originally owned all the land (now subject to native title).

344 Freehold title to real estate (land).

345 Title for land that vests it completely in the owner and her heirs.

346 A temporary land title for a periodic or fixed term for which rent is paid.

347 A security over real estate for a loan.

has leases and mortgages over it, there is a central registration system known as the Torrens title system[348] which originated in South Australia.

An alternative system of land tenure is by a crown lease[349], and where that is for the particular purpose of grazing stock such as sheep or cattle it may be known as a pastoral lease.[350] In this arrangement the government grants the lease to a landowner for say 25 years or 50 years at a fairly low rental and will usually renew it without any difficulty at the end of its term. In Australia there are some huge cattle stations held under Pastoral Leases. Some of these are nearly as big as England.

All this land tenure is based on the legal assumption that there were no existing legal rights to land when Great Britain took possession of Australia. Australia was 'terra nullius'. Captain Cook visited in 1770 and took possession of the Eastern part of Australia. In 1788 Governor Phillip arrived and confirmed that possession. Legally it was a vacuum and English law applied. The land was within the gift of the Crown to grant to whomever it wanted. There was the population of aboriginal natives but it was convenient to see them as nomadic and with no ownership of the land. Their social organisation and their legal system was oral and was given no ongoing status. To an imperial colonialist power this was obvious and simple, and in accordance with the realities of its power.

Everyone accepted this view of legal reality until the Mabo cases. After them the whole world changed. In the second Mabo case the High Court decided that the doctrine of terra nullius did not apply to Australia and legally across the whole of Australia the Aborigines had a legally recognised title of ownership to all the land of Australia and the islands adjoining Australia where ever they had a continuous occupation. This new title was known as native title. What had happened was that Great Britain in taking possession of Australia had the power to impose land rights superior to that of the Aborigines' native title. Where ever a grant of an estate in fee simple had occurred the native title was eliminated. The *Mabo (No. 2)* case decided that where there had not being a grant of an estate in fee simple, there was the possibility that the original owners had a legally recognised title, known as native title, to their land.

This was very heady stuff. Underpinning economic power and certainty is the ownership of land. Australia had a very clear system of land title. The person who held a registered title owned the land in accordance with that registered title. A person who did not have a registered title had only contractual rights that could be enforce against a landowner personally. The thought that behind this certainty lay a group of original owners who may have a type of title to people's land caused a great deal of consternation.

---

348 A system of registration of land ownership to provide certainty of title and ease of transfer of it, based on the British scheme of ownership for the registration of merchant shipping and named after Sir Robert Torrens, its instigator.

349 A lease of land at a nominal rent from the government, usually for large area stock grazing, known as pastoral properties.

350 A Crown Lease over land for grazing stock, usually a large area of land in a low rainfall district.

Because of its attack on the fundamental certainties of land law and ownership, and its intrusion into race relations, the Mabo decision was probably the most controversial decision the High Court has ever made. The Court received unprecedented criticism, not the least, when a politician, under the protection of parliamentary privilege[351], falsely accusing a homosexual judge of 'cruising' in a government car to pick up young men.

In fact the case actually had nothing to do with Australian Aborigines. Eddie Mabo, the plaintiff, was a member of a group of people known as the Meriam people. They are of the Melanesian race and live on Murray Island and other islands in a group of islands in Torres Strait near the mouth of the Fly River closer to New Guinea than Australia. The islands have total area of about 9 square kilometres. Ethnically and culturally they are closer to the people of New Guinea than Australian Aborigines. The judge at first instance reported:[352]

> "Gardening was important not only from the point of view of subsistence but to provide produce for the consumption or exchange during the various rituals associated with the different aspects of community life. ... The natives are very tenacious of their ownership of the land, and the island is divided into small properties which have been handed down from father to son from generation to generation."

On the facts it was clear that successive generations had maintained this connection with the land notwithstanding the intrusion of colonial administration. The Court at first instance and the High Court recognised that this was a system of ownership of title of land, which the common law would find easy to recognise:[353]

> "Nonetheless, there was undoubtedly a local native system under which the established familial or individual rights of occupation and use were of a kind which far exceed the minimum requirements necessary to found a presumptive common law native title."

This is very different to the position of the Australian Aborigines. It is difficult to generalise. Because European settlement destroyed the culture of the Aborigines quickly and comprehensively much of the knowledge of how they lived has been lost. Some coastal aborigines lived from the sea and used stone fish traps, which are clearly indicative of permanent occupation. Aborigines did not formally cultivate the land but it is clear that they had a very sophisticated understanding of edible plants and how to encourage their growth. One aspect of this was a use of burning of the vegetation to prompt new edible growth. They had clear tribal groupings who lived in consistent geographical areas. However, it is clear that the connection that the Aborigines had with their land was very different from the connection that Eddie Mabo had with his land. Eddie was a gardener following on a long line of gardeners. Europeans can

---

351 Things said by Members of Parliament in Parliament are privileged from defamation or other legal action.

352 *Mabo (No. 2)* op cit at p.188.

353 *Mabo (No. 2)* op cit at pp. 115-6.

understand and recognise that connection to the land. Eddie and his forebears in effect used their land as peasant farmers, which lies at the heart of early European culture.

Aborigines in Australia have a very different connection with their land. It is much more deep-seated and important than gardening. The spirit people came to the land and established the features of it. The spirit people had an animal form and the animals now living on the land are representatives of the spirit people. When a tribal Aboriginal boy is reaching maturity the elders take him into his country. He is taught the secrets of the spirit people. When he becomes a man he will adopt a totem. The totem may be a wallaby, or a snake, or some other animal. His totem will have spiritual association with particular places in the nomadic area in which he lives. His job will be to look after the rituals of his totem and the places where it has importance. This connection to these places is much more fundamental than our understanding of ownership. His relationship to these places is his very reason for living. He needs to preserve their sacred rituals and pass them on to the next generation. In this lies the well being of all. This is a level of commitment to land that is more direct and fundamental than ours, and not really understandable by us. The closest parallel would be if each of us was a priest and our land was the sanctuary of our church. This is a bounden duty for life. The women have their own separate and parallel rituals and association with land.

So it is true that the Aborigines indeed have a connection to their land and it is closer and very different than ours, or that of Eddie Mabo and the Meriam people, whose type of ownership was close enough to ours to be understandable and recognised in our law. Against this background the High Court upheld the claim by Eddie Mabo to have title to his garden, although the Queensland Government would not recognise his title, as a vehicle to recognise the potential for ongoing title for all Aborigines in Australia.

Justice Brennan said this:[354]

> "Thus a Select Committee on Aborigines reported in 1837 to the House of Commons[355] that the state of Australian Aborigines was 'barbarous' and 'so entirely destitute … of the rudest forms of civil polity, that their claims, whether as sovereigns or proprietors of the soil, have been utterly disregarded'. The theory that the indigenous inhabitants of a 'settled' colony had no proprietary interest in the land thus depended on a discriminatory denigration of indigenous inhabitants, their social organisation and customs. As the basis of the theory is false in fact and unacceptable in our society, there is a choice of legal principle to be made in the present case. This Court can either apply the existing authorities and proceed to inquire whether the Meriam people are higher 'in the scale of social organisation' than the Australian Aborigines whose claims were 'utterly disregarded' by the existing authorities or the Court can overrule the existing authorities, discarding the distinction between inhabited colonies that were terra nullius and those that were not."

---

354 *Mabo (No. 2)* op cit at p.40.

355 The lower house in the British Parliament.

Deane and Gaudron JJ said this:[356]

> "The issues raised by this case directly concern the entitlement, under the law of Queensland, of the Meriam people to their homelands in the Murray Islands. Those issues must, however, be addressed in their wider context of the common law of Australia. The resolution requires a consideration of some fundamental questions relating to the rights, past and present, of Australian Aborigines in relation to land on which they traditionally lived or live."

Controversially, because no evidence had been heard on the topic[357], the Court made findings about the history of the Aborigines in Australia to reach this conclusion:[358]

> "The conflagration of oppression and conflict which was, over the (nineteenth) century, to spread across the continent to dispossess, degrade and devastate the Aboriginal peoples and leave a national legacy of unutterable shame."

And:[359]

> "The acts and events by which the (dispossession of the Aboriginal peoples of most of their traditional lands) was carried into practical effect constitute the darkest aspect of the history of this nation. The nation as a whole must remain diminished unless and until there is an acknowledgement of, and retreat from, those past injustices."

There are many in our society who did not wholeheartedly accept this view of Aboriginal history, and even if it is true did not accept that there is any guilt in the present generation for that which happened a century ago. The Court anticipated some of the strident criticism that this judgment generated:[360]

> "... we are conscious that, in those parts of the judgment which deal with the dispossession of Australian Aborigines, we have used language and expressed conclusions which some may think to be unusually emotive for a judgment in this Court. We have not done that in order to trespass into the area of assessment or attribution of moral guilt. As we have endeavoured to make clear the reason which has led us to describe, and express conclusions about, the dispossession of Australian Aborigines is that the full facts of the dispossession is of critical importance to the assessment of the legitimacy of the propositions that the continent was unoccupied for legal purposes and that the unqualified legal and beneficial ownership of all lands of the continent vested in the Crown. It is their association with the dispossession that in our view, precludes those two propositions from acquiring the legitimacy which their acceptance as a basis of

---

356 *Mabo (No. 2)* op cit at p. 77.

357 Under the common law system the choice and delivery of the evidence on any topic to brought to court is in the parties' hands. It is not for the Court to make its own inquiries and to draw conclusions on topics which the parties have not brought to the court. See Chapter 7.

358 *Mabo (No. 2)* op cit at p.104.

359 *Mabo (No. 2)* op cit at p.109.

360 *Mabo (No. 2)* op cit at p.120

the real property law[361] of this country for more than hundred and fifty years would otherwise impart."

For the purposes of the common law they were correct. The common law makes a distinction between colonies acquired by conquest or cession[362], which come with their existing legal system which the conqueror can change, and unoccupied land which is a legal vacuum and the English law immediately comes into force. Australia had always been regarded as the latter. To make this decision, the High Court had to find that there was a settled legal system in place dealing with land tenure. Cultivation of land has long been accepted as an indication of possession of it. To the Court, the cultivated gardens of the Murray Islands were a useful vehicle to undo the principle of terra nullius and by sleight of hand find that Aborigines owned their land as well. The connection that Aborigines had with their land was more fundamental in a sense than that of gardeners, but it would have been harder to argue its recognition as a legal system recognisable at common law.

The practical effect of this decision is not as great as it might at first fear appear. Any grant of freehold title brought native title to an end. This means that all cities and towns and most farms can no longer be subject to native title. Areas of land that are national parks or for other reasons have never been the subject of any grant of land titles may still have native title in place. To establish native title Aborigines need to show that they have maintained a continuous connection to the land. The really controversial areas were the vast tracts of Australia that are subject to pastoral leases and also the relationship of mining titles to native title. A later case of *Wik People v Queensland*[363] effectively found that a pastoral lease is superior to native title although the native title may coexist waiting to revive if ever the pastoral lease expires. In some States such as South Australia the pastoral leases already preserved Aboriginal rights to use the land within the lease for traditional purposes so the coexistence has practical effects even during the term of the lease. In Australia a grant of freehold generally does not include the minerals in the land. Mining titles can be obtained to exploit the mineral content in land, coincident with the usual titles of ownership. Mining usually occurs in remote areas, many of which now are subject to native title, so that a significant effect of native title is the need for miners to negotiate agreements with native title owners.

Along the coastal fringes and the better quality farming land where most white people live and the Aborigines have been totally dispossessed, *Mabo (No. 2)* has nothing to offer the Aboriginal people. In the case of *Yorta Yorta*[364] a claim to large parts of the State of Victoria was rejected. The Court quoted Olney J, the judge at first instance:[365]

---

361 The specialisation of law concerning real estate.

362 From to cede: giving away, as in one country giving a part of its territory to another.

363 (1996) 187 CLR 1.

364 *Members of the Yorta Yorta Aboriginal Community v Victoria* (2001) 110 FCR 244 and *Members of the Yorta Yorta Aboriginal Community v Victoria* (2002) 214 CLR 422.

365 Ibid. Kirby and Gaudron JJ at para 107.

"The facts in this case lead inevitably to the conclusion that before the end of the 19th century the ancestors through whom the claimants claim title had ceased to occupy their traditional lands in accordance with their traditional laws and customs. The tide of history has indeed washed away any real acknowledgement of their traditional laws and any real observance of their traditional customs."

The finding on the facts was that there has been no continuous possession or maintained contact by Aboriginal groups with their land. This will be the case for most of settled Australia where Aboriginal connections to the land was severed long ago. In this sense the High Court were clearly right. The Aborigines were dispossessed.

A special tribunal was established to hear native title claims. In first instance the parties are encouraged to mediate a mutually agreeable result and if they cannot the tribunal will determine the claims. These matters can be expensive, slow and complicated as the connections are oral and by practice and there are often competing and overlapping Aboriginal claims to the same areas. In remote areas of Australia, and in particular, in inland Queensland, the Northern Territory, Western Australia and South Australia, large areas of desert country are now subject to recognised native title and miners and other developers need to reach agreements with the native title owners to successfully proceed with their projects.[366] This is expensive and unfinished legal business. For many it was a necessary process to reconcile Australian society with its past wrongs and with the present Aboriginal people.

Immigration and the power over aliens

51. The Parliament shall, subject to this Constitution, have power to make laws for the peace, order, and good government of the Commonwealth with respect to:

    (xix) naturalization and aliens;

    (xxvii) immigration and emigration.

Australia's non indigenous migration was profoundly affected by the gold rushes that more than doubled the population in ten years with immigrants from all over the world including a significant number of Chinese[367]. This laid the seeds for the racist White Australia policy that prohibited coloured migration to Australia until the policy was progressively abandoned between 1968 and 1973[368].

At Federation in 1901 the population was about 4,000,000 and it had risen to 7,300,000 by 1945[369]. After WWII there was a large European migration to Australia. With Australia's involvement in the Vietnam war and the end of the White Australia policy Australia now has a large Asian population and also significant South American and African and Middle Eastern migrants. At 30 June 2002, Australia's overseas-born

---

366 Native title is a common law right and distinct from separate grants of land rights, such as to Uluru. Where Aborigines remain in place in their land there have been large areas granted to tribal groups.

367 See Chapter 1.

368 Also note s. 25 of the Constitution that recognised the exclusion of people from voting on the basis of race.

369 Ibid.

residents comprised 4.6 million people, 23% of the total estimated resident population (19.6 million)[370]. Over 40% of the population were born overseas or had parents that were born overseas. Australia now has a truly multicultural population.

The Chinese migration to the gold fields later led to the case of *Potter v Minahan*[371]. Griffith CJ recited these facts:

> "The respondent was born in Victoria on 4th October 1876, his mother being a young woman, herself born in Victoria, and bearing a British name. She may be assumed to have been of British race. The birth was registered on 29th November, the mother's name in the column headed "Name and maiden surname of the mother, age and birthplace" being given as "Winifred Minahan, 17, Emerald Hill." Emerald Hill is in Victoria. The column for the name of the father of the child was left blank. It appears, however, that the reputed father was a Chinese named Teung Ming, with whom the mother had lived as his wife in a small country town in Victoria. A Chinese witness who knew him at the time said that her name was Minahan and her other name was Minnie."

The magistrate who first heard the case found they were living in a common law marriage[372]. Ming was in partnership in a country store in Victoria but when James was five years old Ming returned to China with his son. When James was 18 years old Ming died in China having given his son a copy of his birth certificate. James studied in China with the intention of qualifying to teach people of Chinese descent in Australia. He did not graduate and returned to Australia in about 1907. The *Immigration Restriction Act* 1901(Cth) defined prohibited immigrants as including:

> "...any person who fails to pass the dictation test; that is to say, who, when a officer dictates to him not less than 50 words in any prescribed language, fails to write them out in that language."

James Minahan was met by Customs officer who gave him the dictation test. A passage was read to him and he was asked if he could write it. He said he could not. He was charged with being a prohibited immigrant. The magistrate dismissed the charge on the basis that he was not an immigrant at all. In the High Court Barton, O'Connor, Isaacs, and Higgins JJ all found in favour of James on the technical ground that in fact James was never actually given the dictation test to write and so he had not formally failed. In was not sufficient to accept his statement that he could not do it. Griffiths CJ rejected the finding of a common law marriage:

> "Having regard to conditions in Victoria in 1876, and to the relations between Chinese and European women at that time, I think that there is not even a *primâ facie* probability of a legal marriage. And, when to these facts it is added that the child was registered without mention of a father, I think that, so far from there

370 Australian Bureau of Census and Statistics.

371 (1908) 7 CLR 277.

372 A marriage not formalised at law but recognised in practice.

being a high degree of probability in favour of a legal marriage, there is the highest degree of probability in favour of a contrary conclusion."

This was despite evidence that Winifred was known as Mrs Tueng Ming. Barton and O'Connor JJ agreed. It followed that James had taken his mother's British nationality and Victorian domicile and thus he was not an immigrant[373].

The dictation test was used for many decades to exclude unwanted immigrants. The courts were not always sympathetic to it. An example concerned the left-wing Czech novelist Egon Kisch. In 1934 there was a left-wing anti-war conference and Kisch was invited to speak. In accordance with a government campaign against communism the Attorney-General[374] of the day, Robert Menzies, tried to prevent Kisch entering Australia. When he arrived in Melbourne and then Sydney the captain refused him permission to land and he applied to the High Court for a writ of habeas corpus[375], which was granted[376]. He was taken ashore to the police station and subjected to the dictation test in Scottish Gaelic. The Act required the test to be in a European language and all the judges of the High Court held that Scottish Gaelic was so limited in its use it was no longer a European language for the purpose of the test[377]. Rich J held:

> "It is not the recognized speech of a community organized politically, socially or on any other basis. There are very few indeed who now use it as their only tongue and not many, comparatively speaking, who speak it in addition to English. No doubt it is a division of the Celtic branch of the Indo-European languages. It may excite the interest of scholars, and perhaps the enthusiasm of the descendants of the Gauls, but in ordinary practical affairs it plays no greater part than a local dialect might."

This attracted much criticism in the Sydney press. Critical letters asserting the ignorance of the Court in finding Scottish Gaelic was not a European language, published in the *Sydney Morning Herald* by Rev. M. M. Macdonald, and under the pseudonyms "Columbinus" "Aonaghus Dumhnullach" were found to be in contempt but the contempt was excused because there was other balanced comment[378]. However, a later editorial in *The Sun* newspaper was too much. It talked about the judges:[379]

> "Keen, microscopic vision for splits in hairs" and suggested that "when amendments are made we should invite him to jump ashore again to see whether the new Act pleases the High Court any better than the old, or whether the ingenuity of 5 bewigged heads can discover another flaw. ... If the High Court were given some real work to do the bench would not have time to argue for days on the exact length of the split in the hair, and the precise difference between Tweedledum and Tweedledee."

373 *Potter v Minahan* (1908) 7 CLR 277.
374 The minister with responsibility for the law department and courts.
375 A writ or court process to establish a right to freedom from custody.
376 *The King v Carter; ex parte Kisch* (1934) 52 CLR 221.
377 *R v Wilson; ex parte Kisch* (1934) 52 CLR 234.
378 *The King v Fletcher*, (1935) 52 CLR 248.
379 From Blackshield and Williams (1998), op cit p.761.

The editor and the paper were found guilty of contempt of court and fined £50.and £200 respectively[380].

Another instance arose as a result of migration caused by WWII.

> "Mrs O'Keefe, formerly Mrs Maas, was a native of Celebes (Sulawesi in Indonesia). When the Japanese invaded Borneo in 1942, she and the husband, with the eight children, escaped. At that time the island was a Dutch possession and the whole family were Dutch subjects. They were evacuated by an Australian warship. It brought them to Australia, where they had another child. Mrs Maas had not voluntarily chosen to enter Australia, and initially had no intention of permanent settlement. But after her husband, while working for the Dutch intelligence service, was killed in a plane crash in 1944, she and her children stayed on in Melbourne. In 1947 she married John O'Keefe and thus became a British subject."[381]

She obtained a certificate of exemption which entitled her to stay in Australia but in 1949 after it had expired she was declared to be a prohibited immigrant and was required to leave Australia. She applied to the High Court to overturn the decision and the majority held that the whole certificate of exemption procedure as applied to her was technically invalid. Although she could have been required to submit to the dictation test at that time and deported if she failed, she was not, and so she was not liable to be deported at that time when the certificate of extension was granted. Her deportation was based on the expiry of the invalid certificate and was invalid. She was allowed to stay. Two judges dissented[382] and thought she should be deported.

In these cases the Court undid particularly harsh applications of immigration law on technicalities, without contesting the extent of the immigration power to restrict immigration at the point of entry and to deport long term residents, on what now seem capricious grounds.

In the early years of Australia there were very close links with Britain. These led to an assumption that a British subject would not be an alien. However, as Australia and Britain have grown apart legally, this assumption is no longer valid. In *Shaw's Case* in 2003[383] the High Court decided that a British subject was an alien. Mr Shaw was born in the UK in 1972 and migrated to Australia with his family in 1974. Although he never acquired Australian citizenship, he was resident in Australia ever since. In 2001 his visa was cancelled on the grounds that he had an extensive criminal record and so he failed the 'character test' in the *Migration Act* 1958 (Cth). The constitutional issue was whether the power to make laws with respect to 'naturalization and aliens' validly extended to him. The majority (Gleeson CJ, Gummow, Hayne and Heydon JJ) accepted that the applicant was an alien for the purposes of s.51(xix). The constitutional meaning of alien has changed. In 1901 British subjects would not have

---

380 *The King v Dunbabin* (1935) 53 CLR 434.

381 Blackshield and Williams (1998), op cit pp. 777-8.

382 A dissent is a minority judgment, disagreeing with the opinion of the majority, from to dissent.

383 *Shaw v Minister for Immigration and Multicultural Affairs* [2003] HCA 72 (9 December 2003).

been considered aliens, but today they are. The majority held that the passage of the *Australian Citizenship Act* 1948 (Cth) was evidence of the change, while the dissenting judges (McHugh, Callinan and Kirby JJ) ruled that the change came later, after the applicant's birth, but this is an argument over timing, not the principle. These cases show the court following the political and cultural reality of Australia's change from a British colony to an independent nation with more links to the USA and Asia than Great Britain. They also show an increasing reliance on the aliens power in s. 51 (xix) in immigration matters.

The last decade has seen many amendments to the relevant legislation to limit the ability of courts to scrutinise bureaucratic decisions limiting migration. However, the Constitution guarantees a jurisdiction of the High Court in all matters in which a writ of Mandamus or Prohibition or an injunction is sought against an officer of the Commonwealth (s 75(v)) and these jurisdictions cannot be circumscribed.

To avoid international treaty obligations affecting refugees, Australia has declared certain offshore islands, such as Christmas Island, not to be part of Australia for the purpose of arrival in Australia. The so-called Pacific solution involved intercepting refugee boats and taking them to these islands, which Australia controls but are deemed not to be part of Australia and then transporting the people to Pacific island states to be processed by the United Nations. The agreement of the Pacific island states has been ensured by generous aid packages. The result is that in Australian law the refugees have never entered Australia. Of course Australia still regards its offshore islands to be part of Australia for the purpose of entitlements to fishing and mineral rights around them.

The High Court shows no present inclination to interpret the immigration and alien powers in a narrow way, nor to interfere with present government policy in this area. Mr Al-Kateb was a stateless illegal migrant who was put into immigration detention. After he failed to obtain a protection visa he asked to be removed from Australia 'as soon as reasonably possible'[384]. There was no prospect of finding a country to which to deport him and he remained in indefinite detention. An application was made to the court to rule whether the *Migration Act* 1958 (Cth) could authorise indefinite detention.[385] The majority held that the *International Covenant on Civil and Political Rights* did not apply and even if it did the detention was in accordance with law so it had not been breached. Indefinite detention was upheld. This case was contrary to earlier cases in the court below, the Federal Court, which had been more sympathetic to refugees in permanent detention[386]. Kirby and Gummow JJ dissented.

---

384 Under s. 198 of the *Migration Act.*

385 *Al-Kateb v Godwin* (2004) 219 CLR 562.

386 In *B v Minister for Immigration and Multicultural and Indigenous Affairs* (2003) 178 FLR 360, the Federal Court decided it could make decisions about children in immigration detention under incidental powers in the Constitution and in *Minister for Immigration and Multicultural and Indigenous Affairs v Al Masri* (2003) 126 FLR 54 the Federal Court decided that indefinite detention could be unlawful. The latter case was expressly disapproved by the majority in *Al Kateb.*

Conclusion

The extent of a power may not be obvious from the wording of the Constitution and a valid exercise of power may depend on several different heads of power. Thus Commonwealth power over industrial relations depends on the corporations, trade and commerce and external affairs power and not on the industrial relations power itself, which would have limited it. The interpretation of a power may vary over time. This is most obvious with the defence power, which the Court explicitly extends in time of war. The external affairs power has obvious potential to further empower the Commonwealth government by the adoption of international obligations in areas not included in s. 51. However, it is the corporations power, which started with a narrow interpretation, that has now emerged with so wide an interpretation as to change the federal and state balance. If the words of the Constitution are not used by the Court as a means of restraining power other principles will need in time to be found. The most obvious are human rights from international jurisprudence.

Interpretation of the Constitution is a product of the received wisdom of judicial experience, the needs of and pressures from the community at the time, and the personal attitudes of the judges on the bench. When there was a White Australia policy, protected by a dictation test which was sometimes used unfairly to exclude immigrants, the Court on occasions found ways to correct obvious injustices. However, the Court has consistently upheld the underlying laws restricting migration, even now authorising indefinite detention for aliens who do not qualify as refugees and who do not have a country to which they can be returned.

Sometimes the bench can radically change the law, confronting community conscience with its own, as in *Mabo (No.2)* or even more profoundly changing the law by upholding the new industrial relations law for reasons that have the potential to radically change the whole structure of the Constitution. The response to *Mabo (No, 2)* was strident, although in the end the results were probably of more psychological than practical importance, as in most areas native title has been extinguished and where it has not, a manageable process to negotiate with the owners is in place. The results of the *Industrial Relations Case* will involve a much greater long term change with a profound shift in power to the Commonwealth, but this had not attracted the same level of controversy. This shows continuing sensitivity in Australia about racial matters, the importance of the attitude of the press in how debates are exhibited, and that professed conservatives can sometimes be the most radical[387].

[387] The socialist left radical contrasted to capitalist right conservative is a paradigm that still frames much of the Australian debate despite no longer having relevance. In true meaning conservatives resist change but the capitalist right often do not take that position now, nor are the socialist left now always radical, often hankering after a departing state control of the distribution of resources.

Chapter 7:

THE COURTS

The meaning of the Constitution, legislation and whether it is within power and the ability to determine that executive power has exceeded its authority is decided by the High Court. Chapter III defines and protects the Judicature. S.71 vests the judicial power of the Commonwealth in the High Court or such other courts that Parliament may create or invest with judicial power. The High Court has an original jurisdiction set out in s.75 but the other courts of the Commonwealth are creatures of statute, that is the extent of their jurisdiction and power is decided by Parliament. At the moment, in addition to the High Court, the Commonwealth courts are the Federal Court which deals with matters of commonwealth jurisdiction, mainly large commercial disputes, trade practices matters, bankruptcy and more recently a good deal of work in defining the extent of Aboriginal native title, the Family Court which deals with divorce, and the consequences of care and custody of children and the sharing of assets and ongoing financial responsibilities, and more recently the Magistrates Service which deals with lower jurisdiction matters for both the Federal Court and the Family Court. The Commonwealth has also vested its jurisdiction in State Courts, particularly criminal prosecutions. As a general rule at the moment Commonwealth criminal jurisdiction is delegated to the State courts.

The State court systems have a Supreme Court that has an appellate function for all the lower courts and tribunals and does first instance trials, with juries, in serious criminal matters and larger civil disputes, usually without juries. Most States have a District or County Court which performs a similar role to the Supreme Court but without the appellate function. In combination these perform a similar role to the Landgericht in Germany. The lower first instance court is known as the Magistrates Court, which has a larger jurisdiction than the Amtsgericht in Germany and does 90-95% of the case load, with the professional Magistrates sitting alone without juries. Both the Commonwealth and State systems have a variety of specialist tribunals to deal with administrative, tenancy and other matters.

Independence of the judiciary

The proactive power under the Constitution lies in Cabinet which effectively controls the executive power and legislative power through its majority in the lower house of Parliament. To moderate this concentration of power the judiciary must have guarantees of independence. S.72 gives judges a constitutional guarantee to hold their office until seventy years of age, unless by choice they retire earlier. Prior to 1977 there was no retiring age. There was one judge who was appointed by a Labor government during the mid 1940s and clung to judicial office until finally another Labor government came to power in 1972. In his last decade he did little more than to say 'I concur'[388]. This led to general agreement that a retiring age of 70 years was

[388] A judge agreeing with the judgment of another judge in the same case.

appropriate, and this is one constitutional amendment that passed. Although they must retire at 70, Chapter III judges can only be dismissed by an address[389] to both Houses of Parliament, that is a vote for their removal in both Houses of Parliament, and a decision that they be dismissed by the Governor-General in Council. There has only been one process for the removal of a federal Judge[390], the contentious instance of Lionel Murphy which is discussed below. As a further guarantee of independence judges' pay cannot be reduced while they hold office. A special remuneration tribunal fixes the salaries of judges, politicians and the higher members of the public service.

The Lionel Murphy case

Lionel Murphy was a Justice of the High Court of Australia for more than eleven years. Murphy J often dissented from the majority decision of the Court, on issues such as tax avoidance or the constitutionality of funding to private schools. Many of his dissenting opinions are now seen as correct and are quoted in later decisions of the Court. He was also in the minority on a number of high profile criminal cases, perhaps most notably the Lindy Chamberlain appeal. This involved contentious charges against a woman for murdering her baby daughter when there was strong evidence that the child was taken by a dingo whilst the family visited what was then called Ayers Rock, or now Uluru. The prosecution relied heavily on forensic evidence that was later discredited. Murphy's minority view was that there had been a miscarriage of justice and that she should be immediately released. She had to wait some years before a Royal Commissioner drew the same conclusions and she was cleared of the murder.

Lionel Murphy's parents migrated to Australia from Ireland in the late 1900s and Lionel Murphy was born in the Sydney suburb of Kensington in 1922. His father was a publican in Sydney for many years but later turned to property developing. Murphy was dux of his local primary school and had outstanding results in High School as well as being an outstanding athlete and sportsman, a combination much admired in Australia. At university he completed an Honours degree in organic chemistry before turning to law. He was admitted to practice as a lawyer in 1947. He became a prominent barrister[391] for the trade unions and took silk[392] in 1959. This association with the trade union movement led him into politics via a Senate place for NSW in 1960.

In Australia in 1972, after decades of government by the conservative Liberal Country Party, a social democrat Labor government headed by Prime Minister Gough Whitlam came to power. It had many pent up ideas for reform but was short on experience and discipline. Murphy was the Attorney-General and presided over a formidable legislative program in just a three year term. The *Family Law Act* 1975 (Cth) created

---

389 A motion to a house of Parliament that a judge should be removed from office.

390 There are similar provisions in State Constitutions where some judges have been removed by an address to Parliament and a decision by the Governor in Council.

391 A lawyer who only appears in court. They usually do not take instructions direct from a client but receive them from a solicitor.

392 Barristers designated as Queen's Counsel (QCs) were then entitled to have their barrister's robe made out of silk fabric, hence to be appointed as a barrister is "to take silk" and a QC is sometimes known as "a silk".

the Family Court and moved divorce cases from the State courts to that new court and at the same time abolished the notion of fault that was the prior basis of divorce. He also established the Federal Court and set up the Australian Law Reform Commission to advise government on improvements in the legal system generally and the Australian Institute of Criminology to advise on criminal law policy. He introduced a legal aid[393] service for all courts, where previously it had been provided on an ad hoc[394] basis mainly by lawyer organisations for a fraction of normal fees. In addition he established community legal centres[395] that give free legal advice and provide mediation services. He completed the abolition of appeals to the Privy Council to the extent the Constitution permits[396]. The only remaining right lies under section 74 if the High Court gives a certificate, which it has made clear it never will[397]. Other parts of his reform program included legislation outlawing racial and other discrimination, abolishing the death penalty, removing censorship, providing freedom of access to government information, and reforming companies legislation and trade practices legislation. In the area of the review of executive decision making, an Ombudsman service was introduced to deal with complaints about abuse of power and an Administrative Appeals Tribunal that provides an appeal process for government decisions in areas such as the taxation, pension payments and migration visas. He argued with the security service, the Australian Security and Intelligence Organisation (ASIO), who would not report to him as Attorney-General in a way that was in his view sufficient, and he was controversial for mounting a raid on their office and personally inspecting their secret files. He then introduced a more rigorous reporting relationship for the security service to Parliament. He had Australia take action in the International Court to prevent the French from conducting nuclear testing in the Pacific. His last act as Attorney-General was to have the government appoint himself as a judge of the High Court in 1975, shortly before its controversial dismissal because it could not pass the appropriation bill for supply through the Senate.

This immediately shows a weakness in the appointment system for judges. It is too easy for Cabinet to appoint judges for reasons other than merit. In this instance it is generally recognised that Murphy J was an outstanding judge. However, Murphy was seen as an enemy by the right wing of politics and many unfounded attacks were made on him. One person even attacked him as having been dishonest about his parents and said he was really Jewish.

A NSW Police Intelligence Unit were recording phone conversations without first obtaining a warrant[398] to authorise the phone taps[399]. This made them illegal with the important consequence that they could not be received as evidence in any court. However the police leaked them to a journalist and excerpts were published in a daily

[393] State payment for legal representation.

[394] On the facts of the moment.

[395] A free legal advice clinic, giving basic legal advice and providing mediation services.

[396] The *Privy Council (Appeals from the High Court) Act* 1975 (Cth) completed the process started in the earlier Act the *Privy Council (Limitation of Appeals Act)* 1968 (Cth).

[397] *Kirmani v Captain Cook Cruises Pty Ltd (No. 2)* (1985) 159 CLR 461.

[398] A written authority from a court to intrude on citizens' rights such as to permit the recording of phone conversations, authorise a search or to have a person arrested.

[399] Monitoring electronic communications.

newspaper, *The Age*. They became known as *The Age Tapes*. The tapes strongly suggested that Lionel Murphy, code-named 'The Trump', wrongly used his influence to protect his friend and solicitor[400] Morgan Ryan who was also solicitor for crime figure Abe Saffron, code named 'Mr Vice', in reference to his alleged involvement with illegal gambling and prostitution. The allegation was that Murphy used his influence in NSW to help Ryan escape some criminal charges. The publication of the tapes brought further evidence to light. The Chief Magistrate of NSW, Clarrie Briese remembered Murphy approaching him to influence who would hear the case involving Ryan and famously saying to him:

> "And now what about my little mate[401]."

This led to two Senate enquiries as to whether Murphy would be dismissed, and he was charged with corruption offences. He stood aside from his duties as a judge whilst the trial proceeded. After a long delay eventually a jury convicted him. But then he was successful on appeal and he was acquitted. He returned to the Court but by then he was dying of cancer and shortly after he died in October 1986.

The story is instructive to show how dangerous it is when politics intrudes on the judicial work of the Court. It also demonstrates that the protection of independence given to judges by the Constitution is in practice substantial. Powerful people were out to get Lionel Murphy and they had some evidence to go on. Despite this he survived the attacks on a legal basis despite its fatal personal price.

It highlights a substantial defect in the method of appointment of judicial officers, which is the case throughout Australia. In contrast to the American system, where Supreme Court judicial appointments are reviewed in Congress, or at the lower level where many judges are elected, in Australia, in accordance with the British system, judges are chosen by a secret political method. Judges are appointed by Executive Council[402]. In practice this means that the Attorney-General makes inquiries in private about who is appropriate for selection to judicial office, and then takes a recommendation to Cabinet. Although Cabinet discussions are secret, it is widely accepted that in at least two recent instances, Cabinet has not accepted the Attorney-General's recommendation and has imposed its own selection. The process is seen to be, and on occasions is, unduly political. The work of the High Court is by its essence sometimes political and so it is probably inevitable that political factors will intrude into the selection process of High Court judges. However, there should be methods in place to ensure merit, impartiality and legal competence remain paramount factors.

In Australia the same method of appointment applies to all levels of the judiciary and to tribunals, which do not even have the protections of Chapter III, that is their

---

400 A written authority from a court to intrude on citizens' rights such as to permit the recording of phone conversations, authorise a search or to have a person arrested.

401 Australian term of casual acquaintance between males: e.g. "g'day mate" as a greeting: that is "good day mate".

402 s. 72(i).

tenure[403] and pay are not guaranteed. All these appointments are made by the government of the day without any required process. In higher courts merit is often achieved through the barrister tradition. Barristers only do court work and the better ones are recognised by appointment as Queen's Counsel (QC) or Senior Counsel (SC), known as taking silk. The Chief Justice is usually consulted about these appointments in an informal way. He may consult his colleagues about their views of the ability of barristers who appear before the court. Appointments to higher courts are usually made from the silks so in that way the best barristers are appointed and the bench itself has an indirect influence over subsequent appointments. However, the system is criticised as leading to appointments from too narrow a clique because a group merely needs to have the ear of, or be favoured by, the Attorney-General or his staff, and the Chief Justice to have a high chance of selection. Also the adversarial oral skills of eminent barristers are not necessarily a sound basis to use to select for judicial appointment. In the lower courts appointments are made from a wider base, but without the filter of the barrister tradition, so they are more open to patronage rather than merit based selection. Also as the Lionel Murphy appointment shows, the Australian system can lead to overt political appointments. Defenders of the system say it permits the appointment of robust individuals who might be screened out by a more structured process. They might say that it turned out that Murphy J was an outstanding judge whose judgments are increasingly admired. On the other hand, if he was corrupt, which remained unproven, this is not justification enough.

This is a difficult area. It has been said that the German academic merit based appointment from results in the State exam occurs too early to assess important personality traits and gives judges too long a career. The USA congressional hearings can be so political that they might discourage good candidates and the model of elections can lead to populist decisions in the year leading up to an election. The Canadian model of standing commissions to independently make recommendations about potential appointees is an interesting compromise, although it is still criticised as open to political patronage.

Abolition of courts

Another way of attacking the judiciary is by abolishing the court. The High Court is not open to this danger as its position and jurisdiction is guaranteed by the Constitution. However for courts that are created by the Commonwealth Parliament under section 71, and for State courts, the judges may have guaranteed tenure but removing their work can marginalise them. In *Attorney-General (NSW) v. Quinn*[404] the Court permitted the abolition of an industrial relations court and the creation of a new court. Not all the judges were subsequently appointed to the new court. Justice Staples famously attended his work and took his pay until retirement, even though his court was abolished. This is a back door way of the government getting rid of a court that it does not like.

403 The right to hold an office. It also describes an entitlement to land.

404 (1990) 170 CLR 1.

The definition of judicial power

Chapter III gives constitutional guarantees to courts, and the High Court has been rigorous in requiring that the exercise of judicial power is separate from executive power. Hence it is important to understand what constitutes judicial power. Its definition is elusive. Griffith CJ said this: [405]

> "[T]he words 'judicial power' as used in s. 71 of the Constitution mean the power which every sovereign authority must of necessity have to decide controversies between its subjects, or between itself and its subjects, whether the rights relate to life, liberty or property. The exercise of this power does not begin until some tribunal which has power to give a binding and authoritative decision (whether subject to appeal or not) is called upon to take action."

Judicial power: [406]

> "…is a power to make a conclusive finding or an authoritative decision in a dispute affecting the traditional rights of the subject within a framework of judicial standards or judicial discretion."

> "It is a truism that the conception of the judicial function is inseparably bound up with the idea of a suit between parties, whether the Crown and the subject or between subject and subject."[407]

Windeyer J said:[408]

> "the concept seems to defy, perhaps it were better to say transcend, purely abstract conceptual analysis."

Professor Tony Blackshield bravely said:[409]

> "(T)he point is clear. Judicial power is controlled power, in the sense that its exercise must be based on authoritative legal materials; the rules, principles, conceptions and standards applied must be drawn from existing law. But this clear central conception becomes elusive and unhelpful as it shades over into either one of two opposite types of case."

Professor Blackshield then contrasts cases where criteria of justice and equity may allow too much flexibility to characterise the process as a judicial one, in contrast to

---

405 Griffiths CJ in *Huddart Parker Limited v Moorehead* (1908-9) 8 CLR 330 at 357.

406 Lumb, *Australian Constitutionalism* op cit referring to *R.V. Quinn: ex parte Consolidated Food Corp* (1977-78) 138 CLR 1.

407 Lord Simons, Privy Council, *Labour Relations Board of Saskatchewan v John East Iron Works Ltd* (1949) AC 149.

408 *R v Trade Practices Tribunal; ex parte Tasmanian Breweries* (1970) CLR 361 at 394.

409 Blackshield and Williams (1998), op cit at pp. 533-4.

the other extreme where a Tribunal's discretion may be so circumscribed that it is a mere rubber stamp and not exercising a judicial function. He goes on to conclude:

> "What appears to be meant by the insistence on the need to apply 'existing law' is that the application of the authoritative legal materials must leave the judges *some* room for independent interpretive judgment, *but not too much.* The crucial question, 'How much?', is not really approached. ...
>
> The missing ingredient thus elided from the heart of 'judicial power' is perhaps supplied, in two very different ways, by two judgments from other jurisdictions often quoted in the Australian decisions. The first is from Oliver Wendell Holmes.
>
>> 'A judicial inquiry investigates, declares and enforces liabilities as they stand on present or past facts and under laws supposed already to exist. ... (T)he nature of the final act determines the nature of the previous inquiry. As the judge is bound to declare the law he must know or discover the facts that established the law.'[410]
>
> What matters is not whether or not the ultimate decision is *in fact* a predetermined inference from existing rules of law, but whether the judge *believes* and *acts as if*, the principles he applies are derived from the existing legal materials. If this seems a hazardously subjective criteria on which to base an explication of 'judicial power', it is worth recalling how faithfully it parallels Max Weber's insistence on 'subjective interpretation' -- on the explication of 'social action' in terms of the 'subjective meaning' attached to it *by the actor himself* -- as the key to sociological 'understanding'.
>
> The other famous quotation is from Palles CB in *R v Local Government Board* (1902) 2 IR 349 at 373 (emphasis added):
>
>> 'I have always thought that to erect a tribunal into a 'court' or 'jurisdiction', so as to make its determinations judicial, the essential element is that it should have power, *by its determinations* within jurisdiction, to impose liability or affect rights. By this I mean that the liability is imposed, or the right affected *by the determination only,* and not by the fact determined, and so that the liability will exist, or the right will be affected, although the determination be wrong in law or in fact.'
>
> The key to 'judicial power' is neither in law nor in facts, but in the 'determination' by the judge, which is interposed between these. He went on to reiterate even more clearly what for him what was the real significance of 'judicial power': that a judge's decision within jurisdiction (and hence validly exercising 'judicial power') will have binding force and effect on the parties *even if the underlying interpretation of the law or the facts is wrong.*"

---

410 *Prentice v Atlantic Coastline Co* (1908) 211 US 210 at pp. 266-7.

One of the underlying reasons why judicial power is hard to define is that it has no separate source of power. Political power once had as its source the notion of divine right, but once the beheading of kings revealed that to be a false claim, its legitimacy relies on the social contract with the people who control the power over them by the electoral process. Judicial power is a gift by the powerful of part of their power to an independent institution to ensure that disputes are determined in an acceptable way. To be acceptable the determinations must be in accordance with an established set of principles, or laws. In European history, from Justinian onwards, courts have appeared in many guises and each has been a construct of the powerful. With the collapse of central power in the Middle Ages there were the Church courts, Guild courts, Manor courts of the feudal landowners, the Kings courts, and more recently the courts of the nation state with which we are familiar. They now have a central role in the constitutional arrangement, but their source of power is executive government, which provides them with their powers to compel witness and to enforce judgments, and with their resources. The reason judicial power is so hard to define is that it is not really a different power but a construct of political power to legitimise its own exercise. The purpose of judges is to handle disputes in a credible way so that the disputes do not harm those in executive and legislative power and in turn to ensure they do not exceed their power. To fulfil these roles courts must have the gift of power but they depend for their legitimacy on the way they exercise it.

For an institution with power over people to be a court, it must then have the following:

- It must have institutional independence,
- It must observe procedural fairness;

and the key elements of the exercise of judicial power must be present, namely:

- an adjudication between parties;
- the relation to existing rights and obligations; and
- the result of a binding decision.

The High Court has been jealous in keeping a strict separation of judicial power. One thing that follows from this is that any body that is not constituted as a court under Chapter III, which purports to exercise Federal judicial power, is liable to have its decisions nullified.

The difficulty in defining judicial power can make it hard to decide when a tribunal is, or is not, a court. In *Shell Co of Australia Ltd v Commissioner) of Taxation (Cth)*[411], the Privy Council observed that just because a tribunal has many attributes of a court, such as making a final decision and the power to summons witnesses and with an appeal lying to a court, it may still be an administrative body. In that case a taxation review tribunal was held to be administrative largely because its decisions substituted for the decision of the Commissioner of Taxation and his decisions were clearly administrative. In contrast the High Court in *Brandy v Human Rights & Equal*

[411] (1930) 44 CLR 530.

Opportunity Commission[412], held that the Commission's power to determine whether the past conduct of a person violated the *Racial Discrimination Act* 1975 (Cth) and to order the payment of damages was an exercise of judicial power because its decisions were enforceable as if they were an order of the Federal Court. The decision of the tribunal to award damages for racial discrimination in a hotel was held to be not enforceable as the tribunal was exercising judicial power when the basis of appointment of tribunal members did not comply with Chapter III. The ability to enforce decisions, directly or by automatic transfer to a court's machinery of enforcement is obviously a key feature of what constitutes a court under these cases, because it effectively gives the tribunal in question actual power over the parties.

An exception to insisting that only a Chapter III court exercise judicial power has been permitted for armed services disciplinary tribunals which have been permitted to exercise judicial power without complying with Chapter III on the justification of the particular needs of defence discipline and their validity has been upheld under the defence power. A member of the Australian navy was charged with 6 counts of an act of indecency without consent and one of assault in the alternative. The alleged incidents occurred whilst she and the alleged victims were off duty and away from Commonwealth property. She claimed the right to be tried by a jury[413] not by a military tribunal[414]. The majority upheld the long established Chapter III exception for military tribunals. Kirby J in a minority judgment argued that the court should distinguish between matters required to maintain service discipline, which could be heard in a military tribunal, and conduct that amounted to serious criminal conduct which should be heard in a Chapter III court.

Another matter that follows from the separation of judicial power is that courts cannot themselves exercise administrative power. The leading example of this was the *Boilermaker's Case*[415]. Here the High Court disallowed enforcement proceedings in the Conciliation & Arbitration Court because it had administrative functions and it was impermissible to mix enforcement and punishment, judicial functions, with them.

Functions incompatible with judicial office

It follows from the strict separation of powers that it may be incompatible for judges to perform some functions. An example of this occurred in a very controversial case in South Australia. At the mouth of the Murray River is a small island known as Hindmarsh Island. It was connected to mainland only by a ferry. A developer borrowed a large amount of money from a finance company connected with the State government. To assist its finance company when this large loan was transferred to a private financier the State government committed itself to building a bridge to the island. The State government finance company lost a huge amount of money and the government lost office as a result, but the commitment remained to build the bridge. A group of Aboriginal women from the Ngarrindjeri tribe claimed that the bridge would

412 (1995) 183 CLR 245.

413 S. 80.

414 *White v the Director of Military Prosecutions* HCA (2007) 29 delivered 19th June 2007.

415 (1956) 94 CLR 254. The same view was taken in the Privy Council: see Chapter 2.

interfere with secret women's information concerning the creation and renewal of life. This information could not be discussed with men. Whether this 'secret women's business' as it became known, was a sincerely held belief or whether it was made up became a matter of great controversy. There were competing claims from Ngarrindjeri groups, and pro and anti development lobbies joined in. A female, Professor Saunders, was appointed to report on the matter. She accepted the authenticity of the women's business and some evidence on the point was placed in sealed envelopes, not to be viewed by men[416]. This happened in 1994. Based on the Saunders report the government of the day made a declaration under the *Aboriginal and Torres Strait Islander Heritage Protection Act* 1984 (Cth), effectively stopping the bridge from being built. This decision then was overturned due to defects in the processes leading to Professor Saunders report, and the minister's failure to make his own independent decision.

The South Australian government appointed a retired female judge Iris Stevens to hold a Royal Commission into the Ngarrindjeri claims. Those who claimed knowledge of the secret women's business refused to give evidence and unsurprisingly the judge then found on the basis of the evidence of those who thought it was a fabrication, that it was a fabrication. The Commonwealth government minister for Aboriginal affairs then thought it appropriate to appoint Justice Matthews of the Federal Court to prepare another report to the government into the secret women's business. The High Court held that her appointment to give an advisory opinion to the executive on a matter of law was incompatible with a judicial office. They approved an opinion from the Supreme Court of the United States in *Mistretta*:[417]

> "The legitimacy of the Judicial Branch ultimately depends upon its reputation for impartiality and non partisanship. That reputation may not be borrowed by the political branches to cloak their work in the neutral colours of judicial action."

The majority concluded:[418]

> "The capacity of Chapter III judges to perform their judicial duties throughout the terms of their appointment independently of the political branches of government cannot be prejudiced by their appointment to a non-judicial office or to perform non-judicial functions. If appointment to a non-judicial office or performance of a non-judicial function prejudices that capacity it is incompatible with the office and function of a Chapter III judge. And that is inconsistent with section 72 of the Constitution.

---

416 A male adviser to the Commonwealth government minister at the time has subsequently admitted he read the content of the sealed envelopes.

417 (1989) 488 US 361, at p. 407 quoted in *Wilson v Minister for Aboriginal and Torres Strait Islander Affairs* (1997) 189 CLR 1, at p. 9.

418 Ibid. Brennan CJ, Dawson, Toohey, McHugh and Gummow JJ in *Wilson*, at p. 16. See also *Grollo* (1995) 184 CLR 348.

In the event there was no valid declaration under the *Aboriginal and Torres Strait Heritage Protection Act* 1984 (Cth) and the bridge was built. Whether or not the secret women's business was a fabrication remains to some a deep controversy.

Court administrative arrangements

It is one thing to have notional independence but it may be another thing to have actual independence. Financial independence is one aspect of actual independence. In recent years courts in Australia have placed emphasis on having control over their administrative establishment. The High Court, the Federal Court, and the Family Court receive a negotiated sum of money each year from Federal government and make their own decisions on how the money is spent. In South Australia the State courts have a governing body known as the Courts Administration Authority (CAA) constituted by the *Courts Administration Act* 1993 (SA)[419]. A council comprising the head and the deputy head of each jurisdiction administers the Authority. Every year when the budget session of Parliament meets the Chief Justice goes to Parliament and presents the annual budget of the CAA and answers questions about it. Once the budget is approved the CAA determines how it is spent. However, many other State courts remain dependant on government departments for their administrative establishment. To some extent this administrative separation is tokenism, in that the total of the budget is still controlled by the executive, but it is an important statement of the importance of independence and there are real benefits in courts being able to control the allocation of their budgets. It allows innovation and creates a greater collegiate sense between the constituent courts. This is important in Australia where the court system is much more fragmented than the system in Germany.

Comparisons of court systems

In Australia each State has established its own courts and tribunals and then there is an overlay of the Federal courts and tribunals. Each of these has the individual capacity to establish its own code of practice and procedure so there are many different forms and approaches according to the jurisdiction. This may seem chaotic, but it does have an advantage of permitting and assessing innovations in small tribunals and courts before committing the whole system to change. The following table sets out the courts and tribunals in South Australia with an analysis of their judicial establishment and cases loads. The first four are Federal courts and tribunals and the rest are State courts and tribunals. Since this table was prepared the Federal government has added the Federal Magistrates Service as an additional court to do the bulk of the lesser first instance work of the Federal Court and Family Court.

---

[419] http://www.parliament.sa.gov.au/Catalog/legislation/Acts/c/1993.11.un.htm (accessed 3 May 2007).

Table 1: Courts and Tribunals in South Australia, December 1998

Court or Tribunal	*full time judicial officers*	*part time judicial officers*	*FTE judicial officers*	*Civil cases per year*
Federal Court	4		4	450
Family Court	5		5	5,258
Administrative Appeals Tribunal	2	4	2.5	951
Human Rights & Equal Opportunity Tribunal		1	0.5	33
Supreme Court	17		17	1,080
District Court	21		21	1,886
District Court Appeals tribunal			counted elsewhere	464
Youth Court	4		4	Not applicable
Environment Resources and Development Court	5	24	5	337
Magistrates Court	33		33	4,861
Industrial Relations Court and Commission	14		14	Court 1,141 Comm. 1,565
Workers Compensation Tribunal	15		15	7,441
Residential Tenancy Tribunal	1	15	5	8,098
Guardianship Board	1	unknown	4	1,743
Coroners Court	1		1	60
State Ombudsman	1		1	3,651
TOTALS			132	39,019

Sources: SA Law Calendar, CAA Annual Report 1998, various judicial officers and registrars in these courts and tribunals, and annual reports. FTE is an acronym for Full Time Equivalent. Ombudsmen, judicial registrars and tribunal members are all included for comparative purposes with Germany where all such jurisdictions are within the court system. Figures for the Supreme, District, Environment Resources and Development, Magistrates and Coroners Courts are for the financial year 1998/9. Uncontested debt claims are not included. The Federal and Family Courts are figures for SA 1998 calendar year. The ERD court figures exclude criminal matters and s.38 documents. The Coroner considers about 3000 matters a year but proceeds to an oral inquest only in about 60. The other matters have been left out in similar fashion to uncontested debt. The Guardianship Board figures are for 1999. It counts hearing outcomes at 4,099 but the lower figure of applications have been taken (one applications often has multiple hearings dealing with different aspects. Part time members have been reduced to FTEs by assuming a full time replacement at 40hrs per week for 50 weeks, if anything understating the figure. No distinction has been made between judges and magistrates who do criminal and civil cases. The workload statistics are for civil disputes for comparative purposes in Table 2.

It is possible to extrapolate these and compare them to comparative data from Germany and The Netherlands as follows:[420]

Table 2: Judges, Lawyers and Claims filed per 100,000 of population in The Netherlands, West Germany and South Australia.

	The Netherlands	*North Rhine-Westphalia*	*South Australia*
Judges	12	24	9
Lawyers	51	110	161
Civil claims filed	2,258	3,535	2,601
Civil claims per judge	188	147	289
Civil claims per lawyer	44	32	16

The figures for The Netherlands and North Rhine-Westphalia are adapted from figures published by Prof. Erhard Blankenburg.[421] He used North Rhine-Westphalia as representative of the former West Germany because of its cultural similarity to The Netherlands and to remove the effect of inclusion of data from the former GDR. The figures are for 1992.[422] His figures have been modified by adding prosecutors to lawyers. The German figures do not include the Mahnverfahren (uncontested debt) procedure which are another 10,588 claims per 100,000. The SA figures are reduced on a population of 1.5million in June 1998 (Australian Bureau of Statistics). The cases in the Magistrates Court likewise exclude uncontested debt cases which were another 46,932. The figures for judges and lawyers include all of them regardless of whether they do criminal or civil work. The number of cases are only non criminal proceedings. Lawyers include all with a current practicing certificate- June 1998, 2,419, June 1999, 2,423 (Law Society Annual Report). In South Australia prosecutors are counted as lawyers.

Taking North Rhine Westphalia as indicative of Germany and South Australia of Australia the differences in judicial methods are expressed in the resources used. The

420 These figures have been previously published in Cannon, "Comparisons of Judicial and Lawyer Resources to Resolve Civil Disputes in the Civil Code and Common Law Methods" (May 2001) 10 JJA 4 at p. 245.

421 Blankenburg, Professor Erhard, "The Infrastructure for Avoiding Civil Litigation: Comparing Cultures of Legal Behaviour in The Netherlands and West Germany" 28(4) *Law and Society Review* 789, 1994.

422 Figures in 2004 for judges are virtually the same. Per 100,000 population, for the whole of Germany there were 25 judges, and for the Netherlands 12 judges. There were more lawyers, 154/80 but the ratio of lawyers between Germany and the Netherlands at about 2/1 remains the same. It is notable in these more up to date figures that England and Wales had 3 judges and 1305 lawyers, emphasising the different role of the judge discussed in the text: CEPEJ, European judicial systems, Edition 2006 (2004 data), www.coe.int/cepej (accessed 29 July 2007).

common law method leaves the control over the gathering of evidence, preparation for trial and the presentation of evidence at the trial, in the hands of the parties' lawyers. Even though juries are rarely used in civil cases in Australia the oral jury tradition with complicated rules of evidence at the climatic trial drives the fact finding method. In Germany and the The Netherlands, although the method is adversary in civil matters, it is very different from the common law method. A major difference is a much greater control exercised by the judges over the fact finding process. Hence there are many more lawyers and less judges per capita in the common law system than in the civil code system because the lawyers do more of the work in each file. For the same reason each lawyer handles many more claims under the civil code system compared to the common law method, which is resource intensive for lawyers.

Professor Blankenburg explained the differences between The Netherlands and Germany as a result of the tight lawyer monopoly and high rates of cost insurance in Germany and a wider culture of solving disputes outside the court system in The Netherlands[423]. He suggests that ensuring use of courts to determine disputes is a last resort is desirable. Underpinning the differences is the different method of calculating cost shifting in Germany compared to The Netherlands. The BRAGO[424] that was in place when these comparisons were made, provided certainty of cost shifting, which allowed clearer actuary calculations by legal cost insurers and discouraged unnecessary activity by lawyers. In The Netherlands the cost calculation was uncertain and the level of costs was based on the extent of the activity of the lawyer rather than the stage of the process. This is the method of calculation in most jurisdictions in Australia, as it is in England. The method of costs calculation can profoundly affect how courts are used. The increasing cost of litigation in common law courts is a major challenge to their role. There is little point in having a court edifice if it cannot be accessed by any but the indigent or the very rich. Hence it is important to consider how cost shifting[425] affects accessibility to courts.

Cost shifting policies[426]

Whether it is desirable to have cost shifting

Economic modelling suggests that cost shifting encourages settlement of disputes rather than determination at trial[427]. Empirical research supports this. In Florida cost shifting

---

423 Blankenburg op cit.

424 Now the *RVG*.

425 The rule that the unsuccessful litigant in a court case pays the successful litigant some costs.

426 For a more detailed discussion see Cannon, "Designing Cost Policies to Provide Sufficient Access to Lower Courts" (July 2002) 23 *Civil Justice Quarterly*, p.198 Sweet & Maxwell, London.

427 The LPG approach to pre-trial negotiation strategies was developed by Landes, Posner and Gould (Landes, W. M., "An Economic Analysis of the Courts", 14 *Journal of Law and Economics*, 61, 1971, Posner, R.A. "An Economic Approach to Legal Procedure and Judicial Administration",2(2) *Journal of Legal Studies*, 1973. and Gould, J., "The Economics of Legal Conflict", 2(2) *Journal of Legal Studies* 279 1973). It works on the assumption that trials are caused by different expectations of the result. This has been developed to suggest that with cost shifting (the 'English' rule) there is less likelihood of trials than with no cost shifting (the 'American rule') because the anticipated costs can be shared between the parties to their mutual benefit (Main *op.cit. supra* n. 1 at p.12).

was introduced in medical negligence cases. This resulted in some large cost awards for plaintiffs and as a result representations from the medical defence lobby the rule was later changed back to the usual no cost shifting rule for the USA. Research[428] based on slightly more than 10,000 medical negligence cases supported the view that cost shifting led to fewer trials. There were 57 trials per 1,000 with cost shifting compared to 107 per 1,000 cases without it[429]. The research suggested that cost shifting encouraged the commencement of more high merit, low value cases but adverse information would cause these to be dropped. No cost shifting encouraged more low merit cases. The amount of cost incurred on each case increased with cost shifting[430].

In litigation in common law lower courts, actual costs are often equal to, or exceed the amount in dispute[431]. Without cost shifting plaintiffs with assets would be discouraged from suing because most or all of the success would be taken by their own lawyer's non shifted costs. Plaintiffs without assets could still sue if they could find a way of funding their own lawyer, but contingency fee arrangements would be unattractive except for large claims. Defendants with a good defence may as well offer substantial settlement because event when they win they will still have to pay their lawyer. Put simply, no-one could afford a trial in any but the largest cases unless someone else was paying the legal costs. The sensible policy at first instance is to impose the burden of paying the winner's legal costs on the loser. The counter argument is that some speculative claims are healthy for the system, by permitting judges to explore the boundaries of the present law. However, that this still occurs with cost shifting is borne out by the development of the law of negligence[432] under the regime of cost shifting in the English courts.

The research suggests that an effect of cost shifting is to discourage low merit cases from being commenced and from proceeding to trial, which is a benefit for the court and defendants. Discouraging plaintiffs with low merit claims is reasonable policy. After all, cost shifting substantially advantages plaintiffs in lower courts with a meritorious claim, because their costs are shifted, in part or whole, to the defendant. Having crossed this Rubicon it is important to recognise that the method of cost shifting can profoundly affect the way that litigants use court systems.

---

428 Snyder, E. A. and J.W. Hughes, "The English Rule for Allocating Legal Costs: Evidence Confronts Theory", 6(2) *Journal of Law, Economics and Organisation*, 1990. Hughes, J.W. and Snyder, E. A. "Litigation and Settlement Under the English and American Rules: Theory and Evidence", 28(1) *Journal of Law and Economics,* 1995.

429 Ibid. 1990, Figure 3, p.365.

430 Ibid. 1990, Table 6, p.375.

431 Woolf, Lord, *Access to Justice: Interim Report to the Lord Chancellor on the civil justice system in England and Wales*, (HMSO June 1995) p.35 and Cannon, Andrew, *An evaluation of some ways of limiting and reducing the costs to parties of conducting litigation in the Magistrates Court (civil division) in South Australia* (unpublished LL.M. (Hons) thesis, Uni of Wollongong, 1996) p.70.

432 The principle that each citizen owes a duty of care to her or his neighbour, which if breached gives rise to rights of compensation.

The effect of activity based scales

In Northern Ireland, which has a court system that is very similar to England, the cost shifting is to provide a fixed fee at the commencement of court proceedings that does not increase regardless of when or how the case is finalised. Surveys by the Civil Justice Reform Group led them to conclude that:[433]

> "Our studies appear to suggest that the cost of litigation in the province is usually lower- and in the case of the county court litigation, often significantly lower- than comparable proceedings in England and Wales."

The activity based scales that are now in place in England were progressively introduced during the 1700s. Christopher Brooks has done an analysis of litigation in English society between 1200 and 1996[434]. He identified a significant decline in litigation in the 1700s and concludes that one reason was the increase in legal fees[435]. Brooks explains that prior to the decline, costs to attorneys were awarded on a fixed fee basis per action (not unlike the concept in the Northern Ireland scale mentioned above), but as the fixed fee did not increase, attorneys began to charge for other activity in pursuing each case:[436]

> "Similarly the fee books of Cambridgeshire practitioner Joshua Eversden show that, in the years around 1710, he supplemented the standard attorney's fee by making a number of additional charges for each piece of work done for a client. He charged for journeys undertaken to consult with litigants, to speak to witnesses and, in what becomes a common phrase in fee books of the eighteenth century, as much as £2 for his 'troubles' in a matter.
>
> Coupled with what appears to be a greater reluctance of lawyers to allow litigants to conduct their business on credit, these seemingly trivial changes in the way fees were taken not only help to explain the contraction of court business in the eighteenth century, they also amount to a profound watershed in the way legal services were financed in England. They mark the replacement of the principle of a fixed tariff by a system of remuneration in which attorneys[437] and solicitors charged essentially on the basis of some kind of calculation of how much time and effort they had expended."

There is research by George Shepherd on pre-trial discovery[438] in 369 federal civil cases in the United States that ended in 1962. He subjected earlier surveys on these cases to econometric modelling and amongst other things concluded that:[439]

---

433 The Civil Justice Reform Group, *Review of the Civil Justice System in Northern Ireland, Interim Report,* Belfast, April 1999 p.37.

434 Brooks, Christopher W., *Lawyers, Litigation and English Society Since 1450*, the Hambledon Press, London and Rio Grande, 1998, Chapter 4.

435 Ibid. p. 92.

436 Ibid. p. 94.

437 Another word for lawyer, more commonly used historically in the English system, or in the USA.

438 A disclosure to the other party to litigation of the documentary evidence in the knowledge of the party and where it might be found. In the USA the term also covers wider powers to require examination of witnesses before trial.

"... (T)he nature of the attorney's fee arrangement influences the attorney's discovery behaviour substantially. For example, plaintiff's attorneys who are paid by the hour conduct in excess of 5 more days of discovery than plaintiff's attorneys who are paid on contingency. This may be due to differing principal-agent incentives between attorney and client. Similarly, each litigant's discovery responds to other client characteristics, such as the client's wealth or whether the client is a business, as well as to characteristics of the adversary."

The author's own research on the comparison between the fixed rate cost scale he introduced into the South Australian Magistrates Court, compared to activity based scales in the higher courts also supports the conclusion that fixed rate cost shifting encourages lawyers to cut their cloth to the price so that unnecessary activity is discouraged:[440]

"The unambiguous conclusion from the interviews was that the policies in the magistrates rules have been successful in limiting the legal costs of litigation in the Court. The fixed rate cost scale has been the driving force in maintaining a cost saving culture in the Court. The other policies have allowed that to happen but as the pleading experience demonstrates the same rules in different environs can lead to vastly different results (i.e. there is much less argument over particulars of pleadings in the Magistrates Court where the cost scale does not reward the arguments). There is no reason to quarrel with the view of the lawyers interviewed that the difference is primarily the result of the cost scale which does not reward activity."

Some conclusions[441] are that:

- Cost shifting is necessary to allow access and to discourage low merit claims. An identified adverse effect is to increase the cost to parties. It follows that cost shifting rules should include policies to discourage unnecessary costs being incurred.
- Fixed rate cost shifting scales discourage unnecessary activity and reduce costs.
- Fixed rate cost shifting scales allow the parties to predict the cost shifting at any stage.
- Cost shifting and actual costs should not be so low that too ready access to courts is encouraged. Some barriers to use of courts are important to encourage a diverse system of dispute resolution.

---

439 Shepherd, George, B., "An Empirical Study of the Economics of Pretrial Discovery", 19(2) *International Review of Law and Economics,* 245, 1999, at p. 262.

440 Ibid. p. 74.

441 Special problems are posed by class actions. In Australia the High Court has recently permitted private enterprise litigation funding of class actions. They take a percentage of the damages and pay the other side's costs if the party they are funding loses: *Campbells Cash and Carry Pty Ltd v Fostif Pty Ltd and others* (2006) HCA 42 (30 August 2006).

The other matter highlighted by the comparative data is the differences in the judicial method between the civil code and common law systems. This is now briefly discussed.

Two types of adversary system

The German court system for deciding civil disputes is adversarial, as is the common law system in Australia, but they are very different. The following are the key similarities between the two systems in civil cases:[442]

- the parties are entitled to be served,
- the parties define the dispute,
- the parties can end the dispute by agreement,
- the parties nominate the evidence to be brought to the court,
- the parties can question witnesses and can be heard on all issues,
- proceedings are conducted in open court in the presence of the parties and their legal advisers, and
- reasons for judgment are given, are subject to appeal and have an effect of res judicata.

These are essentials for an adversary court process between the parties rather than an inquisition by the court. The fact that the parties must be notified of a dispute, their ability to define its boundaries, the evidence that is brought to bear and to end the dispute, leaves the ultimate control of it in their hands. This much must be in the parties' hands for it to be an adversary contest between them. These are the features that make the process adversarial, rather than an errand, or inquiry imposed upon them, by an intermeddler, the court[443]. Their opportunity to test the evidence and be heard on all issues ensures the process is fair, which is essential for a judicial process. Due process ensures fairness but does not define whether the process is inquisitorial or adversarial.

The fact that a process occurs in an open forum, the decision must be justified and the process and the decision is subject to appeal ensures that departures from due process, and other errors can be corrected by the appeal court. The fact that the decision is final, subject only to appeal, ensures that this adversary process determines the dispute and is not just an adversary skirmish.

The common law method *is* different to the German court method in civil disputes, but much of this difference is based on its design for jury trials. The jury trial fact finding method dictates a procedure that ends with a climatic trial when all the evidence that is required is presented, mostly orally, to this disparate group of twelve unconnected people who have been assembled do their work and then return to their lives. The

442 See Cannon, "A Diary of Two German Civil Cases" (March 2002) 76 Australian Law Journal 3 at p. 186.

443 If the Court can determine the boundaries, subject matter and direction of an enquiry then it becomes an inquisitorial process.

pretrial processes are in the control of the lawyers[444], so that they can be properly prepared for the trial. The trial is highly managed, the protagonists wear special costumes, and in this way the method is theatrical in its presentation. It can be highly combative. There are elaborate rules of evidence, many of which have as their basis, the need to protect the jury from falling into error by placing reliance on hearsay, or second hand reports. Rather than permitting this evidence and giving it weight according to the reliability of its source, it is rejected. These rules have become highly technical and they sustain the skilled barrister tradition, from which the judiciary are primarily drawn. They sensibly support the merits of the system that sustains them.

A core difference between the systems is the control over the gathering and presentation of the evidence that the common law method gives to the parties and their lawyers. This is sometimes wrongly asserted as essential for a process to be adversarial. The common law method carries the risk that the judge is choosing between the two cases presented and no-one in court has the responsibility to find the substantive truth, nor even the formal truth[445].

Some differences between the systems are:

- The early disclosure by parties of evidence both to each other and to the court, in the German system. In the Australian common law system there are highly developed rules of discovery requiring the parties to disclose documents[446] to each other, but they do not disclose them to the court.
- German judges are more directly involved in settlement negotiations, whereas in the Australian system settlement is encouraged in well developed alternative dispute resolution systems provided both outside the court and by non judicial mediators within the court system.
- German judges manage the presentation of evidence, whereas in Australia the parties bring the witnesses and other evidence to court and question them in a highly structured way. The oral evidence tradition has very careful rules to ensure that the initial questioning of a witness is by open questions so that the answers are not suggested, and then the witness can be cross examined.
- There is a much greater emphasis on oral evidence in the Australian courts.
- The German courts are much less formal than the courts in Australia.
- In Australia the evidence of the party is often the centre point of the case, whereas in Germany the parties do not give evidence. In Germany the parties must have lawyers and can be active in the proceedings. In Australia, there is much less legal

---

444 Pretrial processes are managed by solicitors who refer the matter to barristers to draft the pleadings in civil matters and for advise on evidence.

445 In Germany courts distinguish between the *substantive* or *material truth (materielle Wahrheit)* in criminal matters and the *formal truth* in civil matters where the judge is constrained by the parties' control over the evidence. This distinction is not known to the common law where the difference is only expressed by the burden of proof, beyond reasonable doubt and balance of probabilities. In civil matters in principle the court makes a decision between the cases the parties put before the court.

446 Discovery in Australia refers to document discovery and is not as broad as the USA where the concept may include witness statements and oral evidence as part of the discovery process.

cost insurance and legal aid, so parties are often unrepresented and this can be very unsatisfactory in a such a highly technical process. Where they have lawyers, the parties sit in the body of the court and play no part in the proceedings.

- In Australia there is very little use by courts of their own experts to assist in the determination of technical issues[447] in contrast to Germany where the court retains its own expert. Experts can be fallible which is a good reason to permit conflicting expert evidence to be ventilated but too often in Australia the court is only presented with competing expert opinions that may be slanted towards the party that pays them.
- The common law tradition puts great reliance on individual case precedents. Australian statutes tend to be very prescriptive to corral[448] the reluctant judges into following Parliament's wishes. In contrast German legislation is more open textured and the courts turn to the code first and then commentaries on the developments from cases to provide the detail.

The core of any judicial process must be accurate fact finding. Anything less makes the determination of disputes a sham. The common law and civil code systems can, and are learning from each other. New statute law is becoming more important in both systems as new prescriptions are necessary to meet the challenges of changing economic and social systems. Precedent is increasingly recognised in Germany and less centrally important in Australia as statute law codifies more areas that were once the preserve of the common law alone. Australian courts would benefit from more control by the court over the presentation of the evidence in cases as happens in Germany. Without this there is the chance that no-one in the process will seek an accurate version of the facts. Common law discovery procedures and the methods of questioning witnesses are highly developed and offer benefits in ascertaining the accurate facts.

Conclusion

Courts are a creation of the powerful to legitimise their power by ensuring its exercise is fair and excesses are restrained. The judiciary interpret the Constitution and ensure legislation and executive acts are within power. To do this they must have a high degree of independence to allow them to make credible decisions in controversial matters.

Actual independence requires the appointment of people of merit and integrity. In Australia this is ensured by appointees being drawn from the barristers who have demonstrated their court skills, but the appointment method is defective due to the process being secret and subject to patronage and manipulation by cliques. Independence once an appointment is made is ensured by guarantees of tenure and salary and judicial control over the administrative establishment of their courts.

---

447 For a discussion of this see Cannon, "Courts using their own experts" (2004) 13 (3) *JJA* p.182.

448 To confine choices as with livestock by herding them into an enclosure from which they cannot escape.

To perform their role courts must be accessible and able to perform their core role of accurate fact finding. This is best achieved with fixed rate cost shifting and a higher degree of judicial control over the presentation of evidence than occurs under the traditional common law jury method. However, there should be sufficient barriers to use of courts and a diverse ADR system to encourage dispute resolution outside the court system.

Chapter 8:

CONCLUSION

The Australian Constitution was a pragmatic power sharing arrangement primarily designed to protect the interests of the member states whilst they surrendered sufficient power to the new central authority to allow for effective national government. It is an amalgam of the British arrangements for the sharing and moderation of governmental power and the USA arrangements for the purpose of a federal system and a written constitution, but without the high sounding ideals and Bill of Rights. It has worked well, without substantial amendment for more than one hundred years, in an admittedly fairly benign political and economic environment compared to Europe.

Although the theory of the British system is a separation of powers between the three arms of government, the legislature, the executive and the judiciary, the pre-eminence of the political party system and the central role of Cabinet has resulted in the reality of executive and legislative power both residing in Cabinet which controls Parliament for legislation (with some restrictions in the Senate) and also has executive power. The remaining restraint is the independent judiciary. In the final analysis the effective restraints on abuses of power lie in the political process, the independent judicial system and the press. The Constitution makes the government accountable to Parliament that is in turn accountable to the people through the electoral process, which gives the capacity to the people to end the reign of a government. The Constitution guarantees the electoral process by prescribing the nature of electorates and the requirements that Parliament must sit so that the government can be subject to questioning and that it must submit to an election at least every three years. To be effective this depends on a free press that can bring bad government and abuses of power, and judicial decisions, to the attention of the voting public. In the Australian Constitution there is no guarantee of the freedom of the press, but the High Court has been vigilant in protecting the ability of the press and others to engage in frank political discussion. This points to the key role of the judiciary in protecting a civil political process.

The central role of the judiciary in preserving a civil society is demonstrated in the Australian decisions. It is the judiciary who decide whether legislation is within power. Thus the High Court in the post war period would not permit one government to nationalise the banking system, nor another to proscribe the communist party. The fact that the founding fathers of the Constitution cannot influence events from the grave is demonstrated by the narrow protection the High Court has given to the freedom and non establishment of religion guaranteed in the Constitution, permitting the stopping of worship in the church of the Jehovah's Witnesses and government subsidising religious schools. On the other hand the High Court has found a freedom of discussion of political matters from the ether of the common law. The mere words in the Constitution give no protection; it is in the meaning given to them by the High Court that any protection from abuse of power lies. The judiciary are the guardians of the liberty in a constitutional arrangement.

Despite the importance the Constitution attached to the protection of State rights in fact there has been a substantial shift of power from the States to the Commonwealth as a result of a shift of financial power, particularly taxation. Again the High Court has had a central role in sanctioning the shift in power, mainly to meet the needs of war, but once the power shifts it does not return. Constitutional draftsmen cannot impose their view on the future. They can do no more than establish a structure that is likely to maintain a civil society as it meets the unknown challenges of destiny.

The examples in this text also show that the judges often shroud their reasons in a cloak of the certainty of the application of legalism as if it were a science. In fact, interpretation of the Constitution is a product of the received wisdom of judicial experience, the needs of and pressures from the community at the time and the personal attitudes of the judges on the bench. The extent of a power may not be obvious from the wording of the Constitution and an exercise of power may depend on several different heads of power. Thus Commonwealth power over industrial relations now depends on the corporations, trade and commerce and external affairs power and is far more extensive than would be permitted by the industrial relations power itself. The interpretation of a power may vary over time. This is most obvious with the defence power, which the Court explicitly extends in time of war, but can also be seen in the interpretation of other powers, such as the corporations power that has steadily increased according to the composition of the Court and the needs of the community.

The High Court has become more sophisticated in the tests it uses to interpret the Constitution, but underlying these is disagreement over the extent that the judiciary should be adventurous in its interpretations and more fundamentally the extent to which it should be open and honest in identifying the underlying policy reasons that influence the interpretations they make. One consistent, but unstated, policy appears to be the protection of private property as in the *Bank Nationalisation Case* against the apparent meaning of the Constitution, the *Goulden Case* where life insurance funds were protected in apparent discrimination against the blind and the *Jehovah's Witnesses Case*, where more protection was given to property than to religious freedom. In *Mabo (No.2)* the Court departed from this principle, and confronted community conscience with its own, threatening land property rights. When it did this, the Court put at risk its unspoken pact with the powerful in society and brought a storm of protest onto its heads. The contrast with the relative silence over the much more profound constitutional shift in the *Industrial Relations Case*, which had the sympathy of business, underlines this relationship. It emphasises the importance of the attitude of the press. It also shows that professed conservatives can sometimes be agents of radical change.

Courts are a creation of the powerful to legitimise their power by ensuring its exercise is fair and excesses are restrained. The judiciary interpret the Constitution and ensure legislation and executive acts are within power. To do this they must have a high degree of independence to allow them to make credible decisions in controversial matters. Unlike the executive, which has a basis of legitimacy for the exercise of its power through being elected, the judiciary has no separate legitimacy other than its credibility, through its decisions, as an independent guardian of the constitutional arrangement. When they inaccurately minimise the nature of their role by pretending that their decisions are an inevitable application of the words of the Constitution they diminish their integrity and credibility by the pretence.

Judicial independence requires the appointment of people of merit and integrity. In Australia this is ensured by appointees being drawn from the barristers who have demonstrated their court skills, but the appointment method is defective due to the process being secret and subject to patronage. A protection against patronage lies in the independence of the judiciary, which is ensured by guarantees of tenure, salary, a generous pension scheme and control over the administrative establishment of their courts. Once in place a judge can ignore any favours of appointment.

The role of courts is to enforce the obligations, criminal and civil, that society requires of its members. Where people contest court enforcement then the courts must be able to determine an accurate version of the facts. Accurate fact finding needs a higher degree of judicial control over the presentation of evidence than occurs under the traditional common law jury method, which leaves the fact finder to choose between the versions presented by the parties, rather than seeking even the formal truth, and permits abuses driven by activity based cost scales that drive up costs to an extent that access is prohibitively expensive. Fixed rate cost scales encourage more efficient use of court processes. However, there should be sufficient barriers to use of courts and a diverse ADR system to encourage dispute resolution outside the court system.

The power sharing arrangement in the Australian Constitution has often not worked as the draftsmen intended, but the parliamentary and electoral processes have accommodated changes in the power groups that demand a voice in government, and the protection provided by an independent judiciary, and free discussion of political matters in the press, have thus far maintained a civil democracy in Australia for more than a hundred years. However, any constitutional arrangement is a human construction and requires the courage of good people to keep the corruption that power inevitably brings in its wake, at bay. Mere words in a statute will not suffice.

APPENDIX

An Act to constitute the Commonwealth of Australia [9th July 1900][449]

WHEREAS the people of New South Wales, Victoria, South Australia, Queensland, and Tasmania, humbly relying on the blessing of Almighty God, have agreed to unite in one indissoluble Federal Commonwealth under the Crown of the United Kingdom of Great Britain and Ireland, and under the Constitution hereby established:

And whereas it is expedient to provide for the admission into the Commonwealth of other Australasian Colonies and possessions of the Queen:

Be it therefore enacted by the Queen's most Excellent Majesty, by and with the advice and consent of the Lords Spiritual and Temporal, and Commons, in this present Parliament assembled, and by the authority of the same, as follows:

1 Short title [*see* Note 1]
This Act may be cited as the Commonwealth of Australia Constitution Act.

2 Act to extend to the Queen's successors
The provisions of this Act referring to the Queen shall extend to Her Majesty's heirs and successors in the sovereignty of the United Kingdom.

3 Proclamation of Commonwealth [*see* Note 2]
It shall be lawful for the Queen, with the advice of the Privy Council, to declare by proclamation that, on and after a day therein appointed, not being later than one year after the passing of this Act, the people of New South Wales, Victoria, South Australia, Queensland, and Tasmania, and also, if Her Majesty is satisfied that the people of Western Australia have agreed thereto, of Western Australia, shall be united in a Federal Commonwealth under the name of the Commonwealth of Australia. But the Queen may, at any time after the proclamation, appoint a Governor-General for the Commonwealth.

4 Commencement of Act
The Commonwealth shall be established, and the Constitution of the Commonwealth shall take effect, on and after the day so appointed. But the Parliaments of the several colonies may at any time after the passing of this Act make any such laws, to come into operation on the day so appointed, as they might have made if the Constitution had taken effect at the passing of this Act.

5 Operation of the Constitution and laws [*see* Note 3]
This Act, and all laws made by the Parliament of the Commonwealth under the Constitution, shall be binding on the courts, judges, and people of every State and of every part of the Commonwealth, notwithstanding anything in the laws of any State; and the laws of the Commonwealth shall be in force on all British ships, the

[449] This version, with notes, was prepared by the Office of Legislative Drafting, Attorney-General's Department, Canberra. Amendments are shown in bold, with deletions struck through.

Queen's ships of war excepted, whose first port of clearance and whose port of destination are in the Commonwealth.

6 Definitions

The Commonwealth shall mean the Commonwealth of Australia as established under this Act.

The States shall mean such of the colonies of New South Wales, New Zealand, Queensland, Tasmania, Victoria, Western Australia, and South Australia, including the northern territory of South Australia, as for the time being are parts of the Commonwealth, and such colonies or territories as may be admitted into or established by the Commonwealth as States; and each of such parts of the Commonwealth shall be called *a State*.

Original States shall mean such States as are parts of the Commonwealth at its establishment.

7 Repeal of Federal Council Act [*see* Note 4]

The Federal Council of Australasia Act, 1885, is hereby repealed, but so as not to affect any laws passed by the Federal Council of Australasia and in force at the establishment of the Commonwealth.

Any such law may be repealed as to any State by the Parliament of the Commonwealth, or as to any colony not being a State by the Parliament thereof.

8 Application of Colonial Boundaries Act

After the passing of this Act the Colonial Boundaries Act, 1895, shall not apply to any colony which becomes a State of the Commonwealth; but the Commonwealth shall be taken to be a self-governing colony for the purposes of that Act.

9 Constitution [*see* Note 1]

The Constitution of the Commonwealth shall be as follows:

The Constitution	
This Constitution is divided as follows:	
Chapter	I—The Parliament
Part	I—General
Part	II—The Senate
Part	III—The House of Representatives
Part	IV—Both Houses of the Parliament
Part	V—Powers of the Parliament
Chapter	II—The Executive Government
Chapter	III—The Judicature
Chapter	IV—Finance and Trade
Chapter	V—The States
Chapter	VI—New States
Chapter	VII—Miscellaneous
Chapter	VIII—Alteration of the Constitution
The Schedule	

Chapter I—The Parliament

Part I—*General*

1 Legislative power
The legislative power of the Commonwealth shall be vested in a Federal Parliament, which shall consist of the Queen, a Senate, and a House of Representatives, and which is hereinafter called *The Parliament*, or *The Parliament of the Commonwealth*.

2 Governor-General
A Governor-General appointed by the Queen shall be Her Majesty's representative in the Commonwealth, and shall have and may exercise in the Commonwealth during the Queen's pleasure, but subject to this Constitution, such powers and functions of the Queen as Her Majesty may be pleased to assign to him.

3 Salary of Governor-General
There shall be payable to the Queen out of the Consolidated Revenue fund of the Commonwealth, for the salary of the Governor-General, an annual sum which, until the Parliament otherwise provides, shall be ten thousand pounds.
The salary of a Governor-General shall not be altered during his continuance in office.

4 Provisions relating to Governor-General
The provisions of this Constitution relating to the Governor-General extend and apply to the Governor-General for the time being, or such person as the Queen may appoint to administer the Government of the Commonwealth; but no such person shall be entitled to receive any salary from the Commonwealth in respect of any other office during his administration of the Government of the Commonwealth.

5 Sessions of Parliament. Prorogation and dissolution
The Governor-General may appoint such times for holding the sessions of the Parliament as he thinks fit, and may also from time to time, by Proclamation or otherwise, prorogue the Parliament, and may in like manner dissolve the House of Representatives.
Summoning Parliament
After any general election the Parliament shall be summoned to meet not later than thirty days after the day appointed for the return of the writs.
First session
The Parliament shall be summoned to meet not later than six months after the establishment of the Commonwealth.

6 Yearly session of Parliament
There shall be a session of the Parliament once at least in every year, so that twelve months shall not intervene between the last sitting of the Parliament in one session and its first sitting in the next session.

7 The Senate [*see* Note 5]

The Senate shall be composed of senators for each State, directly chosen by the people of the State, voting, until the Parliament otherwise provides, as one electorate.

But until the Parliament of the Commonwealth otherwise provides, the Parliament of the State of Queensland, if that State be an Original State, may make laws dividing the State into divisions and determining the number of senators to be chosen for each division, and in the absence of such provision the State shall be one electorate.

Until the Parliament otherwise provides there shall be six senators for each Original State. The Parliament may make laws increasing or diminishing the number of senators for each State, but so that equal representation of the several Original States shall be maintained and that no Original State shall have less than six senators.

The senators shall be chosen for a term of six years, and the names of the senators chosen for each State shall be certified by the Governor to the Governor-General.

8 Qualification of electors

The qualification of electors of senators shall be in each State that which is prescribed by this Constitution, or by the Parliament, as the qualification for electors of members of the House of Representatives; but in the choosing of senators each elector shall vote only once.

9 Method of election of senators [*see* Note 6]

The Parliament of the Commonwealth may make laws prescribing the method of choosing senators, but so that the method shall be uniform for all the States. Subject to any such law, the Parliament of each State may make laws prescribing the method of choosing the senators for that State.

Times and places [*see* Note 6]

The Parliament of a State may make laws for determining the times and places of elections of senators for the State.

10 Application of State laws

Until the Parliament otherwise provides, but subject to this Constitution, the laws in force in each State, for the time being, relating to elections for the more numerous House of the Parliament of the State shall, as nearly as practicable, apply to elections of senators for the State.

11 Failure to choose senators

The Senate may proceed to the despatch of business, notwithstanding the failure of any State to provide for its representation in the Senate.

12 Issue of writs

The Governor of any State may cause writs to be issued for elections of senators for the State. In case of the dissolution of the Senate the writs shall be issued within ten days from the proclamation of such dissolution.

13 Rotation of senators

As soon as may be after the Senate first meets, and after each first meeting of the Senate following a dissolution thereof, the Senate shall divide the senators chosen for each State into two classes, as nearly equal in number as practicable; and the places of the senators of the first class shall become vacant at the expiration of ~~the third year~~ *three years,* and the places of those of the second class at the expiration of ~~the sixth year~~ *six years,* from the beginning of their term of service; and afterwards the places of senators shall become vacant at the expiration of six years from the beginning of their term of service.

The election to fill vacant places shall be made ~~in the year at the expiration of which~~ *within one year before* the places are to become vacant.

For the purposes of this section the term of service of a senator shall be taken to begin on the first day of ~~January~~ *July* following the day of his election, except in the cases of the first election and of the election next after any dissolution of the Senate, when it shall be taken to begin on the first day of ~~January~~ *July* preceding the day of his election.

14 Further provision for rotation [*see* Note 7]

Whenever the number of senators for a State is increased or diminished, the Parliament of the Commonwealth may make such provision for the vacating of the places of senators for the State as it deems necessary to maintain regularity in the rotation.

~~15 Casual vacancies~~

~~If the place of a senator becomes vacant before the expiration of his term of service, the House of Parliament of the State for which he was chosen shall, sitting and voting together, choose a person to hold the place until the expiration of the term, or until the election of a successor as hereinafter provided, whichever first happens. But if the Houses of Parliament of the State are not in session at the time when the vacancy is notified, the Governor of the State, with the advice of the Executive Council thereof, may appoint a person to hold the place until the expiration of fourteen days after the beginning of the next session of the Parliament of the State, or until the election of a successor, whichever first happens.~~

~~At the next general election of members of the House of Representatives, or at the next election of senators for the State, whichever first happens, a successor shall, if the term has not then expired, be chosen to hold the place from the date of his election until the expiration of the term.~~

~~The name of any senator so chosen or appointed shall be certified by the Governor of the State to the Governor-General.~~

15 Casual vacancies [*see* Note 8]

If the place of a senator becomes vacant before the expiration of his term of service, the Houses of Parliament of the State for which he was chosen, sitting and voting together, or, if there is only one House of that Parliament, that House, shall choose a person to hold the place until the expiration of the term. But if the Parliament of the State is not in session when the vacancy is notified, the Governor of the State, with the advice of the Executive Council thereof, may appoint a person to hold the place until the expiration of fourteen days from the beginning of the next session of the Parliament of the State or the expiration of the term, whichever first happens.

Where a vacancy has at any time occurred in the place of a senator chosen by the people of a State and, at the time when he was so chosen, he was publicly recognized by a particular political party as being an endorsed candidate of that party and publicly represented himself to be such a candidate, a person chosen or appointed under this section in consequence of that vacancy, or in consequence of that vacancy and a subsequent vacancy or vacancies, shall, unless there is no member of that party available to be chosen or appointed, be a member of that party.

Where:

(a) in accordance with the last preceding paragraph, a member of a particular political party is chosen or appointed to hold the place of a senator whose place had become vacant; and

(b) before taking his seat he ceases to be a member of that party (otherwise than by reason of the party having ceased to exist);

he shall be deemed not to have been so chosen or appointed and the vacancy shall be again notified in accordance with section twenty-one of this Constitution.

The name of any senator chosen or appointed under this section shall be certified by the Governor of the State to the Governor-General.

If the place of a senator chosen by the people of the State at the election of senators last held before the commencement of the *Constitution Alteration (Senate Casual Vacancies) 1977* became vacant before that commencement and, at that commencement, no person chosen by the House or Houses of Parliament of the State, or appointed by the Governor of the State, in consequence of that vacancy, or in consequence of that vacancy and a subsequent vacancy or vacancies, held office, this section applies as if the place of the senator chosen by the people of the State had become vacant after that commencement.

A senator holding office at the commencement of the *Constitution Alteration (Senate Casual Vacancies) 1977*, being a senator appointed by the Governor of a State in consequence of a vacancy that had at any time occurred in the place of a senator chosen by the people of the State, shall be deemed to have been appointed to hold the place until the expiration of fourteen days after the beginning of the next session of the Parliament of the State that commenced or commences after he was appointed and further action under this section shall be taken as if the vacancy in the place of the senator chosen by the people of the State had occurred after that commencement.

Subject to the next succeeding paragraph, a senator holding office at the commencement of the *Constitution Alteration (Senate Casual Vacancies) 1977* who was chosen by the House or Houses of Parliament of a State in consequence of a vacancy that had at any time occurred in the place of a senator chosen by the people of the State shall be deemed to have been chosen to hold office until the expiration of the term of service of the senator elected by the people of the State.

If, at or before the commencement of the *Constitution Alteration (Senate Casual Vacancies) 1977*, a law to alter the Constitution entitled "*Constitution Alteration (Simultaneous Elections) 1977*" came into operation, a senator holding office at the commencement of that law who was chosen by the House or Houses of Parliament of a State in consequence of a vacancy that had at any time occurred in the place of a senator chosen by the people of the State shall be deemed to have been chosen to hold office:
(a) if the senator elected by the people of the State had a term of service expiring on the thirtieth day of June, One thousand nine hundred and seventy-eight—until the expiration or dissolution of the first House of Representatives to expire or be dissolved after that law came into operation; or
(b) if the senator elected by the people of the State had a term of service expiring on the thirtieth day of June, One thousand nine hundred and eighty-one—until the expiration or dissolution of the second House of Representatives to expire or be dissolved after that law came into operation or, if there is an earlier dissolution of the Senate, until that dissolution.

16 Qualifications of senator
The qualifications of a senator shall be the same as those of a member of the House of Representatives.

17 Election of President
The Senate shall, before proceeding to the despatch of any other business, choose a senator to be the President of the Senate; and as often as the office of President becomes vacant the Senate shall again choose a senator to be the President.
The President shall cease to hold his office if he ceases to be a senator. He may be removed from office by a vote of the Senate, or he may resign his office or his seat by writing addressed to the Governor-General.

18 Absence of President
Before or during any absence of the President, the Senate may choose a senator to perform his duties in his absence.

19 Resignation of senator

A senator may, by writing addressed to the President, or to the Governor-General if there is no President or if the President is absent from the Commonwealth, resign his place, which thereupon shall become vacant.

20 Vacancy by absence

The place of a senator shall become vacant if for two consecutive months of any session of the Parliament he, without the permission of the Senate, fails to attend the Senate.

21 Vacancy to be notified

Whenever a vacancy happens in the Senate, the President, or if there is no President or if the President is absent from the Commonwealth the Governor-General, shall notify the same to the Governor of the State in the representation of which the vacancy has happened.

22 Quorum

Until the Parliament otherwise provides, the presence of at least one-third of the whole number of the senators shall be necessary to constitute a meeting of the Senate for the exercise of its powers.

23 Voting in the Senate

Questions arising in the Senate shall be determined by a majority of votes, and each senator shall have one vote. The President shall in all cases be entitled to a vote; and when the votes are equal the question shall pass in the negative.

Part III—*The House of Representatives*

24 Constitution of House of Representatives

The House of Representatives shall be composed of members directly chosen by the people of the Commonwealth, and the number of such members shall be, as nearly as practicable, twice the number of the senators.

The number of members chosen in the several States shall be in proportion to the respective numbers of their people, and shall, until the Parliament otherwise provides, be determined, whenever necessary, in the following manner:

(i) a quota shall be ascertained by dividing the number of the people of the Commonwealth, as shown by the latest statistics of the Commonwealth, by twice the number of the senators;
(ii) the number of members to be chosen in each State shall be determined by dividing the number of the people of the State, as shown by the latest statistics of the Commonwealth, by the quota; and if on such division there is a remainder greater than one-half of the quota, one more member shall be chosen in the State.
But notwithstanding anything in this section, five members at least shall be chosen in each Original State.

25 Provision as to races disqualified from voting

For the purposes of the last section, if by the law of any State all persons of any race are disqualified from voting at elections for the more numerous House of the Parliament of the State, then, in reckoning the number of the people of the State or of the Commonwealth, persons of that race resident in that State shall not be counted.

26 Representatives in first Parliament

Notwithstanding anything in section twenty-four, the number of members to be chosen in each State at the first election shall be as follows:

New South Wales	twenty-three;
Victoria	twenty;
Queensland	eight;
South Australia	six;
Tasmania	five;

Provided that if Western Australia is an Original State, the numbers shall be as follows:

New South Wales	twenty-six;
Victoria	twenty-three;
Queensland	nine;
South Australia	seven;
Western Australia	five;
Tasmania	five.

27 Alteration of number of members

Subject to this Constitution, the Parliament may make laws for increasing or diminishing the number of the members of the House of Representatives.

28 Duration of House of Representatives

Every House of Representatives shall continue for three years from the first meeting of the House, and no longer, but may be sooner dissolved by the Governor-General.

29 Electoral divisions *[see Note 9]*

Until the Parliament of the Commonwealth otherwise provides, the Parliament of any State may make laws for determining the divisions in each State for which members of the House of Representatives may be chosen, and the number of members to be chosen for each division. A division shall not be formed out of parts of different States.

In the absence of other provision, each State shall be one electorate.

30 Qualification of electors

Until the Parliament otherwise provides, the qualification of electors of members of the House of Representatives shall be in each State that which is prescribed by the law of the State as the qualification of electors of the more numerous House of Parliament of the State; but in the choosing of members each elector shall vote only once.

31 Application of State laws

Until the Parliament otherwise provides, but subject to this Constitution, the laws in force in each State for the time being relating to elections for the more numerous House of the Parliament of the State shall, as nearly as practicable, apply to elections in the State of members of the House of Representatives.

32 Writs for general election

The Governor-General in Council may cause writs to be issued for general elections of members of the House of Representatives.

After the first general election, the writs shall be issued within ten days from the expiry of a House of Representatives or from the proclamation of a dissolution thereof.

33 Writs for vacancies

Whenever a vacancy happens in the House of Representatives, the Speaker shall issue his writ for the election of a new member, or if there is no Speaker or if he is absent from the Commonwealth the Governor-General in Council may issue the writ.

34 Qualifications of members

Until the Parliament otherwise provides, the qualifications of a member of the House of Representatives shall be as follows:

(i) he must be of the full age of twenty-one years, and must be an elector entitled to vote at the election of members of the House of Representatives, or a person qualified to become such elector, and must have been for three years at the least a resident within the limits of the Commonwealth as existing at the time when he is chosen;

(ii) he must be a subject of the Queen, either natural-born or for at least five years naturalized under a law of the United Kingdom, or of a Colony which has become or becomes a State, or of the Commonwealth, or of a State.

35 Election of Speaker

The House of Representatives shall, before proceeding to the despatch of any other business, choose a member to be the Speaker of the House, and as often as the office of Speaker becomes vacant the House shall again choose a member to be the Speaker.

The Speaker shall cease to hold his office if he ceases to be a member. He may be removed from office by a vote of the House, or he may resign his office or his seat by writing addressed to the Governor-General.

36 Absence of Speaker
Before or during any absence of the Speaker, the House of Representatives may choose a member to perform his duties in his absence.

37 Resignation of member
A member may by writing addressed to the Speaker, or to the Governor-General if there is no Speaker or if the Speaker is absent from the Commonwealth, resign his place, which thereupon shall become vacant.

38 Vacancy by absence
The place of a member shall become vacant if for two consecutive months of any session of the Parliament he, without the permission of the House, fails to attend the House.

39 Quorum
Until the Parliament otherwise provides, the presence of at least one-third of the whole number of the members of the House of Representatives shall be necessary to constitute a meeting of the House for the exercise of its powers.

40 Voting in House of Representatives
Questions arising in the House of Representatives shall be determined by a majority of votes other than that of the Speaker. The Speaker shall not vote unless the numbers are equal, and then he shall have a casting vote.

Part IV—*Both Houses of the Parliament*

41 Right of electors of States
No adult person who has or acquires a right to vote at elections for the more numerous House of the Parliament of a State shall, while the right continues, be prevented by any law of the Commonwealth from voting at elections for either House of the Parliament of the Commonwealth.

42 Oath or affirmation of allegiance
Every senator and every member of the House of Representatives shall before taking his seat make and subscribe before the Governor-General, or some person authorised by him, an oath or affirmation of allegiance in the form set forth in the schedule to this Constitution.

43 Member of one House ineligible for other
A member of either House of the Parliament shall be incapable of being chosen or of sitting as a member of the other House.

44 Disqualification
Any person who:
(i) is under any acknowledgment of allegiance, obedience, or adherence to a foreign power, or is a subject or a citizen or entitled to the rights or privileges of a subject or a citizen of a foreign power; or

(ii) is attainted of treason, or has been convicted and is under sentence, or subject to be sentenced, for any offence punishable under the law of the Commonwealth or of a State by imprisonment for one year or longer; or

(iii) is an undischarged bankrupt or insolvent; or

(iv) holds any office of profit under the Crown, or any pension payable during the pleasure of the Crown out of any of the revenues of the Commonwealth; or

(v) has any direct or indirect pecuniary interest in any agreement with the Public Service of the Commonwealth otherwise than as a member and in common with the other members of an incorporated company consisting of more than twenty-five persons;

shall be incapable of being chosen or of sitting as a senator or a member of the House of Representatives.

But subsection (iv) does not apply to the office of any of the Queen's Ministers of State for the Commonwealth, or of any of the Queen's Ministers for a State, or to the receipt of pay, half pay, or a pension, by any person as an officer or member of the Queen's navy or army, or to the receipt of pay as an officer or member of the naval or military forces of the Commonwealth by any person whose services are not wholly employed by the Commonwealth.

45 Vacancy on happening of disqualification

If a senator or member of the House of Representatives:

(i) becomes subject to any of the disabilities mentioned in the last preceding section; or

(ii) takes the benefit, whether by assignment, composition, or otherwise, of any law relating to bankrupt or insolvent debtors; or

(iii) directly or indirectly takes or agrees to take any fee or honorarium for services rendered to the Commonwealth, or for services rendered in the Parliament to any person or State;

his place shall thereupon become vacant.

46 Penalty for sitting when disqualified

Until the Parliament otherwise provides, any person declared by this Constitution to be incapable of sitting as a senator or as a member of the House of Representatives shall, for every day on which he so sits, be liable to pay the sum of one hundred pounds to any person who sues for it in any court of competent jurisdiction.

47 Disputed elections

Until the Parliament otherwise provides, any question respecting the qualification of a senator or of a member of the House of Representatives, or respecting a vacancy in either House of the Parliament, and any question of a disputed election to either House, shall be determined by the House in which the question arises.

48 Allowance to members

Until the Parliament otherwise provides, each senator and each member of the House of Representatives shall receive an allowance of four hundred pounds a year, to be reckoned from the day on which he takes his seat.

49 Privileges etc. of Houses

The powers, privileges, and immunities of the Senate and of the House of Representatives, and of the members and the committees of each House, shall be such as are declared by the Parliament, and until declared shall be those of the Commons House of Parliament of the United Kingdom, and of its members and committees, at the establishment of the Commonwealth.

50 Rules and orders

Each House of the Parliament may make rules and orders with respect to:
(i) the mode in which its powers, privileges, and immunities may be exercised and upheld;
(ii) the order and conduct of its business and proceedings either separately or jointly with the other House.

Part V—*Powers of the Parliament*

51 Legislative powers of the Parliament [*see* Notes 10 and 11]

The Parliament shall, subject to this Constitution, have power to make laws for the peace, order, and good government of the Commonwealth with respect to:
(i) trade and commerce with other countries, and among the States;
(ii) taxation; but so as not to discriminate between States or parts of States;
(iii) bounties on the production or export of goods, but so that such bounties shall be uniform throughout the Commonwealth;
(iv) borrowing money on the public credit of the Commonwealth;
(v) postal, telegraphic, telephonic, and other like services;
(vi) the naval and military defence of the Commonwealth and of the several States, and the control of the forces to execute and maintain the laws of the Commonwealth;
(vii) lighthouses, lightships, beacons and buoys;
(viii) astronomical and meteorological observations;
(ix) quarantine;
(x) fisheries in Australian waters beyond territorial limits;
(xi) census and statistics;
(xii) currency, coinage, and legal tender;
(xiii) banking, other than State banking; also State banking extending beyond the limits of the State concerned, the incorporation of banks, and the issue of paper money;
(xiv) insurance, other than State insurance; also State insurance extending beyond the limits of the State concerned;
(xv) weights and measures;
(xvi) bills of exchange and promissory notes;
(xvii) bankruptcy and insolvency;
(xviii) copyrights, patents of inventions and designs, and trade marks;
(xix) naturalization and aliens;
(xx) foreign corporations, and trading or financial corporations formed within the limits of the Commonwealth;
(xxi) marriage;

(xxii) divorce and matrimonial causes; and in relation thereto, parental rights, and the custody and guardianship of infants;
(xxiii) invalid and old-age pensions;
(xxiiiA) the provision of maternity allowances, widows' pensions, child endowment, unemployment, pharmaceutical, sickness and hospital benefits, medical and dental services (but not so as to authorize any form of civil conscription), benefits to students and family allowances;
(xxiv) the service and execution throughout the Commonwealth of the civil and criminal process and the judgments of the courts of the States;
(xxv) the recognition throughout the Commonwealth of the laws, the public Acts and records, and the judicial proceedings of the States;
(xxvi) the people of any race~~, other than the aboriginal race in any State,~~ for whom it is deemed necessary to make special laws;
(xxvii) immigration and emigration;
(xxviii) the influx of criminals;
(xxix) external affairs;
(xxx) the relations of the Commonwealth with the islands of the Pacific;
(xxxi) the acquisition of property on just terms from any State or person for any purpose in respect of which the Parliament has power to make laws;
(xxxii) the control of railways with respect to transport for the naval and military purposes of the Commonwealth;
(xxxiii) the acquisition, with the consent of a State, of any railways of the State on terms arranged between the Commonwealth and the State;
(xxxiv) railway construction and extension in any State with the consent of that State;
(xxxv) conciliation and arbitration for the prevention and settlement of industrial disputes extending beyond the limits of any one State;
(xxxvi) matters in respect of which this Constitution makes provision until the Parliament otherwise provides;
(xxxvii) matters referred to the Parliament of the Commonwealth by the Parliament or Parliaments of any State or States, but so that the law shall extend only to States by whose Parliaments the matter is referred, or which afterwards adopt the law;
(xxxviii) the exercise within the Commonwealth, at the request or with the concurrence of the Parliaments of all the States directly concerned, of any power which can at the establishment of this Constitution be exercised only by the Parliament of the United Kingdom or by the Federal Council of Australasia;
(xxxix) matters incidental to the execution of any power vested by this Constitution in the Parliament or in either House thereof, or in the Government of the Commonwealth, or in the Federal Judicature, or in any department or officer of the Commonwealth.

52 Exclusive powers of the Parliament
The Parliament shall, subject to this Constitution, have exclusive power to make laws for the peace, order, and good government of the Commonwealth with respect to:

(i) the seat of government of the Commonwealth, and all places acquired by the Commonwealth for public purposes;
(ii) matters relating to any department of the public service the control of which is by this Constitution transferred to the Executive Government of the Commonwealth;
(iii) other matters declared by this Constitution to be within the exclusive power of the Parliament.

53 Powers of the Houses in respect of legislation
Proposed laws appropriating revenue or moneys, or imposing taxation, shall not originate in the Senate. But a proposed law shall not be taken to appropriate revenue or moneys, or to impose taxation, by reason only of its containing provisions for the imposition or appropriation of fines or other pecuniary penalties, or for the demand or payment or appropriation of fees for licences, or fees for services under the proposed law.
The Senate may not amend proposed laws imposing taxation, or proposed laws appropriating revenue or moneys for the ordinary annual services of the Government.
The Senate may not amend any proposed law so as to increase any proposed charge or burden on the people.
The Senate may at any stage return to the House of Representatives any proposed law which the Senate may not amend, requesting, by message, the omission or amendment of any items or provisions therein. And the House of Representatives may, if it thinks fit, make any of such omissions or amendments, with or without modifications.
Except as provided in this section, the Senate shall have equal power with the House of Representatives in respect of all proposed laws.

54 Appropriation Bills
The proposed law which appropriates revenue or moneys for the ordinary annual services of the Government shall deal only with such appropriation.

55 Tax Bill
Laws imposing taxation shall deal only with the imposition of taxation, and any provision therein dealing with any other matter shall be of no effect.
Laws imposing taxation, except laws imposing duties of customs or of excise, shall deal with one subject of taxation only; but laws imposing duties of customs shall deal with duties of customs only, and laws imposing duties of excise shall deal with duties of excise only.

56 Recommendation of money votes
A vote, resolution, or proposed law for the appropriation of revenue or moneys shall not be passed unless the purpose of the appropriation has in the same session been recommended by message of the Governor-General to the House in which the proposal originated.

57 Disagreement between the Houses

If the House of Representatives passes any proposed law, and the Senate rejects or fails to pass it, or passes it with amendments to which the House of Representatives will not agree, and if after an interval of three months the House of Representatives, in the same or the next session, again passes the proposed law with or without any amendments which have been made, suggested, or agreed to by the Senate, and the Senate rejects or fails to pass it, or passes it with amendments to which the House of Representatives will not agree, the Governor-General may dissolve the Senate and the House of Representatives simultaneously. But such dissolution shall not take place within six months before the date of the expiry of the House of Representatives by effluxion of time.

If after such dissolution the House of Representatives again passes the proposed law, with or without any amendments which have been made, suggested, or agreed to by the Senate, and the Senate rejects or fails to pass it, or passes it with amendments to which the House of Representatives will not agree, the Governor-General may convene a joint sitting of the members of the Senate and of the House of Representatives.

The members present at the joint sitting may deliberate and shall vote together upon the proposed law as last proposed by the House of Representatives, and upon amendments, if any, which have been made therein by one House and not agreed to by the other, and any such amendments which are affirmed by an absolute majority of the total number of the members of the Senate and House of Representatives shall be taken to have been carried, and if the proposed law, with the amendments, if any, so carried is affirmed by an absolute majority of the total number of the members of the Senate and House of Representatives, it shall be taken to have been duly passed by both Houses of the Parliament, and shall be presented to the Governor-General for the Queen's assent.

58 Royal assent to Bills

When a proposed law passed by both Houses of the Parliament is presented to the Governor-General for the Queen's assent, he shall declare, according to his discretion, but subject to this Constitution, that he assents in the Queen's name, or that he withholds assent, or that he reserves the law for the Queen's pleasure.

Recommendations by Governor-General

The Governor-General may return to the house in which it originated any proposed law so presented to him, and may transmit therewith any amendments which he may recommend, and the Houses may deal with the recommendation.

59 Disallowance by the Queen

The Queen may disallow any law within one year from the Governor-General's assent, and such disallowance on being made known by the Governor-General by speech or message to each of the Houses of the Parliament, or by Proclamation, shall annul the law from the day when the disallowance is so made known.

60 Signification of Queen's pleasure on Bills reserved

A proposed law reserved for the Queen's pleasure shall not have any force unless and until within two years from the day on which it was presented to the

Governor-General for the Queen's assent the Governor-General makes known, by speech or message to each of the Houses of the Parliament, or by Proclamation, that it has received the Queen's assent.

Chapter II—The Executive Government

61 Executive power

The executive power of the Commonwealth is vested in the Queen and is exercisable by the Governor-General as the Queen's representative, and extends to the execution and maintenance of this Constitution, and of the laws of the Commonwealth.

62 Federal Executive Council

There shall be a Federal Executive Council to advise the Governor-General in the government of the Commonwealth, and the members of the Council shall be chosen and summoned by the Governor-General and sworn as Executive Councillors, and shall hold office during his pleasure.

63 Provisions referring to Governor-General

The provisions of this Constitution referring to the Governor-General in Council shall be construed as referring to the Governor-General acting with the advice of the Federal Executive Council.

64 Ministers of State

The Governor-General may appoint officers to administer such departments of State of the Commonwealth as the Governor-General in Council may establish.

Such officers shall hold office during the pleasure of the Governor-General. They shall be members of the Federal Executive Council, and shall be the Queen's Ministers of State for the Commonwealth.

Ministers to sit in Parliament

After the first general election no Minister of State shall hold office for a longer period than three months unless he is or becomes a senator or a member of the House of Representatives.

65 Number of Ministers

Until the Parliament otherwise provides, the Ministers of State shall not exceed seven in number, and shall hold such offices as the Parliament prescribes, or, in the absence of provision, as the Governor-General directs.

66 Salaries of Ministers

There shall be payable to the Queen, out of the Consolidated Revenue Fund of the Commonwealth, for the salaries of the Ministers of State, an annual sum which, until the Parliament otherwise provides, shall not exceed twelve thousand pounds a year.

67 Appointment of civil servants

Until the Parliament otherwise provides, the appointment and removal of all other officers of the Executive Government of the Commonwealth shall be vested in the

Governor-General in Council, unless the appointment is delegated by the Governor-General in Council or by a law of the Commonwealth to some other authority.

68 Command of naval and military forces
The command in chief of the naval and military forces of the Commonwealth is vested in the Governor-General as the Queen's representative.

69 Transfer of certain departments
On a date or dates to be proclaimed by the Governor-General after the establishment of the Commonwealth the following departments of the public service in each State shall become transferred to the Commonwealth:
posts, telegraphs, and telephones;
naval and military defence;
lighthouses, lightships, beacons, and buoys;
quarantine.
But the departments of customs and of excise in each State shall become transferred to the Commonwealth on its establishment.

70 Certain powers of Governors to vest in Governor-General
In respect of matters which, under this Constitution, pass to the Executive Government of the Commonwealth, all powers and functions which at the establishment of the Commonwealth are vested in the Governor of a Colony, or in the Governor of a Colony with the advice of his Executive Council, or in any authority of a Colony, shall vest in the Governor-General, or in the Governor-General in Council, or in the authority exercising similar powers under the Commonwealth, as the case requires.

Chapter III—The Judicature

71 Judicial power and Courts
The judicial power of the Commonwealth shall be vested in a Federal Supreme Court, to be called the High Court of Australia, and in such other federal courts as the Parliament creates, and in such other courts as it invests with federal jurisdiction. The High Court shall consist of a Chief Justice, and so many other Justices, not less than two, as the Parliament prescribes.

72 Judges' appointment, tenure, and remuneration
The Justices of the High Court and of the other courts created by the Parliament:
(i) shall be appointed by the Governor-General in Council;
(ii) shall not be removed except by the Governor-General in Council, on an address from both Houses of the Parliament in the same session, praying for such removal on the ground of proved misbehaviour or incapacity;
(iii) shall receive such remuneration as the Parliament may fix; but the remuneration shall not be diminished during their continuance in office.
The appointment of a Justice of the High Court shall be for a term expiring upon his attaining the age of seventy years, and a person shall not be appointed as a Justice of the High Court if he has attained that age.

The appointment of a Justice of a court created by the Parliament shall be for a term expiring upon his attaining the age that is, at the time of his appointment, the maximum age for Justices of that court and a person shall not be appointed as a Justice of such a court if he has attained the age that is for the time being the maximum age for Justices of that court.
Subject to this section, the maximum age for Justices of any court created by the Parliament is seventy years.
The Parliament may make a law fixing an age that is less than seventy years as the maximum age for Justices of a court created by the Parliament and may at any time repeal or amend such a law, but any such repeal or amendment does not affect the term of office of a Justice under an appointment made before the repeal or amendment.
A Justice of the High Court or of a court created by the Parliament may resign his office by writing under his hand delivered to the Governor-General.
Nothing in the provisions added to this section by the *Constitution Alteration (Retirement of Judges) 1977* affects the continuance of a person in office as a Justice of a court under an appointment made before the commencement of those provisions.
A reference in this section to the appointment of a Justice of the High Court or of a court created by the Parliament shall be read as including a reference to the appointment of a person who holds office as a Justice of the High Court or of a court created by the Parliament to another office of Justice of the same court having a different status or designation.

73 Appellate jurisdiction of High Court
The High Court shall have jurisdiction, with such exceptions and subject to such regulations as the Parliament prescribes, to hear and determine appeals from all judgments, decrees, orders, and sentences:
(i) of any Justice or Justices exercising the original jurisdiction of the High Court;
(ii) of any other federal court, or court exercising federal jurisdiction; or of the Supreme Court of any State, or of any other court of any State from which at the establishment of the Commonwealth an appeal lies to the Queen in Council;
(iii) of the Inter-State Commission, but as to questions of law only;
and the judgment of the High Court in all such cases shall be final and conclusive.
But no exception or regulation prescribed by the Parliament shall prevent the High Court from hearing and determining any appeal from the Supreme Court of a State in any matter in which at the establishment of the Commonwealth an appeal lies from such Supreme Court to the Queen in Council.
Until the Parliament otherwise provides, the conditions of and restrictions on appeals to the Queen in Council from the Supreme Courts of the several States shall be applicable to appeals from them to the High Court.

74 Appeal to Queen in Council [*see* Note 12]
No appeal shall be permitted to the Queen in Council from a decision of the High Court upon any question, howsoever arising, as to the limits inter se of the Constitutional powers of the Commonwealth and those of any State or States, or as to the limits inter se of the Constitutional powers of any two or more States, unless

the High Court shall certify that the question is one which ought to be determined by Her Majesty in Council.

The High Court may so certify if satisfied that for any special reason the certificate should be granted, and thereupon an appeal shall lie to Her Majesty in Council on the question without further leave.

Except as provided in this section, this Constitution shall not impair any right which the Queen may be pleased to exercise by virtue of Her Royal prerogative to grant special leave of appeal from the High Court to Her Majesty in Council. The Parliament may make laws limiting the matters in which such leave may be asked, but proposed laws containing any such limitation shall be reserved by the Governor-General for Her Majesty's pleasure.

75 Original jurisdiction of High Court

In all matters:

(i) arising under any treaty;

(ii) affecting consuls or other representatives of other countries;

(iii) in which the Commonwealth, or a person suing or being sued on behalf of the Commonwealth, is a party;

(iv) between States, or between residents of different States, or between a State and a resident of another State;

(v) in which a writ of Mandamus or prohibition or an injunction is sought against an officer of the Commonwealth;

the High Court shall have original jurisdiction.

76 Additional original jurisdiction

The Parliament may make laws conferring original jurisdiction on the High Court in any matter:

(i) arising under this Constitution, or involving its interpretation;

(ii) arising under any laws made by the Parliament;

(iii) of Admiralty and maritime jurisdiction;

(iv) relating to the same subject-matter claimed under the laws of different States.

77 Power to define jurisdiction

With respect to any of the matters mentioned in the last two sections the Parliament may make laws:

(i) defining the jurisdiction of any federal court other than the High Court;

(ii) defining the extent to which the jurisdiction of any federal court shall be exclusive of that which belongs to or is invested in the courts of the States;

(iii) investing any court of a State with federal jurisdiction.

78 Proceedings against Commonwealth or State

The Parliament may make laws conferring rights to proceed against the Commonwealth or a State in respect of matters within the limits of the judicial power.

79 Number of judges

The federal jurisdiction of any court may be exercised by such number of judges as the Parliament prescribes.

80 Trial by jury

The trial on indictment of any offence against any law of the Commonwealth shall be by jury, and every such trial shall be held in the State where the offence was committed, and if the offence was not committed within any State the trial shall be held at such place or places as the Parliament prescribes.

Chapter IV—Finance and Trade

81 Consolidated Revenue Fund

All revenues or moneys raised or received by the Executive Government of the Commonwealth shall form one Consolidated Revenue Fund, to be appropriated for the purposes of the Commonwealth in the manner and subject to the charges and liabilities imposed by this Constitution.

82 Expenditure charged thereon

The costs, charges, and expenses incident to the collection, management, and receipt of the Consolidated Revenue Fund shall form the first charge thereon; and the revenue of the Commonwealth shall in the first instance be applied to the payment of the expenditure of the Commonwealth.

83 Money to be appropriated by law

No money shall be drawn from the Treasury of the Commonwealth except under appropriation made by law.

But until the expiration of one month after the first meeting of the Parliament the Governor-General in Council may draw from the Treasury and expend such moneys as may be necessary for the maintenance of any department transferred to the Commonwealth and for the holding of the first elections for the Parliament.

84 Transfer of officers

When any department of the public service of a State becomes transferred to the Commonwealth, all officers of the department shall become subject to the control of the Executive Government of the Commonwealth.

Any such officer who is not retained in the service of the Commonwealth shall, unless he is appointed to some other office of equal emolument in the public service of the State, be entitled to receive from the State any pension, gratuity, or other compensation, payable under the law of the State on the abolition of his office.

Any such officer who is retained in the service of the Commonwealth shall preserve all his existing and accruing rights, and shall be entitled to retire from office at the time, and on the pension or retiring allowance, which would be permitted by the law of the State if his service with the Commonwealth were a continuation of his service with the State. Such pension or retiring allowance shall be paid to him by the Commonwealth; but the State shall pay to the Commonwealth a part thereof, to be calculated on the proportion which his term of service with the State bears to his whole term of service, and for the purpose of the calculation his salary shall be taken to be that paid to him by the State at the time of the transfer.

Any officer who is, at the establishment of the Commonwealth, in the public service of a State, and who is, by consent of the Governor of the State with the advice of the Executive Council thereof, transferred to the public service of the Commonwealth, shall have the same rights as if he had been an officer of a department transferred to the Commonwealth and were retained in the service of the Commonwealth.

85 Transfer of property of State

When any department of the public service of a State is transferred to the Commonwealth:

(i) all property of the State of any kind, used exclusively in connexion with the department, shall become vested in the Commonwealth; but, in the case of the departments controlling customs and excise and bounties, for such time only as the Governor-General in Council may declare to be necessary;

(ii) the Commonwealth may acquire any property of the State, of any kind used, but not exclusively used in connexion with the department; the value thereof shall, if no agreement can be made, be ascertained in, as nearly as may be, the manner in which the value of land, or of an interest in land, taken by the State for public purposes is ascertained under the law of the State in force at the establishment of the Commonwealth;

(iii) the Commonwealth shall compensate the State for the value of any property passing to the Commonwealth under this section; if no agreement can be made as to the mode of compensation, it shall be determined under laws to be made by the Parliament;

(iv) the Commonwealth shall, at the date of the transfer, assume the current obligations of the State in respect of the department transferred.

86 Customs, excise, and bounties [*see* Note 13]

On the establishment of the Commonwealth, the collection and control of duties of customs and of excise, and the control of the payment of bounties, shall pass to the Executive Government of the Commonwealth.

87 Revenue from customs and excise duties [*see* Note 13]

During a period of ten years after the establishment of the Commonwealth and thereafter until the Parliament otherwise provides, of the net revenue of the Commonwealth from duties of customs and of excise not more than one-fourth shall be applied annually by the Commonwealth towards its expenditure.

The balance shall, in accordance with this Constitution, be paid to the several States, or applied towards the payment of interest on debts of the several States taken over by the Commonwealth.

88 Uniform duties of customs

Uniform duties of customs shall be imposed within two years after the establishment of the Commonwealth.

89 Payment to States before uniform duties
Until the imposition of uniform duties of customs:
(i) the Commonwealth shall credit to each State the revenues collected therein by the Commonwealth;
(ii) the Commonwealth shall debit to each State:
(a) the expenditure therein of the Commonwealth incurred solely for the maintenance or continuance, as at the time of transfer, of any department transferred from the State to the Commonwealth;
(b) the proportion of the State, according to the number of its people, in the other expenditure of the Commonwealth;
(iii) the Commonwealth shall pay to each State month by month the balance (if any) in favour of the State.

90 Exclusive power over customs, excise, and bounties
On the imposition of uniform duties of customs the power of the Parliament to impose duties of customs and of excise, and to grant bounties on the production or export of goods, shall become exclusive.
On the imposition of uniform duties of customs all laws of the several States imposing duties of customs or of excise, or offering bounties on the production or export of goods, shall cease to have effect, but any grant of or agreement for any such bounty lawfully made by or under the authority of the Government of any State shall be taken to be good if made before the thirtieth day of June, one thousand eight hundred and ninety-eight, and not otherwise.

91 Exceptions as to bounties
Nothing in this Constitution prohibits a State from granting any aid to or bounty on mining for gold, silver, or other metals, nor from granting, with the consent of both Houses of the Parliament of the Commonwealth expressed by resolution, any aid to or bounty on the production or export of goods.

92 Trade within the Commonwealth to be free
On the imposition of uniform duties of customs, trade, commerce, and intercourse among the States, whether by means of internal carriage or ocean navigation, shall be absolutely free.
But notwithstanding anything in this Constitution, goods imported before the imposition of uniform duties of customs into any State, or into any Colony which, whilst the goods remain therein, becomes a State, shall, on thence passing into another State within two years after the imposition of such duties, be liable to any duty chargeable on the importation of such goods into the Commonwealth, less any duty paid in respect of the goods on their importation.

93 Payment to States for five years after uniform tariffs
During the first five years after the imposition of uniform duties of customs, and thereafter until the Parliament otherwise provides:
(i) the duties of customs chargeable on goods imported into a State and afterwards passing into another State for consumption, and the duties of excise paid on goods produced or manufactured in a State and afterwards passing into another State for

consumption, shall be taken to have been collected not in the former but in the latter State;
(ii) subject to the last subsection, the Commonwealth shall credit revenue, debit expenditure, and pay balances to the several States as prescribed for the period preceding the imposition of uniform duties of customs.

94 Distribution of surplus
After five years from the imposition of uniform duties of customs, the Parliament may provide, on such basis as it deems fair, for the monthly payment to the several States of all surplus revenue of the Commonwealth.

95 Customs duties of Western Australia
Notwithstanding anything in this Constitution, the Parliament of the State of Western Australia, if that State be an Original State, may, during the first five years after the imposition of uniform duties of customs, impose duties of customs on goods passing into that State and not originally imported from beyond the limits of the Commonwealth; and such duties shall be collected by the Commonwealth.
But any duty so imposed on any goods shall not exceed during the first of such years the duty chargeable on the goods under the law of Western Australia in force at the imposition of uniform duties, and shall not exceed during the second, third, fourth, and fifth of such years respectively, four-fifths, three-fifths, two-fifths, and one-fifth of such latter duty, and all duties imposed under this section shall cease at the expiration of the fifth year after the imposition of uniform duties.
If at any time during the five years the duty on any goods under this section is higher than the duty imposed by the Commonwealth on the importation of the like goods, then such higher duty shall be collected on the goods when imported into Western Australia from beyond the limits of the Commonwealth.

96 Financial assistance to States
During a period of ten years after the establishment of the Commonwealth and thereafter until the Parliament otherwise provides, the Parliament may grant financial assistance to any State on such terms and conditions as the Parliament thinks fit.

97 Audit
Until the Parliament otherwise provides, the laws in force in any Colony which has become or becomes a State with respect to the receipt of revenue and the expenditure of money on account of the Government of the Colony, and the review and audit of such receipt and expenditure, shall apply to the receipt of revenue and the expenditure of money on account of the Commonwealth in the State in the same manner as if the Commonwealth, or the Government or an officer of the Commonwealth, were mentioned whenever the Colony, or the Government or an officer of the Colony, is mentioned.

98 Trade and commerce includes navigation and State railways
The power of the Parliament to make laws with respect to trade and commerce extends to navigation and shipping, and to railways the property of any State.

99 Commonwealth not to give preference

The Commonwealth shall not, by any law or regulation of trade, commerce, or revenue, give preference to one State or any part thereof over another State or any part thereof.

100 Nor abridge right to use water

The Commonwealth shall not, by any law or regulation of trade or commerce, abridge the right of a State or of the residents therein to the reasonable use of the waters of rivers for conservation or irrigation.

101 Inter-State Commission

There shall be an Inter-State Commission, with such powers of adjudication and administration as the Parliament deems necessary for the execution and maintenance, within the Commonwealth, of the provisions of this Constitution relating to trade and commerce, and of all laws made thereunder.

102 Parliament may forbid preferences by State

The Parliament may by any law with respect to trade or commerce forbid, as to railways, any preference or discrimination by any State, or by any authority constituted under a State, if such preference or discrimination is undue and unreasonable, or unjust to any State; due regard being had to the financial responsibilities incurred by any State in connexion with the construction and maintenance of its railways. But no preference or discrimination shall, within the meaning of this section, be taken to be undue and unreasonable, or unjust to any State, unless so adjudged by the Inter-State Commission.

103 Commissioners' appointment, tenure, and remuneration

The members of the Inter-State Commission:
(i) shall be appointed by the Governor-General in Council;
(ii) shall hold office for seven years, but may be removed within that time by the Governor-General in Council, on an address from both Houses of the Parliament in the same session praying for such removal on the ground of proved misbehaviour or incapacity;
(iii) shall receive such remuneration as the Parliament may fix; but such remuneration shall not be diminished during their continuance in office.

104 Saving of certain rates

Nothing in this Constitution shall render unlawful any rate for the carriage of goods upon a railway, the property of a State, if the rate is deemed by the Inter-State Commission to be necessary for the development of the territory of the State, and if the rate applies equally to goods within the State and to goods passing into the State from other States.

105 Taking over public debts of States

The Parliament may take over from the States their public debts~~as existing at the establishment of the Commonwealth~~, or a proportion thereof according to the respective numbers of their people as shown by the latest statistics of the

Commonwealth, and may convert, renew, or consolidate such debts, or any part thereof; and the States shall indemnify the Commonwealth in respect of the debts taken over, and thereafter the interest payable in respect of the debts shall be deducted and retained from the portions of the surplus revenue of the Commonwealth payable to the several States, or if such surplus is insufficient, or if there is no surplus, then the deficiency or the whole amount shall be paid by the several States.

105A Agreements with respect to State debts

(1) The Commonwealth may make agreements with the States with respect to the public debts of the States, including:

(a) the taking over of such debts by the Commonwealth;

(b) the management of such debts;

(c) the payment of interest and the provision and management of sinking funds in respect of such debts;

(d) the consolidation, renewal, conversion, and redemption of such debts;

(e) the indemnification of the Commonwealth by the States in respect of debts taken over by the Commonwealth; and

(f) the borrowing of money by the States or by the Commonwealth, or by the Commonwealth for the States.

(2) The Parliament may make laws for validating any such agreement made before the commencement of this section.

(3) The Parliament may make laws for the carrying out by the parties thereto of any such agreement.

(4) Any such agreement may be varied or rescinded by the parties thereto.

(5) Every such agreement and any such variation thereof shall be binding upon the Commonwealth and the States parties thereto notwithstanding anything contained in this Constitution or the Constitution of the several States or in any law of the Parliament of the Commonwealth or of any State.

(6) The powers conferred by this section shall not be construed as being limited in any way by the provisions of section one hundred and five of this Constitution.

Chapter V—The States

106 Saving of Constitutions

The Constitution of each State of the Commonwealth shall, subject to this Constitution, continue as at the establishment of the Commonwealth, or as at the admission or establishment of the State, as the case may be, until altered in accordance with the Constitution of the State.

107 Saving of Power of State Parliaments

Every power of the Parliament of a Colony which has become or becomes a State, shall, unless it is by this Constitution exclusively vested in the Parliament of the Commonwealth or withdrawn from the Parliament of the State, continue as at the establishment of the Commonwealth, or as at the admission or establishment of the State, as the case may be.

108 Saving of State laws

Every law in force in a Colony which has become or becomes a State, and relating to any matter within the powers of the Parliament of the Commonwealth, shall, subject to this Constitution, continue in force in the State; and, until provision is made in that behalf by the Parliament of the Commonwealth, the Parliament of the State shall have such powers of alteration and of repeal in respect of any such law as the Parliament of the Colony had until the Colony became a State.

109 Inconsistency of laws

When a law of a State is inconsistent with a law of the Commonwealth, the latter shall prevail, and the former shall, to the extent of the inconsistency, be invalid.

110 Provisions referring to Governor

The provisions of this Constitution relating to the Governor of a State extend and apply to the Governor for the time being of the State, or other chief executive officer or administrator of the government of the State.

111 States may surrender territory

The Parliament of a State may surrender any part of the State to the Commonwealth; and upon such surrender, and the acceptance thereof by the Commonwealth, such part of the State shall become subject to the exclusive jurisdiction of the Commonwealth.

112 States may levy charges for inspection laws

After uniform duties of customs have been imposed, a State may levy on imports or exports, or on goods passing into or out of the State, such charges as may be necessary for executing the inspection laws of the State; but the net produce of all charges so levied shall be for the use of the Commonwealth; and any such inspection laws may be annulled by the Parliament of the Commonwealth.

113 Intoxicating liquids

All fermented, distilled, or other intoxicating liquids passing into any State or remaining therein for use, consumption, sale, or storage, shall be subject to the laws of the State as if such liquids had been produced in the State.

114 States may not raise forces. Taxation of property of Commonwealth or State

A State shall not, without the consent of the Parliament of the Commonwealth, raise or maintain any naval or military force, or impose any tax on property of any kind belonging to the Commonwealth, nor shall the Commonwealth impose any tax on property of any kind belonging to a State.

115 States not to coin money

A State shall not coin money, nor make anything but gold and silver coin a legal tender in payment of debts.

116 Commonwealth not to legislate in respect of religion

The Commonwealth shall not make any law for establishing any religion, or for imposing any religious observance, or for prohibiting the free exercise of any religion, and no religious test shall be required as a qualification for any office or public trust under the Commonwealth.

117 Rights of residents in States

A subject of the Queen, resident in any State, shall not be subject in any other State to any disability or discrimination which would not be equally applicable to him if he were a subject of the Queen resident in such other State.

118 Recognition of laws etc. of States

Full faith and credit shall be given, throughout the Commonwealth to the laws, the public Acts and records, and the judicial proceedings of every State.

119 Protection of States from invasion and violence

The Commonwealth shall protect every State against invasion and, on the application of the Executive Government of the State, against domestic violence.

120 Custody of offenders against laws of the Commonwealth

Every State shall make provision for the detention in its prisons of persons accused or convicted of offences against the laws of the Commonwealth, and for the punishment of persons convicted of such offences, and the Parliament of the Commonwealth may make laws to give effect to this provision.

Chapter VI—New States

121 New States may be admitted or established

The Parliament may admit to the Commonwealth or establish new States, and may upon such admission or establishment make or impose such terms and conditions, including the extent of representation in either House of the Parliament, as it thinks fit.

122 Government of territories

The Parliament may make laws for the government of any territory surrendered by any State to and accepted by the Commonwealth, or of any territory placed by the Queen under the authority of and accepted by the Commonwealth, or otherwise acquired by the Commonwealth, and may allow the representation of such territory in either House of the Parliament to the extent and on the terms which it thinks fit.

123 Alteration of limits of States

The Parliament of the Commonwealth may, with the consent of the Parliament of a State, and the approval of the majority of the electors of the State voting upon the question, increase, diminish, or otherwise alter the limits of the State, upon such terms and conditions as may be agreed on, and may, with the like consent, make provision respecting the effect and operation of any increase or diminution or alteration of territory in relation to any State affected.

124 Formation of new States

A new State may be formed by separation of territory from a State, but only with the consent of the Parliament thereof, and a new State may be formed by the union of two or more States or parts of States, but only with the consent of the Parliaments of the States affected.

Chapter VII—Miscellaneous

125 Seat of Government

The seat of Government of the Commonwealth shall be determined by the Parliament, and shall be within territory which shall have been granted to or acquired by the Commonwealth, and shall be vested in and belong to the Commonwealth, and shall be in the State of New South Wales, and be distant not less than one hundred miles from Sydney.

Such territory shall contain an area of not less than one hundred square miles, and such portion thereof as shall consist of Crown lands shall be granted to the Commonwealth without any payment therefore.

The Parliament shall sit at Melbourne until it meet at the seat of Government.

126 Power to Her Majesty to authorise Governor-General to appoint deputies [*see* Note 14]

The Queen may authorise the Governor-General to appoint any person, or any persons jointly or severally, to be his deputy or deputies within any part of the Commonwealth, and in that capacity to exercise during the pleasure of the Governor-General such powers and functions of the Governor-General as he thinks fit to assign to such deputy or deputies, subject to any limitations expressed or directions given by the Queen; but the appointment of such deputy or deputies shall not affect the exercise by the Governor-General himself of any power or function.

~~127 Aborigines not to be counted in reckoning population~~

~~In reckoning the numbers of people of the Commonwealth, or of a State or other part of the Commonwealth, aboriginal natives shall not be counted.~~

Chapter VIII—Alteration of the Constitution

128 Mode of altering the Constitution [*see* Note 1]

This Constitution shall not be altered except in the following manner:

The proposed law for the alteration thereof must be passed by an absolute majority of each House of the Parliament, and not less than two nor more than six months after its passage through both Houses the proposed law shall be submitted in each State and Territory to the electors qualified to vote for the election of members of the House of Representatives.

But if either House passes any such proposed law by an absolute majority, and the other House rejects or fails to pass it, or passes it with any amendment to which the first-mentioned House will not agree, and if after an interval of three months the first-mentioned House in the same or the next session again passes the proposed law by an absolute majority with or without any amendment which has been made or agreed to by the other House, and such other House rejects or fails to pass it or passes it with any amendment to which the first-mentioned House will not agree, the Governor-General may submit the proposed law as last proposed by the first-mentioned House, and either with or without any amendments subsequently agreed to by both Houses, to the electors in each State and Territory qualified to vote for the election of the House of Representatives.

When a proposed law is submitted to the electors the vote shall be taken in such manner as the Parliament prescribes. But until the qualification of electors of members of the House of Representatives becomes uniform throughout the Commonwealth, only one-half the electors voting for and against the proposed law shall be counted in any State in which adult suffrage prevails.

And if in a majority of the States a majority of the electors voting approve the proposed law, and if a majority of all the electors voting also approve the proposed law, it shall be presented to the Governor-General for the Queen's assent.

No alteration diminishing the proportionate representation of any State in either House of the Parliament, or the minimum number of representatives of a State in the House of Representatives, or increasing, diminishing, or otherwise altering the limits of the State, or in any manner affecting the provisions of the Constitution in relation thereto, shall become law unless the majority of the electors voting in that State approve the proposed law.

In this section, *Territory* means any territory referred to in section one hundred and twenty-two of this Constitution in respect of which there is in force a law allowing its representation in the House of Representatives.

Schedule

OATH

I, *A.B.*, do swear that I will be faithful and bear true allegiance to Her Majesty Queen Victoria, Her heirs and successors according to law.

SO HELP ME GOD!

AFFIRMATION

I, *A.B.*, do solemnly and sincerely affirm and declare that I will be faithful and bear true allegiance to Her Majesty Queen Victoria, Her heirs and successors according to law.

(NOTE: *The name of the King or Queen of the United Kingdom of Great Britain and Ireland for the time being is to be substituted from time to time.*)

Notes

Note 1

The Commonwealth of Australian Constitution Act (the Constitution) as shown in this compilation comprises the Constitution amended as indicated in the Tables below.

Table of Acts

Act	*Number and year*	*Date of Assent*
Constitution Alteration (Senate Elections) 1906	1, 1907	3 Apr 1907
Constitution Alteration (State Debts) 1909	3, 1910	6 Aug 1910
Constitution Alteration (State Debts) 1928	1, 1929	13 Feb 1929
Constitution Alteration (Social Services) 1946	81, 1946	19 Dec 1946
Constitution Alteration (Aboriginals) 1967	55, 1967	10 Aug 1967
Constitution Alteration (Senate Casual Vacancies) 1977	82, 1977	29 July 1977
Constitution Alteration (Retirement of Judges) 1977	83, 1977	29 July 1977
Constitution Alteration (Referendums) 1977	84, 1977	29 July 1977

Table of Amendments

ad. = added or inserted rep. = repealed	am. = amended rs. = repealed and substituted
Provision affected	*How affected*
S. 13	am. No. 1, 1907
S. 15	rs. No. 82, 1977
S. 51	am. No. 81, 1946; No. 55, 1967
S. 72	am. No. 83, 1977
S. 105	am. No. 3, 1910
S. 105A	ad. No. 1, 1929
S. 127	rep. No. 55, 1967
S. 128	am. No. 84, 1977

Note 2
Covering Clause 3—The Proclamation under covering clause 3 was made on 17 September 1900 and published in *Gazette* 1901.

Note 3
Covering Clause 5—*see also* the *Statute of Westminster Adoption Act 1942*.

Note 4
Covering Clause 7—The following Acts have repealed Acts passed by the Federal Council of Australasia:
Defence Act 1903 (No. 20, 1903), s. 6
Pearl Fisheries Act 1952 (No. 8, 1952), s. 3 (*Pearl Fisheries Act 1952* repealed by *Continental Shelf (Living Natural Resources) Act 1968*, s. 3)
Service and Execution of Process Act 1901 (No. 11, 1901), s. 2 (subsequently repealed by *Service and Execution of Process Act 1963*, s. 3).

Note 5
Section 7—The number of senators for each State was increased to 12 by the *Representation Act 1983*, s. 3.

Note 6
Section 9—The following State Acts have been passed in pursuance of the powers conferred by s. 9:

State	*Number*	*Short title*	*How affected*
New South Wales	No. 73, 1900	Federal Elections Act 1900	Ss. 2, 3, 4, 5 and 6 and the Schedule repealed by No. 9, 1903; wholly repealed by No. 41, 1912
	No. 9, 1903	Senators' Elections Act 1903	*(still in force)*
Victoria	No. 1715	Federal Elections Act 1900	Repealed by No. 1860
	No. 1860	Senate Elections (Times and Places) Act 1903	Repealed by No. 2723
	No. 2399	Senate Elections (Times and Places) Act 1912	Repealed by No. 2723
	No. 2723	Senate Elections (Times and Places) Act 1915	Repealed by No. 3769
	No. 3769	Senate Elections (Times and Places) Act 1928	Repealed by No. 6365
	No. 6365	Senate Elections Act 1958	*(still in force)*

State	*Number*	*Short title*	*How affected*
Queensland	64 Vic. No. 25	The Parliament of the Commonwealth Elections Act and the Elections Acts 1885 to 1898 Amendment Act of 1900	Operation exhausted
	3 Edw. VII. No. 6	The Election of Senators Act of 1903	Repealed by 9 Eliz. II. No. 20
	9 Eliz. II. No. 20	The Senate Elections Act of 1960	*(still in force)*
South Australia	No. 834	The Election of Senators Act 1903	*(still in force)*
Western Australia	No. 11, 1903	Election of Senators Act 1903	*(still in force)*
Tasmania	64 Vic. No. 59	The Federal Elections Act 1900	Repealed by 26 Geo. V. No. 3
	3 Edw. VII. No. 5	The Election of Senators Act 1903	Repealed by 26 Geo. V. No. 3
	26 Geo. V. No. 3	Senate Elections Act 1935	*(still in force)*

Note 7
Section 14—For the provisions applicable upon the increase in the number of senators to 12 made by the *Representation Act 1983*, *see* s. 3 of that Act.

Note 8
Section 15—The proposed law to alter the Constitution entitled "*Constitution Alteration (Simultaneous Elections) 1977*" was submitted to the electors in each State of the Commonwealth on 21 May 1977: it was not approved by a majority of all the electors voting in a majority of the States. *See Gazette* 1977, No. S100.

Note 9
Section 29—The following State Acts were passed in pursuance of the powers conferred by s. 29, but ceased to be in force upon the enactment of the *Commonwealth Electoral Act 1902*:

State	*Number*	*Short title*
New South Wales	No. 73, 1900	Federal Elections Act 1900
Victoria	No. 1667	Federal House of Representatives Victorian Electorates Act 1900
Queensland	64 Vic. No. 25	The Parliament of the Commonwealth Elections Act and The Elections Acts 1885 to 1898 Amendment Act of 1900
Western Australia	64 Vic. No. 6	Federal House of Representatives Western Australian Electorates Act 1900

Note 10
Section 51—The following Imperial Acts extended the legislative powers of the Parliament:
Whaling Industry (Regulations) Act 1934, s. 15
Geneva Convention Act, 1937, s. 2
Emergency Powers (Defence) Act 1939, s. 5
Army and Air Force (Annual) Act 1940, s. 3.

Note 11
Section 51 (xxxvii)—The following Acts have been passed by the Parliaments of the States to refer matters to the Parliament under section 51 (xxxvii):

State	*Number*	*Short title*	*How affected*
New South Wales	No. 65, 1915	Commonwealth Powers (War) Act 1915	Expired 9 Jan 1921; *see* s. 5
	No. 33, 1942	Commonwealth Powers Act 1942	Expired; *see* s. 4
	No. 18, 1943	Commonwealth Powers Act 1943	Expired; *see* s. 4
	No. 48, 1983	Commonwealth Powers (Meat Inspection) Act 1983	*(still in force)*
	No. 182, 1986	Commonwealth Powers (Family Law–Children) Act 1986	*(still in force)*
	No. 61, 1992	Mutual Recognition (New South Wales) Act 1992	*(still in force)*

State	*Number*	*Short title*	*How affected*
	No. 104, 1992	Commonwealth Powers (State Banking) Act 1992	*(still in force)*
	No. 100, 1993	Commonwealth Powers (Poultry Processing) Act 1993	*(still in force)*
	No. 1, 2001	Corporations (Commonwealth Powers) Act 2001	*(still in force)*
	No. 114, 2002	Terrorism (Commonwealth Powers) Act 2002	*(still in force)*
Victoria	No. 3108	Commonwealth Powers (Air Navigation) Act 1920	Repealed by No. 4502
	No. 3658	Commonwealth Arrangements Act 1928 (Part III)	Part III Repealed by No. 4502: Parts I & II Repealed by No. 6223
	No. 4009	Debt Conversion Agreement Act 1931 (No. 2)	*(still in force)*
	No. 4950	Commonwealth Powers Act 1943	Not proclaimed to come into operation and cannot now be so proclaimed
	No. 92, 1986	Commonwealth Powers (Family Law–Children) Act 1986	*(still in force)*
	No. 2, 1993	Mutual Recognition (Victoria) Act 1993	*(still in force)*
	No. 59, 1996	Commonwealth Powers (Industrial Relations) Act 1996	*(still in force)*
	No. 6, 2001	Corporations (Commonwealth Powers) Act 2001	*(still in force)*
	No. 14, 2003	Terrorism (Commonwealth Powers) Act 2003	*(still in force)*

State	*Number*	*Short title*	*How affected*
Queensland	12 Geo. V. No. 30	The Commonwealth Powers (Air Navigation) Act 1921	Repealed by 1 Geo. VI. No. 8
	22 Geo. V. No. 30	The Commonwealth Legislative Power Act 1931	Repealed by No. 46, 1983
	7 Geo. VI. No. 19	Commonwealth Powers Act 1943	Expired; *see* s. 4
	14 Geo. VI. No. 2	The Commonwealth Powers (Air Transport) Act 1950	*(still in force)*
	No. 37, 1990	Commonwealth Powers (Family Law–Children) Act 1990	*(still in force)*
	No. 67, 1992	Mutual Recognition (Queensland) Act 1992	*(still in force)*
	No. 43, 2001	Corporations (Commonwealth Powers) Act 2001	*(still in force)*
	No. 79, 2002	Terrorism (Commonwealth Powers) Act 2002	*(still in force)*
South Australia	No. 1469, 1921	Commonwealth Powers (Air Navigation) Act 1921	Repealed by No. 2352, 1937
	No. 2061, 1931	Commonwealth Legislative Power Act 1931	*(still in force)*
	No. 3, 1943	Commonwealth Powers Act 1943	Expired; *see* s. 5
	No. 89, 1986	Commonwealth Powers (Family Law) Act 1986	*(still in force)*
	No. 72, 1993	Mutual Recognition (South Australia) Act 1993	*(still in force)*
	No. 21, 2001	Corporations (Commonwealth Powers) Act 2001	*(still in force)*

State	*Number*	*Short title*	*How affected*
	No. 50, 2002	Terrorism (Commonwealth Powers) Act 2002	*(still in force)*
Western Australia	No. 4, 1943	Commonwealth Powers Act 1943	Repealed by No. 58, 1965
	No. 57, 1945	Commonwealth Powers Act 1945	Repealed by No. 58, 1965
	No. 30, 1947	Commonwealth Powers Act 1943, Amendment Act 1947	Repealed by No. 58, 1965
	No. 31, 1947	Commonwealth Powers Act 1945, Amendment Act 1947	Repealed by No. 58, 1965
	No. 73, 1947	Commonwealth Powers Act 1945, Amendment Act (No. 2), 1947	Repealed by No. 58, 1965
	No. 81, 1947	Commonwealth Powers Act 1945-1947, Amendment (Continuance) Act 1947	Repealed by No. 58, 1965
	No. 53, 1995	Mutual Recognition (Western Australia) Act 1995	*(still in force)*
	No. 7, 2001	Corporations (Commonwealth Powers) Act 2001	*(still in force)*
	No. 53, 2002	Terrorism (Commonwealth Powers) Act 2002	*(still in force)*
Tasmania	11 Geo. V. No. 42	Commonwealth Powers (Air Navigation) Act 1920	Repealed by 1 Geo. VI. No. 14
	No. 46, 1952	Commonwealth Powers (Air Transport) Act 1952	*(still in force)*
	No. 62, 1966	Commonwealth Powers (Trade Practices) Act 1966	Expired; *see* s. 2
	No. 5, 1987	Commonwealth Powers (Family Law) Act 1987	*(still in force)*

State	*Number*	*Short title*	*How affected*
	No. 33, 1993	Mutual Recognition (Tasmania) Act 1993	*(still in force)*
	No. 20, 1994	Commonwealth Powers (Family Law) Amendment Act 1994	*(still in force)*
	No. 39, 2001	Corporations (Commonwealth Powers) Act 2001	*(still in force)*
	No. 68, 2002	Terrorism (Commonwealth Powers) Act 2002	*(still in force)*

Note 12
Section 74—*See Privy Council (Limitation of Appeals) Act 1968*, *Privy Council (Appeals from the High Court) Act 1975* and Kirmani v Captain Cook Cruises Pty. Ltd [No. 2] (1985) 159 CLR 461.

Note 13
Sections 86 and 87—the headings for these sections have been added for compilation purposes.

Note 14
S. 126—*See* clause IV of the Letters Patent relating to the Office of Governor-General, published in *Gazette* 1984, S334.

GLOSSARY

abscond, to:	to leave in breach of bail.
Act:	legislation passed by both Houses of Parliament and with the Royal assent.
address:	a motion to a house of Parliament that a judge should be removed from office.
ad hoc:	on the facts of the moment.
adjourn, to:	to put a court case off to another time, hence the noun adjournment.
ADR:	Alternative Dispute Resolution. This covers any dispute resolution other than determination by a court.
affidavit:	a written statement that is sworn on oath so that it can be received as evidence by a court.
agenda:	program, often used to describe the outline of issues to be discussed at a meeting.
amalgamation:	a joining, or merging of two things to create a new thing. Thus there might be an amalgamation of two companies, or two court cases might be amalgamated, or joined, into a single action.
appropriation:	the Act to authorise the annual budget for the collection of taxes (supply) and spending of money by the executive government.
as he then was:	a politeness to acknowledge that judge who is quoted later was promoted, or elevated, to a higher judicial office.
assess, to:	to decide the amount of something, typically to assess the value of damages, or to assess on taxation a lawyer's entitlement to costs, hence assessment.
assent:	consent by the Queen, or her representative the Governor-General.
associate:	a graduate lawyer who works with a judge for experience.
attorney:	another word for lawyer, more commonly used historically in the English system, or in the USA
Attorney-General:	The minister with responsibility for the law department and courts.
award:	a fixing of minimum wages and conditions for a class of workers.
bail:	the conditional release of a person charged with an offence into the community, to return to court at a future time.
barrister:	a lawyer who only appears in court. They usually do not take instructions direct from a client but receive them from a solicitor.
bench:	the judge or group of judges or magistrates. The seat in the court room where the judge(s) sit.

bi-cameral: a Parliament with two houses, as in Australia, the lower house, the House of Representatives and the upper house, the Senate.

Bill: legislation that has been presented to Parliament but not yet passed.

bond: an undertaking to be of good behaviour and do other things ordered by the court in return for a sentence not being carried out (hence good behaviour bond). Also in commercial law it is a particular kind of undertaking to pay money in a future event.

borough: an older English term for a property or area that had parliamentary representation.

breach: fail to comply with a condition of bail or of a good behaviour bond.

British Commonwealth: a loose grouping of nations that were formerly British colonies.

case law: legal principles established from cases under the common law method.

Cabinet: the chief ministers of the government meeting as a governing group.

case stated: a set of questions on law that a lower court refers to a higher court for guidance.

certiorari: an order of a court overturning, or quashing an executive decision.

cession: from to cede: giving away, as in one country giving a part of its territory to another.

clerk: a court officer who keeps the court records.

common law marriage: a marriage not formalised at law but recognised in practice.

Commonwealth: a political grouping as in a nation state. It is also used to describe the loose organisation of nations that used to be British colonies: see British Commonwealth.

community legal centre: A free legal advice clinic, giving basic legal advice and providing mediation services.

compel, to: to force, hence compulsion.

complaint: a process to start a criminal prosecution in a lower court.

compliance: the extent of performance of conditions, as bail or a good behaviour bond.

conciliation: a process of discussion and negotiation of a dispute where the facilitator may express views about the merits of each case and the likely outcome if it goes to court (in contrast to mediation).

concur, to: a judge agreeing with the judgment of another judge in the same case, as "I concur".

confederation: an alliance of States, usually with the surrender of less power than in a Federation.

confidence:	commanding the majority vote in the lower House of Parliament, as 'a vote of confidence'.
Congress:	the legislative House of Parliament of the USA.
contempt:	disrespect for a court that can be punished with a fine or imprisonment.
convene, to:	bring people together for a meeting.
conventions:	unwritten rules of political and constitutional conduct. Also a meeting to draft laws as in a constitutional convention.
convicted:	the formal recording of guilt of a criminal charge. Sometimes in view of a defendant's prior good character, even where a charge is proved it might be dealt with without a conviction.
corral, to:	to confine choices as with livestock by herding them into an enclosure from which they cannot escape.
cost scales:	the basis for calculating legal costs, both between the litigants to a court case, known as party party costs, or as between the lawyer and the client, known as solicitor client costs.
cost shifting:	the rule that the unsuccessful litigant in a court case pays the successful litigant some costs.
counsel:	a barrister or barristers.
counterclaim:	a claim by a defendant that the plaintiff in fact owes the defendant money arising out of the circumstances of the plaintiff's claim.
crayfish:	a large edible saltwater lobster, without claws, which are common in Australian waters.
Crown:	an impersonal way to describe the Queen or King. The Head of State.
crown lease:	A lease of land at a nominal rent from the government, usually for large area stock grazing, known as pastoral properties.
curfew:	a period during which a person must be at home, typically as part of bail conditions.
custody:	keeping a person in gaol. More generally: care or control, as in custody of children.
deadlock:	when the two House of Parliament cannot agree on a Bill.
debenture:	a special type of mortgage over the assets of a company, usually a floating charge, i.e. it remains in the background, or floats, unless the company defaults and then it crystallises to have immediate effect as a mortgage on all the company's stock, debts and goodwill. At this point the company's affairs will be taken over by a receiver who will run the business for the benefit of the debenture holder.

defamation:	a right to recover damages for harm to character caused by published unfair statements. If the publication is oral it is called slander. If the words are written it is called libel.
demerit points:	points accrued from speeding (3 points) and other bad driving. If a driver exceeds twelve points in any 3 year period the licence is suspended.
detention:	a form of custody. This word is used for juveniles and people will mental health disorders to avoid the negative connotations of custody and gaol.
detoxification:	abstinence from drugs or alcohol during which withdrawal symptoms are experienced.
directions hearing:	a pretrial hearing where the court ensures the parties are progressing the action. Pretrial processes in common law systems are more party controlled and complicated than under the ZPO.
discovery:	a disclosure to the other party to litigation of the documentary evidence in the knowledge of the party and where it might be found. In the USA the term also covers wider powers to require examination of witnesses before trial.
dispatch, to:	to send on an errand.
dissent:	a minority judgment, disagreeing with the opinion of the majority, from to dissent.
dissolution:	ending a Parliament and submitting the members to election. In Australia this involves all members of the House of Representatives and half the members of the upper house, the Senate. In a double dissolution, all the Senators submit to election.
distinguish, to:	to find a case is different on the facts, or some other basis, so it is not necessary to follow the ratio decidendi.
Dominion:	A nation that was previously a British colony and that still has the English crown as its head of state.
double dissolution:	a dissolution where all members of both houses submit to election.
double jeopardy:	being prosecuted twice for the same criminal offence.
DPP:	Director of Public Prosecutions, the officer in charge of prosecuting services for the government. Used generically to describe the prosecution in serious cases. In minor cases the police sometimes prosecute.
eligible:	suitable, satisfies all the requirements for a program.
emancipists:	freed convicts. Used generally for groups who seek freedom and rights.
enable, to:	to authorise or make possible.
Establish, to:	in normal use to set up but it has a particular meaning of the adoption by the State of a religion in preference to others.

estate in fee simple:	freehold title to real estate (land).
evidence:	information that can be admitted at a trial to prove a fact in issue. In the common law the rules of evidence emphasise oral evidence, having grown up around the jury trial method, and are very complicated.
Executive Council:	the Governor-General (or Governor of a State) and key ministers of Cabinet.
exegesis:	an obscure word meaning explanation.
ex parte:	in the absence of a party.
expulsion:	the ejection of a person from a program or place.
federation:	a binding alliance of States who surrender some of their power to the new central authority created.
female suffrage:	the right for women to vote.
firearm:	a gun.
first instance:	the first trial in a case, in Australia generally the facts are decided at the first level and the appeal is only as to procedural faults and the law.
fiscally:	financially
forfeiture:	the loss of the right to possess something, as in a firearm for example because an offence has been committed with it.
fortnight:	two consecutive weeks.
freehold:	title for land that vests it completely in the owner and her heirs.
found:	the decision of a court, viz: "the High Court *found*". *Held* is used in the same way.
Governor:	the Queen of England's representative in a State in Australia.
Governor- General:	the Queen of England's representative in Australia.
grant:	of land is the creation of the freehold title to land by the Crown, which originally owned all the land (now subject to native title).
grant, to:	to give someone a particular power or authority.
habeas corpus:	a writ or court process to establish a right to freedom from custody.
hang on, to:	follow from, as in "nothing hangs on that proposition".
harass, to:	to annoy continually.
hearing:	the trial, or other formal attendance, in a court.
held:	the decision of a court, viz: "the High Court *held*". *Found* is used in the same way.
High Court of Australia:	the ultimate court of appeal and the constitutional court in Australia.
HMS:	Her/His Majesty's Ship. A designation for all English naval vessels. HMAS, for Her Majesty's Australian Ship.
Home Office:	the British Department of the Secretary of State for Home Affairs that had responsibility for administering colonies.

House of Commons:	the lower house in the British Parliament.
House of Lords:	the upper house in the British Parliament, and also its legal part, which is the highest court of appeal in the British legal system.
House of Representatives:	the lower house in the Australian Parliament. The upper house is the Senate.
hung jury:	a jury that cannot reach a verdict. Usually jury verdicts must be unanimous, so if one juror disagrees with the other 11 it is a hung jury.
ibid:	abbreviation of Latin ibi with the suffix dem = ibidem meaning in the same place. Used in footnotes to refer to the immediately preceding footnote.
illicit:	illegal, as in illicit drugs as opposed to drugs from the chemist shop.
impairment:	disability.
Imperial Parliament:	the English Parliament exercising authority over its colonies and dominions, abbreviated (Imp).
impugned:	under attack, as in criticising legislation as invalid under the Constitution.
Inc:	abbreviation for incorporated, that is an artificial legal entity such as a company.
incarcerate, to:	to gaol, hence incarceration.
incentive:	reward.
indictment:	the written statement of charges for serious criminal matters (known as indictable offences). Lesser charges (known as summary offences) are commenced on a complaint.
injunction:	a court order forbidding something being done.
instalment:	a regular payment.
invalid:	not effective, not legally binding. In a non legal sense it means someone who is so ill as to be incapacitated.
irrevocable:	cannot be cancelled, usually an agreement for a future payment of money.
jingoistic:	excessively patriotic or chauvinistic.
John Doe and Richard Roe:	fictitious people sometimes used to mask the identity of a party to a legal action.
joint sitting:	The House of Representatives and the Senate sitting together.
judgment:	the decision of a court, sometimes used to describe the reasons given and sometimes the enforceable result, or in German terms, an enforceable title.
jury:	a group of lay people, usually twelve in number who decide a case.
Keynesian:	an economic policy for government to fund projects from borrowings to take an economy out of depression; after the English economist John Maynard Keynes.

kinship:	family relationships, used especially to describe relationships in Aboriginal groups.
labour/Labor:	Labour with the 'u' is the correct spelling of manual work (except in the USA where it is labor). The Australian Labor Party, the party whose origins lie in the trade union movement, have dropped the 'u' from the spelling.
lackey:	a follower of a leader who tries to seek the favours of the leader.
lapse, to:	to fall into disuse.
lease:	a temporary land title for a periodic or fixed term for which rent is paid.
legal aid:	State payment for legal representation.
legislation:	A law duly passed by both Houses of Parliament, assented to by the Queen and proclaimed to come into operation.
Legislative Council:	The upper house in a State Parliament.
Letters Patent:	an open letter of appointment by the Crown.
levy:	a form of tax, usually for a particular purpose, such as the victims of crime levy which is charged to everyone convicted of a criminal offence.
libel:	defamation which is published in writing.
lie, to:	to place before, as a regulation is to lie before a committee of Parliament for 15 sitting days. Also to be an available legal conclusion, as: 'an action may lie in negligence'. The common meaning is to tell an intentional falsehood.
litigant:	a party to a court case.
local government:	the lowest level of government for the town or suburb of a city. Also known as the local council or municipal council.
lodge, to:	to file with the court, hence lodgements the collective noun for court files.
Magistrates Court:	the lower court, equivalent to the Amtsgericht.
Magna Carta:	a guarantee of basic liberties forced on King John of England by his Barons in 1215 at Runnymede.
malice:	in defamation a deliberate intention to harm someone's reputation that invalidates the defence of qualified privilege.
mandamus:	an order requiring an action to be taken.
mate:	Australian term of casual acquaintance between males: e.g. "g'dday mate" as a greeting: that is "good day mate".
material:	relevant.
mediation:	a process of discussion and negotiation of a dispute where a facilitator assists the parties, but without suggesting any outcome or view on the merits.

mores:	deductions (obscure), also morals.
mortgage:	a security over real estate for a loan.
mutual:	reciprocal.
native title:	a type of ownership of land vested in Aboriginal tribal groups by the High Court in *Mabo (No. 2)v the State of QLD.*
negligence:	the principle that each citizen owes a duty of care to her or his neighbour, which if breached gives rise to rights of compensation.
no:	abbreviation of number.
no bans clause:	a requirement in an award for workers that prevents the union from putting bans on any type of work or overtime.
obiter dicta:	expressions of views and rulings on the law in a judgment that are not essential for the decision in the particular case. They are not binding on later cases.
offence:	(USA offense) a breach of the criminal law.
office:	position in a government.
onus:	obligation, used in relation to proving something: eg 'the plaintiff bears the onus of proof'.
op. cit.:	in the work quoted (L. *opera citato*): used in footnotes to refer to a earlier citation of a source. Where it is cited immediately preceding *ibid.* is preferred.
opinion:	a formal statement of the law by a barrister.
ordinance:	legislation by an authority lesser than a State, such as a Territory or a local council.
pamphlet:	leaflet, a short document giving information.
parliamentary privilege:	the protection against any legal liability that might otherwise be attracted to statements made by members of Parliament in parliamentary sessions, and witnesses in select committee hearings.
pastoral lease:	a leasehold title over land for grazing stock, usually a large area of land in a low rainfall district.
pawn, to:	to give property as security for a small debt, usually at usurious (very high) rates of interest.
per:	by or by means of.
persuade, to:	to convince by argument, hence persuasive.
per se:	taken alone, by itself.
plead, to:	in the common law system the defendant in a criminal case is asked if they plead guilty or not guilty of the charge, hence a guilty plea. A guilty plea may be on a factual basis agreed by the prosecutor and defendant and the court will generally accept that as the facts for sentencing. Also it is the verb to describe the drafting of a statement of claim or defence, which may be called a pleading, or collectively the pleadings.
plebiscite:	a vote of the all electors.

prerogative:	an exclusive or special power or privilege.
Premier:	the head of government of a State.
presiding:	conducting a court, eg the presiding judge.
pretrial conference:	a court hearing before a trial where possible outcomes are discussed with a view to narrowing or agreeing all the issues without a trial.
Prime Minister:	the head of government of Australia.
principal:	the most senior person in an organisation.
principle:	the underlying proposition, the basis. (note principal and principle are pronounced in the same way).
private international law:	an area of law that resolves which law applies between competing laws, eg if a contract made in one State for the export of goods is breached in another State which has different contract law.
Privy Council:	the Queen's council of ministers and advisors. More often in the Australian context used to describe the judicial wing of the House of Lords constituted to hear appeals from colonies and Dominions.
proclaim, to:	the act of announcing that legislation has come into effect, done by publishing a notice in the government gazette.
prohibition:	a court order to prohibit an action being taken.
province:	area of responsibility. This word can also mean a political region much the same as a State, especially in Canada.
provision:	a section of legislation.
pursuant to:	in reliance upon, as in "pursuant to the *Motor Vehicles Act …*"
qualified privilege:	a defence to an action in defamation available for statements published to a small group to serve a legitimate purpose of the group, e.g. commenting to a selection panel about an employee's suitability for promotion. The defence is lost if the statement can be shown to have been made with malice.
quash, to:	to overturn or undo a decision.
Queen in Council:	the Queen with her council of key ministers, in Australia the Executive Council.
Queen's Counsel:	an honorary designation that a barrister has high ability. Usually abbreviated to QC (or KC if a King is the monarch at the time). Now in some States designated SC for Senior Counsel.
Question Time:	a special session of Parliament when the members can question Ministers.
ratify, to:	to adopt something to give it effect, as in an international treaty obligation enacted to apply in the country.
ratio decidendi:	the principle reason for judicial decision (see in contrast *obiter dicta*). It is binding a lower court.

real estate: land.

real property law: the specialisation of law concerning real estate.

receiver: a person appointed under authority of a debenture to run the affairs of a company that defaulted on the debenture. An appointment of this sort may be made by a court to enforce orders against a debtor.

recidivism: committing repeat offences, hence recidivist, a regular criminal.

refer, to: to grant power to the Commonwealth under s. 51 (xxxvii) of the Constitution. It can also be used to describe the reference of a matter for decision by an arbitrator or referee, and further to allude or point to.

relapse: going back to addictive drugs after a period of abstinence.

representative: elected as in representative government, or my local member of parliament is my representative.

Regina: the Queen, from Latin.

regulate, to: Parliament when passing legislation often permits detail to be provided in subordinate regulations, which regulate the matters authorised.

regulations: subordinate legislation as to detail authorised by an Act of Parliament.

remand, to: to require the defendant in a criminal case to return at a later time, to adjourn.

remit, to: to send back to a lower court from a higher court.

reside, to: to live, often at a specified address in a bail condition.

residual: what is left after a specified list.

restrain, to: to order that a person not do certain things. This often occurs in family violence situations where a court may make a restraining order, limiting contact by one partner and imposing other conditions.

retrial: a rehearing of trial due to error or other reasons.

retrospective: legislation which backdates changes to the law.

Royal Commission: a special inquiry with powers of inquisition established by the Queen on advice of the government, headed by a Royal Commissioner who is usually a judge.

sack, to to dismiss.

scales: basis for calculating legal costs. Scales are also used to represent the weighing of matters to arrive at justice, believed to be derived from the Egyptian Goddess Maat who used scales to measure the souls of the deceased against the weight of a feather.

scrutiny: close inspection.

search warrant: a document from a court authorising someone, usually a police officer, to enter private property and search and seize items of a specified type.

secession: withdrawal from a federation.

select committee:	a committed formed by a House of Parliament, usually the Senate, to enquire into a particular topic or specially consider legislation that is before it.
Senate:	the upper house of the Australian Parliament.
silk:	Barristers designated as Queen's Counsel (QCs) were then entitled to have their barrister's robe made out of silk fabric, hence to be appointed as a barrister is "to take silk" and a QC is sometimes known as "a silk".
slander:	defamation by spoken, not written words.
solicitor:	a lawyer who does not appear in court.
southern cross:	a kite shaped star constellation, visible only in the Southern Hemisphere from which the direction due South can readily be established.
stare decisis:	the foundation principle of the common law system of precedent that a judge is bound by the ratio decidendi of a judgment of higher court, but a judgment at the same level, or obiter dicta in any judgment, is only of persuasive value.
State:	in Australia the constituent legal entities that make up the federation of the Commonwealth of Australia, as in German: Lander. In a broader context it can be used to describe any geographically defined group of people under a sovereign government.
statute:	an Act of Parliament, or legislation.
strand:	a thread of argument or a line of cases.
subrogate, to:	to give one person the right to exercise another's rights, as when an insurer has paid a claim, it may have the right under the insurance policy to recover the loss in the name of the insured person. This is known as a right of subrogation.
suffrage:	the right to vote, hence Suffragettes were the group of women campaigning for the right to vote.
summary:	lower court procedure. The lower court is known as the Magistrates Court or Local Court.
summons:	a document directing someone to attend at court at a specified time.
supply:	the sum of money granted by Parliament by the annual *Appropriation Act* to permit the executive to govern.
Supply Bill:	the Bill for the annual budget, also known as the Appropriation Bill.
Supreme Court:	in Australia the highest court in a State (as opposed to the USA where it describes the highest court of the Federal Government. In Australia this is the High Court).
taking silk:	being appointed a Queen's Counsel (see "silk").
tap, to:	to monitor an electronic communication.

taxation:	the process of assessing a lawyer's proper entitlement to costs in a legal action. (The common meaning is the government levies on the community such as taxation of income.)
tenure:	the right to hold an office, or land.
terra nullius:	Latin for vacant land; the principle that the Aboriginal people had no legally enforceable rights to the land they occupied in Australia.
title:	the legal right to ownership and/or possession of property, especially land.
Torrens title system:	a system of registration of land ownership to provide certainty of title and ease of transfer of it, based on the British scheme of ownership for the registration of merchant shipping and named after Sir Robert Torrens, its instigator.
trade unions:	associations of workers to negotiate better conditions and rights.
Treasurer:	the minister with responsibility for government finances.
troopers:	soldiers.
uphold, to:	to confirm a decision, particularly a higher court upholds the decision of a lower court (past tense "upheld").
vacate, to:	to leave empty, as in a house, or to adjourn a trial date (as in adjourn it to another date).
viz:	namely, from the Latin videlicet.
warder:	a person who guards prisoners, a gaoler.
warrant:	a written authority from a court to intrude on citizens' rights such as to permit the recording of phone conversations, authorise a search or to have a person arrested.
withdraw, to:	to recall or abandon an allegation.
writ:	a document that commences a civil case in a higher court. The document in a lower court is called a claim or a summons.
WWII:	World War two.